William Henry Schofield

Studies on the Libeaus Desconus

William Henry Schofield

Studies on the Libeaus Desconus

ISBN/EAN: 9783337778675

Printed in Europe, USA, Canada, Australia, Japan

Cover: Foto ©Thomas Meinert / pixelio.de

More available books at **www.hansebooks.com**

STUDIES AND NOTES

IN

PHILOLOGY AND LITERATURE

Vol. IV

Studies on the Libeaus Desconus

BY

WILLIAM HENRY SCHOFIELD

PUBLISHED UNDER THE DIRECTION OF THE
MODERN LANGUAGE DEPARTMENTS OF HARVARD UNIVERSITY
By GINN & COMPANY, 13 Tremont Place, Boston
1895

CONTENTS.

	PAGE
Introduction	1
Comparison of the Four Poems	4
I. Introduction	4
II. At the Court	6
III. The Adventure at the Ford	12
IV. The Fight with the Three Avengers	16
V. The Adventure with the Giants	18
VI. The Sparrow-hawk Adventure	25
VII. The Dispute about the Dog	32
VIII. At the Ile d'Or	36
IX. The Adventure with Lampart	42
X. The Rescue of the Enchanted Lady	47
XI. The Conclusion	53
XII. Continuation of BI	54
Wherein the Poems agree	56
LD-Car. opposed to BI	56
LD-Car.-Wig. opposed to BI	58
Relation of LD to BI	59
I. Proper Names	59
II. Borrowings of BI from *Erec*	60
Changes introduced by Renaud	106
Renaud's Use of the *Perceval*	139
Renaud's Knowledge of *Tristan*	145

	PAGE
The Origin and Development of the Story	145
Comparison with *Peredur*	147
Version A	154
Version B	157
The Sparrow-hawk Adventure	164
The Adventure with the Dog	171
Heads on Poles	175
Gliglois	180
Carduino	183
The Stay with the Enchantress	197
Disenchantment by Means of a Kiss	199
Wigalois	208
The French Prose Redaction	239
Wolfram's *Parzival*	240
References to LD in Later English Literature	241
Appendix. Proper Names in *Le Bel Inconnu*	243

STUDIES ON THE LIBEAUS DESCONUS.

IN the following investigation[1] attention will be directed mainly to the following four poems: the Middle English *Libeaus Desconus*, the old French *Guinglain* or *Le Bel Inconnu*, the Italian *Carduino*, and the Middle High German *Wigalois*.[2]

The English poem contains some 2232 lines in tail-rhyme strophe. It is in the dialect of the south of England, probably that of Kent or some neighboring district, and was probably written about 1350. The author may be said to be entirely unknown to us, although Sarrazin[3] and Kaluza[4] hold, on insufficient evidence, that the poem was written in whole or in part by Thomas Chestre, the author of the *Launfal*. It has been four times edited, by Ritson in 1802,[5] by Hippeau in 1860,[6] by Hales and Furnivall in 1868,[7] and by Kaluza from six MSS. in 1890. It is to Kaluza's excellent critical edition that I shall always refer in this investigation.

---

[1] This study, in a form somewhat more extended, was presented on April 30th, 1895, to the Faculty of Arts and Sciences of Harvard University for the acquisition of the degree of Doctor of Philosophy. I take this opportunity of expressing my gratitude to Professors Child and Sheldon for their counsel and encouragement in its preparation. I am, however, especially indebted to Professor Kittredge, whose constant help has been invaluable. He and Professor Sheldon have had the great kindness to read the entire work in proof.

[2] The following contractions are regularly used in this paper: LD for the Middle English *Libeaus Desconus* (or its hero); BI for the Old French *Bel Inconnu* (or its hero); Car. for *Carduino;* Wig. for *Wigalois.*

[3] Sarrazin, *Octavian*, Heilbronn, 1885, *Introd.*, pp. xxv ff.

[4] *Altengl. Bibliothek*, Vol. V, *Introd.*, p. clxiii. For all matters pertaining to the MSS., metre, grammar and the like, see the introduction to this edition. On the question as to Chestre's authorship of LD, see Mennung, *Der Bel Inconnu*, pp. 32-3; Breul, *Engl. Studien*, IX, 459-466; Hausknecht, *Litblatt.*, 1886, col. 138; etc.

[5] *Ancient Engl. Met. Romanceës*, London, 1802, II, 1-90; ed. Goldsmid, Edinb., 1885, II, 35-98.

[6] At the end of his edition of *Le Bel Inconnu*, Paris, 1860, pp. 241-330.

[7] *Percy's Folio MS.*, London, 1868, II, 415-499; cf. *Introd.*, pp. 404-415.

Le Bel Inconnu is preserved in a unique manuscript belonging to the library of the Duc d'Aumale. The poet in concluding gives his name as Renals de Biauju, or, as usually written, Renaud de Beaujeu. He is only known to us otherwise as the author of a song, one stanza of which is preserved in *Le Roman de la Rose ou de Guillaume de Dole*.[1] As Gaston Paris says,[2] this citation shows, however, that he was a knight and that his song was well known before the year 1200. The romance also was probably written in the closing years of the twelfth century. Mennung puts it at about the year 1190.[3] The song, says Paris, "en l'appelant le bon chevalier, confirme bien la conclusion à laquelle amène la lecture de son poème, œuvre d'un homme du monde plutôt que d'un trouveur de profession." *Le Bel Inconnu* has been but once edited, and that in an entirely unsatisfactory manner, by Hippeau in 1860. A new edition has been long promised by Professor Wendelin Foerster.[4]

The Italian *Carduino* is a short poem containing only two *cantari* of thirty-five and seventy-two stanzas respectively in *ottava rima*. As Professors d'Ancona and Rajna believe, it was in all probability written by Antonio Pucci about 1375. It was well edited by Rajna in 1873.[5]

Wigalois was, according to the author's statement, the first work of Wirnt von Gravenberg, and was probably written in Bavaria about 1210. In one form or another it has ever since enjoyed a remarkable popularity. It has been twice edited, by Benecke[6] in 1819 and by Pfeiffer[7] in 1847. The poem contains 11,708 lines.

---

[1] *Soc. des Anciens Textes Français*, ed. Servois, Paris, 1893 (so dated, but in reality 1894). vv. 1454 ff.; cf. Bartsch, *Jahrb. f. rom. u. eng. Lit.*, XI, 161-2; *Hist. Litt.*, XXX, 184.

[2] In the introduction to Servois's edition, pp. cviii ff. Even without external evidence one would at once suspect the song to be written by Renaud. The same ideas are expressed in the same language in the two poems. With the song cf., for example, Bl, 4094, 4457 ff., 4931, 4131, 4734-5.

[3] Mennung, *Der Bel Inconnu*, Halle a. S., 1890, p. 15.

[4] Cf. *Zt. f. rom. Phil.*, II, 78.

[5] *I Cantari di Carduino*, in *Poemetti Cavallereschi*, Bologna, 1873, 1-44; cf. *Introd.*, pp. v-xl.   [6] *Wigalois*, Berlin, 1819.

[7] *Dichtungen des deutschen Mittelalters*, Vol. VI, Leipzig, 1847; see *Introd.*, pp. xiv ff. On Wirnt's indebtedness to his predecessors see Meisner in *Germania*, XX, 421 ff.; cf. Bethge, *Wirnt von Gravenberg*, Berlin, 1881.

Studies on the Libeaus Descouus. 3

The chief matter of dispute as to this cycle of poems concerns the relations between LD and BI. There are two opposite opinions in the matter — that of Gaston Paris, who holds that BI is not the original of LD,[1] and that of Kaluza,[2] who holds that LD is directly derived from BI. The view of Paris was supported by the dissertation of A. Mennung[3] (1890). Kaluza, however, in his review of Mennung,[4] declared himself unshaken in his own opinion. Bülbring[5] and Schröer[6] regard Kaluza's reply to Mennung as entirely adequate; but Paris, in his review of Kaluza and Mennung,[7] maintains his original view. Suchier (1891)[8] declined to take sides, and suggested that the whole question should be subjected to a more rigid examination. This is attempted in the present study. The results, it is believed, may serve to establish the view of Paris and to throw new light on the relations of all the poems in the cycle. It is hoped also that some contributions are made toward the solution of other problems in mediæval literary history.

---

[1] *Romania*, XV, 1-24 (1886), and *Hist. Litt.*, XXX, 171-199. This view was first expressed by Kölbing in *Englische Studien*, I, 121-169; cf. his review (*Engl. Stud.*, IV, 182) of Mebes, *Ueber den Wigalois*, 1879; but Paris was the first to use the Italian poem and so arrive at a complete and consistent theory. Cf. also Stengel in *Zt. f. rom. Phil.*, I, 486, and Rhode in *Engl. Stud.*, VII, 152.

[2] In his edition of the Middle English poem, Leipzig, 1890, cxxxi ff.

[3] *Der Bel Inconnu des Renaut de Beaujeu in seinem Verhältnis zum Lybeaus Disconus, Carduino und Wigalois*, Halle, 1890.

[4] *Litbl. f. germ. u. rom. Phil.*, 1891, coll. 84 ff. The works of Mennung and Kaluza appeared contemporaneously.

[5] *Engl. Stud.*, XVII, 119 f. Cf. also the review of Mennung in *Giorn. Stor.*, XVIII, 396.

[6] Koch's *Zt. f. vergl. Litteraturgesch.*, N. F., V, 412.

[7] *Rom.*, XX, 297-302.

[8] *Lit. Centralbl.*, 1891, pp. 762-3. Furnivall, *Percy's Folio MS.*, II, 407, says: "De Biauju's text *may* have given rise to some lost *later* version which the English adapters handled; but I see no reason why the early French text which M. Hippeau has printed may not have been before our early men." Ward, *Cat. of Romances*, I, 400, speaks of LD as "an abridged translation of the French metrical romance" of Renaud. Pollard in *English Miracle Plays*, Oxford, 1890, p. 216, Brandl in Paul's *Grundriss*, 1892, II, i, 6, and Skeat in his recent edition of Chaucer, Oxford, 1894, V, 199, all accept Kaluza's view.

It is necessary to begin our investigation with a somewhat minute analysis of the incidents in the four poems of the cycle, LD, BI, Car., and Wig.[1]

COMPARISON OF THE FOUR POEMS.

I. INTRODUCTION.

(LD, vv. 1-42; BI, vv. 1-70; Car., i, sts. 1-29.)

1. LD opens with an invocation to Christ and Mary for aid in writing the book. The poet is to tell of *Gingelein*, who was begotten of Sir Gawein "be a forest side." His mother "all for doute of wikked loos" brought him up alone in the forest

> þat he scholde se no kniȝt
> Y-armed in no manere. (17-18.)

He is so fair that she calls him only *Beaufis*. One day he goes hunting in the woods and finds a knight lying dead. He clothes himself in the slain knight's armor and goes to *Glastinbery*, "þer ley þe King Arthour." (42.)

The author of BI begins his poem with an explanation of his reasons for writing the book: he loves a lady "outre mesure," and it is for her sake that he undertakes the work: " mostrer veul que faire sai " (10). Then follows a sixty-line description of the crowning of King Arthur at Charlion, "qui siet sor mer," in the presence of a large and distinguished assembly, and of the coronation feast. A list of kings and others present is given.

> Tant en i ot, ne puis conter,
> Ne les Dames ne puis nommer. (55-6.)
> Mainte i en ot de mainte guise,
> Si com la letre le devise. (69-70.)

They are all seated at table when a young knight approaches,

---

[1] This analysis covers ground already traversed by Kölbing, Paris, Kaluza, and especially Mennung, but it has of course been made from the originals, and in arrangement has been adapted to the special requirements of this paper. In some particulars it will be seen to correct or supplement the work of these scholars.

nothing of whose history has as yet been told us. Indeed, the story of the boy's youth is entirely omitted in this version.

In *Carduino* there is first an introduction telling of the three wise men of the East and their significance, and closing with a prayer for aid in telling the story. There lived with Arthur at Camelot a very noble baron, whom the king especially loved. But certain barons, prompted by jealousy, contrived to murder him secretly. His wife, fearing lest her young son, Carduino, may also be killed, flees to the woods, taking her jewels and treasures with her, and there she lives for more than seven years, none at court knowing her whereabouts. The boy, constantly with the animals in the forest, is brought to believe that no other creatures exist. When he is ten years old, he asks his mother who his father is. She replies "God," and tells him that there are no other human beings besides themselves in the world. One day he finds two spears which have been left in the wood by some hunters. "O padre Iddio, che cosa è questa?" he exclaims, and rushes off to his mother to find out what they are. She tells him God has sent them, and teaches him how they are to be used. Afterwards he takes them with him wherever he goes, and roams about the forest, hunting wild beasts for food and clothing. Attired in skins and "grand e grosso e fiero nel visagio," he appears like a regular forest dweller and is twelve years old before he sees another man. One day the king is hunting in the forest. Car., hearing the strange noise, issues without fear from his lodging with his two spears, and is seen by the hunters, who, with a cry, "Eco un uon selvagio," pursue him; but he escapes by hard running. His mother receives him in her arms and inquires anxiously what is the matter.

> Ed e' rispuose: 'Dolcie madre mia,
> O madre, tummi gabi e tummi incaccia.
> Tu di' c'al mondo nonn' à più giente
> Se non no' due e Cristo 'nipotente.' (19, 8.)

He no longer wishes to dwell in the forest, and so his mother collects her treasures, and they start off together. Soon they come to a great city, where the mother procures for Car. all the equipment necessary for a warrior, and he gives up his covering of skins. In the city he soon gathers about him a group of companions, who,

seeing his valor, urge him to go to Arthur's court, where he is sure
to win honor. He is eager to go to "serve" the king, and his
mother falls in with his request. She tells him that his father's name
was *Dondinelo*, and that he has been murdered by *Mordarette* and
his brothers:

      E se sugietto sarai elleale
      Vendicherai tuo padre naturale. (27, 7-8.)

[Here there is a lacuna of 8 stanzas, in which it was probably told
that the mother advises him to conceal his real name because of his
enemies, and that she herself is of lowly origin. He goes to Arthur
and asks to be made a knight.]

In *Wig.* the introduction is very different from that in the other
versions (see below, pp. 235 ff.).

II. AT THE COURT.

(LD, 43-285; BI, 71-316; Car., i, 30-35, ii, 1-8; Wig., 44, 20-53, 23.)

1. When LD comes to the court, he kneels, greets the knights with
honor, and asks the king if he may " speke a word." He says he is
a child "uncouthe," come from the South, and wishes to be made a
knight. Arthur at once asks his name, and the boy replies that his
mother "in her game" called him *Beaufis*. The king declares he
shall be called *Libeaus Desconus*, " þe faire unknowe"; then he
makes him a knight and gives him armor. He is given over to
Gawein for instruction in knightly ways. LD now makes a request
that he be allowed to undertake the first fight that any one asks of
the king. The latter agrees, although he thinks the boy too young
for any great encounter. They all wash and go to meat.

In BI the knights are all at table, when an unknown warrior rides
into the hall. All salute him. The king bids him dismount; but he
will not do so until he is given a promise that he shall be granted the
first request he shall make. Attendants hasten to remove his arms,
and soon he is clothed in a handsome mantle which Gauvain gives
him. The king remarks on his excellent bearing:

      Tot cil qui l'voient redisoient
      Que si biel homme ne savoient. (99-100.)

He sits down at the table beside Gauvain.

In Car. the king, hearing the boy's words, quickly takes him by the hand and asks him who his father and mother are and what his nationality is. Car. replies that he does not know anything of his father, but that his mother is "d'una vil giente." His wish is to serve the king faithfully. Arthur gives orders for him to be honored. The table is made ready, and all sit down to their meal. The barons marvel at seeing Car.

> tanto grosso e smisurato,
> E l' uno insieme col' altro bisbiglia;
> Per più di sei baroni avie mangiato. (33, 2-4.)

When Wigalois comes to the court, he is given a hearty welcome. The king at once inquires who he is, and he replies that he does not know who his father is (although, like Car., he really does know), but that he wishes to be made a knight. Arthur, delighted by his humble bearing (cf. BI) and courage, makes him a knight and gives him over to Gawein's charge. He is given a sword, shield, shaft, and rich apparel, and later they sit down to a great feast. (In all this Wig. agrees with LD or Car. and is unlike BI.) Wig. also makes a special request, but not until after the messenger has come to court. Arthur grants it before he knows what it is.

2. But soon a beautiful maid, accompanied by a dwarf, rides up to seek help from Arthur for her mistress, who is in distress. This incident is in all four poems. In Wig., however, the feast is not that which was held when the young man first came to court. The lady and the dwarf appeared

> ze den næhsten sunwenden,
> dô der künec ze tische saz. (48, 13-14.)

3. In LD her name is at once given as *Elene*. In BI it is not mentioned until she has been described at length and her mission made known (57 lines). It is then given as *Hélie*. No name is given her in Car. or Wig.

4. Elene is clothed in *tars*, " pelured wiþ blaunner." She is more beautiful than countess or queen, and rides on a milk-white steed. The English poet also adds the graphic detail that she is " all beswette for hete."

Hélie is clothed in samite, and on her head is a "cercle d'or."

Her complexion is as the rose, her eyes are *vairs*, her mouth is laughing, her hands are white, her body is *avenant*, her hair is blond, etc. She rides a palfrey covered with cloth of silk, the *orile* of fine gold, inlaid with precious stones.

In Car. she is *vermiglia, dilicata*, and *piaciente*. She is a sister (!) of the enchanted princess, who is called *Beatricie* " dal viso rosato." (ii, 5, 6.)

In Wig. she rides a white horse. There is no description of her, but only of her dress. (Cf. 48, 40.)

5. The dwarf in LD is clothed in *inde*, "stout and pert," with open surcoat, a beard yellow as wax, his hair hanging to his girdle. His shoes are adorned with gold, and he is "coped as a kniȝt: þat seemed no poverte." He is far famed for his accomplishments.

> Miche he couþe of game:
> Citole. sautrie in same.
> Harpe. fiþele and crouþe.
> He was a noble disour
> Wiþ ladies in her bour,
> A mery man of mouþe. (148 ff.)

In BI he is "cortois et bien apris: Gent ot le cors et biel le vis." His only defect is that he is small. He wears a robe " de *vair* et d'eskerlate," which fits him well.

In Car. he is called " il nano sagio."

In Wig. he rides on a horse behind his lady with both hands on her shoulders. He sings a song so beautifully that all the listeners forget themselves.

6. In LD the name of the dwarf—*Teodelain*—is at once told. In BI it is *Tidogolain*, but is not given until he and Hélie leave the court. He has no name in Car. and Wig.

7. In LD he suggests to Elene, when she reaches the court, that it is time to tell her errand. Afterward he declares that LD will not be worth a farthing to them in the battles he will have to endure, and adds:

> At þe point perilous
> Be þe chapell auntrous,
> Schall be his beginning. (202 ff.)

In BI he says nothing while at court.

In Car., when Arthur selects Car., the dwarf begs the king to send another. Such a wild-looking man will not answer the purpose. He cannot endure what will be before him if he goes.

In Wig. he only sings the song.

8. Elene pleads for the lady of Sinadoun (!), who is in prison; and asks for a knight

> Wiþ herte good and liȝt,
> To winne her wiþ honour.   (167–8.)

LD's duties, except in a very general way, are unknown to him until long after.

Hélie bears greetings from the daughter of King Gringars, and prays that succor may be sent her, for she is in great distress. She asks for one of Arthur's knights, "trestot li millor que tu as" (183), and urges him for God's sake to make haste. The knight, if he succeeds, will win great honor; but he will have to accomplish the *fier baiser*.

In Car. the messenger tells the whole state of affairs, — how the city has been enchanted because its mistress will not marry the enchanter, and how all the inhabitants have been turned into wild beasts. She begs for a warrior "il quale sia valoroso e saciente," to rid the desolate regions of their tormentor, whose evil deeds Arthur must have heard of, for the city is his.

In Wig. there is no mention of any definite undertaking. The messenger says her lady is in distress and needs help. It will be a very bitter fight, — even to the death. It requires the most valiant knight to perform it.

9. In LD the words are hardly out of Elene's mouth before LD has claimed the privilege of doing this deed, and Arthur must needs stick to his promise.

In BI Arthur looks about and waits for some one to offer himself; but instead each one dreads lest he be forced to go.

In Car. all the barons at once offer their services, but Arthur turns to Car. and says he wishes him to go.

Wig. rises immediately and offers himself. The rest of the knights marvel at his request. (Cf. 50, 3 ff.)

10. In LD Arthur at once acknowledges the boy's claim and gives him encouragement.

Arthur tries hard to dissuade BI from going, and offers him a seat at the Round Table.

In Wig. Arthur grants the youth's request and exhorts him to uphold his honor; yet he is sorry to see him undertake such a perilous adventure. He will enrich him if he stays at home.

For Arthur's conduct in Car., see 9.

11. Elene declares that Arthur's fame is lost since he sends a child, "þat is witles and wilde: to dele douȝty dent," when he has such knights as Perceval and Gawein.

Hélie says that she has sought the best, but is given the worst, — one who is of no use to her. She needs a knight who in chivalry is "esprovés et de millor los." (235.)

In Car. she says nothing more.

In Wig. also she is so angry "daz si ze niemen niht ensprach." (50, 30.)

12. In LD Arthur says they shall have no other; if they are not satisfied with LD, let them seek elsewhere.

In BI, however, the king says he cannot help himself: he would if he could.

In Car. the king receives the dwarf's protest with:

> To' quel ch' io ti dono;
> Questi sarà barone ardito e buono.   (ii, 7, 7–8.)

13. During the dispute LD swears that he is not afraid of any man, and that he will never forsake the fight, "as hit is Arthours lawe."

> He þat fleþ for drede,
> I wolde, by way or strete
> His body wer to-drawe.   (211 ff.)

This point is not found in any other version.

14. At Arthur's command four of the best knights, Gawein, Perceval, Iwein, and Agrafain, arm LD with a *gipell* of silk, a bright hauberk, etc. Gawein puts about his neck "a scheld wiþ a griffoun" and a rich steel helmet; Perceval puts on his *croun;* Launcelet bears him a spear and a "fell fauchoun"; Iwein brings him a splendid steed "egre as lioun."

This scene is not described in any of the other poems; yet it is one of the three places where the English poet refers to a French source. ("So seiþ þe frensche tale," 246.) The only one mentioned in BI as assisting the boy to arm is Gawein, who has been sitting beside him.

In Wig. there is a long description of the arming of the young knight. He puts on a coal-black shield with a red gold *rad* raised in the centre (whence his name, *der Ritter mit dem Rade*) and armor which Queen Guinovere has sent him. Gawein aids him, binds on his helmet, attaches a rich banner to his spear, etc.

15. Elene and the dwarf put up with what is offered them, but will eat nothing "for wreþþe and hete" (223), and sit down discontented until dinner is over.

Hélie and the dwarf go away in anger and will have nothing to do with BI.

Car. and the dwarf depart together. The lady follows them.

In Wig. the messenger rides off angry.

16. LD, as soon as he is ready to start, rides to the king and asks his blessing, which Arthur "as corteis kinge and hende" gives with upraised hand.

In BI it is simply said that the boy takes leave of the king.

There is no mention of leave-taking in Car.

Wig., when armed, goes before the king.

> dem milten künege neig er sâ
> und der messenie gar.
> 'herr got, nu bewar
> dem riter sînen schœnen lîp!'
> sprach dâ man unde wîp.
> si wunschten im alle heiles nâch. (51, 15 ff.)

When he takes leave of Gawein,

> vil grôzer jâmer âne spot
> wart zwischen in beiden,
> dô si sich muosen scheiden. (52, 14 ff.)

17. BI is given a squire *Robert*, who plays a very important part in the narrative. There is no hint of this character in LD, Car., or Wig.

18. In LD all three start off together; and, though it is said that Elene chides LD for three days, there is no suggestion of her refusal to accept his services.

Helie and the dwarf having departed, BI and Robert start off, spurring their steeds through a little valley until they overtake the others. Hélie turns round and asks BI where he is going. He says he wishes to accompany her and begs her to cease her railing and have mercy on him. She declares he shall not go with her permission and urges him to return. Under no circumstances will he go back. The dwarf pleads for him, saying no one should be blamed until his cowardice has been proved, and God may be his support. All efforts at dissuasion proving of no avail, they go on together.

When the dwarf in the German poem sees Wig. coming, he tells the maid, and says they ought to have waited for him: he looks like a valiant knight. But his companion says she knows nothing of him, she wanted the famous Gawein of whose valor she has heard so much. While they are speaking, Wig. appears, with his helmet in his hand, and begs permission to join them. At first she refuses, but afterwards assents, and they seem to go on together happily enough. (Cf. 53, 17 ff.)

III. THE ADVENTURE AT THE FORD.

(LD, 286-468; BI, 317-586; Car., ii, 20-25; Wig., 53, 24-55, 29.)

1. The first adventure takes place at a point or pass called *Perilous* (in BI, *Gué Périlleus*) which in LD is "be þe chapell auntrous" (303). It is kept by a knight "þat wiþ ech man will fiȝt" (287) and who is renowned for his valor. In LD he is called *William Salebraunche;* in BI, *Blioblićris* (although the name of one of the three avengers is *Willaume Salebrant*).

2. In BI the dwelling of Blioblićris is described. When he sees them coming, he gives orders to his valets, and the scene is described in which they make ready for him. This is not found elsewhere.

3. In the description of the knight (which is given in LD by Elene, in BI by the author) in LD the most prominent thing is his green shield with three lions of bright gold. In BI his boots of iron, bound with *cordićles*, the "cote de soie d'outremer" over his hauberk, and the horse "covert de ses armes" are especially noticeable.

4. Elene chides LD for not being stronger, but does not try to keep him from going on; while Hélie urges BI not to cross the river, else he will lose his life. LD is always confident of victory.

It never occurs to him to turn back. BI refuses to return because it would seem cowardly.

5. But in LD

> Whan he hadde of hem siȝt,
> To hem he rod full riȝt
>   And seide: 'Welcome, beaufrere!
> Who so rit her day oþer niȝt,
> Wiþ me he mot fiȝt
>   Oþer leave his armes her.'
> Quoþ Libeaus Desconus:
> 'For love of swete Jhesus,
>   Nou lete us passe skere!
> We haveþ forþ to wende
> And beþ fer from our frende,
>   I and þis meide in fere.' (st. 27.)

But BI knows what he is to expect if he crosses the stream. He is nevertheless defiant,

> 'S'il veut joster nos josterons,
> Et s'il désire la bataille
> Jà le porra avoir, sans faille!' (382 ff.)

He calls Robert to help him make ready, mounts his steed, takes his shield and lance, and passes over. He is quickly stopped by the knight, who tells him he shall pay dear for his folly. BI, however, begs to be allowed to pass; he has been sent by King Arthur to succor a lady, he says, and his companion is the messenger who brought news of her distress. But the knight replies:

> 'Avant n'irés-vos, sans bataille;
> Del gué passer est tels l'usage;
> Ensi l'a tenu mes lignages
> Et je certes plus de VII ans
> Maintes gens i ai ans dolens,
> Et maint bon chevalier de pris
> I ai abatu et ocis.' (414 ff.)

6. In the ensuing fight LD, after knocking William over his horse's *croupe*, alights, at William's request, and fights on foot. He shaves his opponent's beard, and the latter, in his effort to return the stroke, breaks his sword in two. He pleads that it would be "greet vilanie" to kill a weaponless man, and LD spares him.

When Bliobliéris is struck from his steed, he gets on an equality with Bl by killing the latter's horse. He is forced to succumb by a blow on the helmet which brings him to his knees, and he is too weak to resist longer.

7. In both poems the knight is forced to promise to go to Arthur. In LD he is to tell that he has been sent by one

> Þat is y-cleped in us,
> Libeaus Desconus,
> Unknowe of keþ and kende. (403 ff.)

Bl does not tell him his name, although Bliobliéris later tells it to others.

8. Bl has here a scene not in LD. The dwarf calls the attention of Hélie to Bl's bravery; but she replies:

> 'Ocis serra: s'ert grans damages;
> Que moult est buens li siens corages.' (497-8.)

Of course Bl refuses to return. Hélie then says they must hurry on, for night approaches. Further, Robert catches the wounded knight's horse and leads it to Bl, who mounts, takes his shield and lance, and they continue their journey.

9. In LD William at once sets out for Arthur's court. By chance he meets three knights "proud in palle." They are his sister's sons. He explains what has happened and where he is going, and they (not he) at once suggest revenge and start off without delay to take it.

In Bl it is told how the valets carry the wounded Bliobliéris to his lodging, take off his armor, and put him to bed; how he expectantly awaits his companions (!), who are "Elins li blans Sires de Graies, li bons chevaliers des Aies," and Willaume de Salebrant. They are to return that night. When they finally appear, he exhorts them to revenge him, and hopes they will bring Bl back and free him from prison. He does not mention Arthur.

10. After this encounter LD and Elene ride on "pas be pas" until it grows dark. They rest together.

> Mercy sche gan him crie,
> Þat sche spak vilanie;
> He forȝaf her þat trespas. (475 ff.)

The dwarf serves them in all things they need. In the morning they encounter the three nephews of William, who are in pursuit.

In BI, for some unhappy reason, Renaud has separated these two adventures. He makes the fight with the giants take place during this night.

11. The adventure in Car. which comes nearest to the one just described, follows the visit to the castle of the enchantress.[1] While Car., the dwarf, and the messenger are riding along, Car. sees a knight coming towards them. This turns out to be Agueriesse, one of the murderers of the boy's father. Seeing the beauty of Car.'s companion, Agueriesse at once demands that she be given over to him: otherwise Car. shall lose his head. Car. says nothing, but immediately takes his spear and strikes him in the breast with it. When the knight falls dead from his horse, the dwarf exclaims: "What have you done? This is the nephew of King Arthur, the man who slew Dondinello." [It is indeed strange that the dwarf should know this.] Car. rejoices in his heart that he has to some extent avenged his father's death, and goes on happier than before.

12. In Wig. this adventure has been influenced by the introduction of one of the features of the fight with the steward (which comes later in the poem, see p. 46, below); viz., the information given Wig. by his companion that if he asks lodging at a castle near by he will first be forced to joust with the lord. If he wins, he will be well received; if not, he will suffer indignity. On the introduction of this feature here, see pp. 226 ff. As evening comes on, the maid asks Wig. where they shall spend the night. He replies: "Where you will." She then tells him the custom of the place. If the knight is defeated, he must depart disgraced without his belongings. It would therefore be better to get rest elsewhere. This speech displeases Wig., who replies that he will meet the test (54, 14 ff.). But the house of the lord is so near that he sees Wig. riding up armed. He does not wait for Wig. to ask for lodging, but orders his arms, mounts his steed, and starts off at once. His attendants follow him past the city ditches. Wig. sees him coming and binds on his helmet. They run at each other. Each protects himself well, but Wig. finally kills his antagonist (55, 13–14). The messenger says it is not safe to

---

[1] It is the visit to the castle of the enchantress which is misplaced.

stay there, and they hasten on, leaving the lord's followers in bitter grief.

IV. THE FIGHT WITH THE THREE AVENGERS.

(LD, 469-588; BI, 947-1259.)

1. There is nothing corresponding to this adventure in Car. or Wig. In BI it follows the rescue of the maiden from the giants.

2. The account differs greatly in LD and BI; indeed, in many cases it is exactly opposite in the two poems, e.g., in LD the hero and his companions meet their foes as they are riding along (484), and it is expressly stated that it is day (481); while in BI it is night and the moon is shining. "Que de cler jor rien n'i avoit" (1028). BI is lying asleep on the grass beside the two maidens when Robert sees the three knights coming and flies to awake his master.

3. The three at once cry out to LD:

> 'Þef, turne aȝain and fiȝt,
> Or leve her by renoun!' (491-2.)

He at once replies that he is ready to ride against them all together, and spurs on his steed (497).

In BI, however, after BI is aroused, there is a little discussion between all in the party, during which Robert keeps urging haste in getting ready. The assailants are robbers and appear "lès le roce de valcolor." They express their joy at finding him whom they were seeking. Hélie reminds them that it is not chivalrous to fight with an unarmed man. Willaume Salebrant speaks in favor of letting him arm, and the others agree. BI puts on his hauberk and laces his helmet; then Hélie girds on his sword. She encourages him, reminds him of his duty to her lady, and hands him his shield after he is mounted. He puts it on his neck, takes his lance, and calls upon God to preserve him. The young ladies kneel and pray for him.

4. In LD the hero overcomes the first assailant, and then the other two attack him at once so that he exclaims: "Allas!"

> 'Oon aȝeines two
> To fiȝte, þat is nouȝt good.' (547-8.)

But in BI they come one at a time (William first); for, as the author says, in those times, when a man fought he had only to care for the one with whom he was engaged. The poet laments in twelve lines the evil customs of his own day, since "Tos est mués en autre guise" (1065).

5. In LD it is *Sir Gower* with whom the hero first fights. LD breaks Gower's thigh and makes him lame forever. He leaves him on the ground groaning with pain. BI pierces William's body, and he falls dead from his horse.

6. Of the second brother the author says:

> He [LD] þrew him in þat place,
> And in þat ilke space
> His *left* arm brast a two.   (556 ff.)

In BI the second knight is unhorsed with such violence that his *right* arm is broken (1116).

7. In LD, when the second brother is wounded the youngest yields at once.

In BI the fight with the last knight is the fiercest, for he is maddened by the fate of his companions. After the first meeting they are both unhorsed; then they fight with their swords, batter each other's helmets, and at dawn are still in conflict. At last BI deprives his foe of his helmet and makes him prisoner.

8. In LD all three are obliged to plight their troth to go to Arthur, yield up "tour and toun," and dwell in his *bandoun* ever without end.

In BI only the last knight is required (on pain of losing his head) to go to the king. One of his companions is dead, and the other so sorely wounded that he must be carried away.

9. When LD fells the eldest brother, the dwarf takes the latter's steed by the rein, leaps into the saddle, and rides quickly to the place where the maid is sitting. She laughs and says:

> 'þis ʒinge kniʒt
> Is chose for champioun.'   (515-6.)

(With this cf. III, 8, p. 14.)

10. LD rides on without any inquiry as to who his opponents are.

BI questions the Sire des Aies, and finds out the names and the purpose of the assailants.

11. BI begs the Sire des Aies to take back Clarie (whom he had

rescued from the giants) to her parents, and the maid departs rejoicing.

This struggle has yet to take place in LD and, as will be seen, Libeaus takes the maiden home himself and she is offered him to wife.

12. The author of BI here inserts (1225 ff.) 35 lines in a digression in which he tells of his own loved one:

> Cil qui se font sage d'amor,
> Cil en sont faus et traïtor.
> Por ço, mius veul faire folie
> Que ne soie loiaus m'amie.
> Ço qu'ele n'est l'ai apelée.
> Que dirai dont? La mult amée.
> S'ensi l'apel. voir en dirai:
> S'amie di, lors mentirai;
> Car moi ne fait ele sanblant,
> Las! por li muir, et por li cant:
> Tos jors serai en sa merci! (1250 ff.)

Never under any circumstances does the personality of the English author appear.

13. In LD they ride on in a wild forest toward Sinadoun. They wish to rest, and

> In Þe grene greves
> Þey di3te a logge of leves
> Wiþ swordes bri3t and broune:
> Þer inne þey dwelde all ni3t. (595 ff.)

In BI they decide to stop in a grassy meadow. Robert performs his duties well. BI and Hélie go to sleep beside each other. The moon is shining, and the nightingales sing above them.

In Car. the young knight and the dwarf, when they come to the wood in the evening, make ready a rich pavilion for the lady in a flower-covered meadow (cf. Wig., p. 19, below).

V. THE ADVENTURE WITH THE GIANTS.

(LD, 589–750; BI, 587–946; Car., ii, 26–39; Wig., 55, 30–60, 20.)

1. This adventure is found in all four versions, in forms closely resembling one another. LD seems to vary most from the original.

In the English poem the dwarf is ever waking up, in fear that the horses may be stolen. His attention is attracted by the sight of a great fire and the smell of roasting. He wakes LD.

BI himself is aroused by the cries of a woman in distress who is calling upon God for help.

In Car. they are all engaged in eating their supper beside a fire they have lighted to warm themselves by, when they hear a voice crying to the Virgin for help.

2. LD does not wait. In a moment, without a word to any one, he is mounted and off to see what is the matter.

BI first assures himself from Hélie, who has been aroused by the noise, that it is not a dream. She brings forward good practical reasons why he should go to sleep again, and not trouble himself about the matter; but BI is a true knight, and will not be dissuaded by reasons of policy, for he cannot resist the cries of a woman calling for aid. He calls to Robert to get his horse, crosses himself, and as soon as the whole company can be got in motion, starts off, with Robert as a guide, in the direction whence the cries come.

Car. asks the dwarf what voice it is he hears. The dwarf replies: "For God's sake do not speak. Let us put out the fire. Keep silence. Alas! we cannot escape. If you should be heard by the giants, all the gold in the world could not save us." Again the voice cries:

'Vergin madre di Dio, ora m' aita
Mandami l' angiel tuo chi mi difenda.' (30, 1–2.)

Hearing this, Car. cannot hold back. He tells the dwarf that though his life be at stake he must defend her who is calling thus. He takes his spear without delay and runs (!) into the wood.

Wig. and his companions stop in a grassy field where the nightingales "singen vaste gegen der naht" (53, 34). In a forest near by, Wig. and the dwarf prepare a lodge for the maiden, the dwarf breaking off green boughs and placing them on the grass. After they have gone to bed they hear a voice crying bitterly in the forest by a lake:

wê! wê! als daz dâ fürhtet den tôt. (56, 20–1.)

Wig. asks his companion if she hears it.

frouwe, ist ez iuwer rât,
sô wil ich rîten dar
daz ich uns rehte ervar
waz ez sî daz dâ klaget. (56, 24 ff.)

She answers: "nu tuot als ir welt" (cf. BI), and Wig. rides off alone. The night is half gone and the moon is shining "gegen dem tage." Wig. rides about a mile "durch dorne und durch gedrenge" (56, 38), until at last he sees two great giants sitting by a fire.

3. LD sees two giants "grisly of chere," one "red and loplich," the other "swart as pich." The black one holds a maid in his embrace.

Robert points them out to BI, and they are described as: "lais et hisdels et mescréans" (700).[1] The maiden is weeping bitterly and crying aloud because one of the giants wishes to kiss her.

> Ja nus hom ne demant plus biele.
> Se ele n' eüst tel paor. (702-3.)

Car. sees the giants by the fire, one of whom is holding the maid in his arms. She seems to be about fifteen years old, and is weeping bitterly.

In Wig. the young lady is trying to get away. The giants cannot still her cries. One of them has her pressed to him with both arms. When Wig. sees this, he desires to free her, for such shame should not continue.

4. In LD we read:

> þe rede geaunt sterne
> A wilde boor gan terne
>   Aboute upon a spite.
> þat fier briȝt gan berne. (625 ff.)

In BI:

> De l'autre part le feu, séoit
> L'autre gaians qui rostissoit,
> Et aveuc son pointe faisoit
> Norrir le feu qui relusoit. (711 ff.)

In Car.:

> e vide un gran giugante
> A un gran fuoco, ch' arostia 'na ciervia
> Con tutto il cuoio e tutte le zanpe. (ii, 31, 2 ff.)

There is no parallel passage in Wig.; but the author puts into his hero's thoughts a series of reflections on the pleasures which women give men (57, 33 ff.).

---

[1] Cf. the giants in *Claris et Laris*, ed. Alton, 22489 ff. with BI, 729 ff.

5. LD, Car., and Wig. go alone to the rescue, and their companions take no part in the scene before the fight.

Robert guides BI, Hélie, and the dwarf to the place where they see the giants. BI points out the young woman to Hélie and says he will fight for her. Hélie replies that if he wishes to die, he had better go on. She informs him that these giants have laid waste the land about and killed the inhabitants, and advises him to flee from the devils.

6. LD attacks first the giant holding the maiden, and strikes him

>þorȝ liver, longe and herte,
>þat never he miȝte arise. (647-8.)

BI deals the same giant such a blow that he falls dead into the burning fire.

In Car. the one who is roasting the meat sees the hero first, rises at once, and raises the roast as high as he can to strike him with it; but the latter eludes the blow and strikes the giant with one of his spears so furiously that it passes through his breast and heart, and the giant falls dead to the earth.

Wig. also chooses first the giant by the fire, and strikes him with his spear so that it pierces his heart.

7. In LD we are here told how the maiden at once rushes off, thanking " hevene quene " for her succor. Elene and the dwarf come up, take her by the hand, and lead her to their lodging, where they pray for LD's safety.

8. The red giant then strikes at LD

>wiþ þe bore : As man þat wolde awede.

He kills LD's horse ; but LD leaps from the saddle and fights with his falchion. The giant's " spite brak atwo " (675), and then

>A tre in honde he cauȝt,
>To fiȝte aȝens his fo,
>And wiþ þe ende of þe tre
>He smitte his scheld a þre. (677 ff.)

Before he raises it up again, however, LD cuts off his right arm (684). He falls to the ground, and LD cuts off his head.

In BI the giant uses a club as a weapon. When he is making a violent onslaught on BI, it strikes a tree with such force as to make the tree quaver and the branches fall. The club flies out of his hands, and before he can get it again BI has seized his opportunity and given him a blow on the head by which he is killed.

In Car. the hero draws near the giant who holds the maiden and addresses him:

> 'Falso traditore,
> Non fare alla donzella disinore.' (ii, 34, 8.)

The giant rises, seizes a great brand of oak from the fire, raises it on high, and strikes a fierce blow at Car. The latter avoids it, and in return strikes the giant on the head with his spear so that the iron passes even to the middle of his heart.

In Wig. the second giant (the one who holds the maiden) also seizes a great branch of a tree. Wig. alights, and they begin to fight. The giant is very strong and forces Wig. to flee into a bush by the lake near by. Finally, however, the giant has to give himself up and to beg for life. Wig. grants this on certain conditions. Then follows a digression on the way men kept their oaths in former times.

9. In LD the hero cuts off the heads of both giants and bears them to the maiden he has freed, who thereupon thanks heaven he has been made a knight.

[This is especially important, because this is one of the three places where the author says he is following a French source:

> In frensche as hit is y-founde,
> Him. þat he ȝaf er wounde.
> He served so, apliȝt. (688 ff.)]

The incident is not found in any other version.

10. In BI Robert disarms his master and performs other duties, such as looking after the horses. The dwarf reproves Hélie for her former treatment of BI and induces her to apologize for her *vilonie*. She does so humbly, and BI graciously grants pardon. This does not occur in the other poems in this connection, but cf. LD at p. 14, above.

11. LD inquires the name and family of the rescued maiden, and she tells him her father is "of riche fame," dwelling near by.

> 'An erl, an old, hore kni3t,
> þat haþ be man of mi3t;
> His name is *Sir Antore*.' (703 ff.)

Her own name is *Violette*. The evening before she had been playing in the garden when the two giants sprang out of a cave and brought her to the fire.

In BI the maiden is ignored for a while, and it is only some time after the fight that she reappears, is described again, and expresses her gratitude to BI, promising to be ever his servant. She falls at his feet. He lifts her up and places her beside him on the grass. In reply to his inquiries she tells BI that her name is *Clarie* and that of her brother *Saigremor*. She was taken by *one* of the giants in her father's garden. He was "desous l'entrée," found the door open, and carried her off to the wood where he met his companion.

In Car. she is represented as a young lady of that land, the daughter of a count "di somo valore"; but no names are given. She has been carried off by the *two* giants from her father,

> per farlle villania e disinore. (32, 4.)

No name is given her in Wig.

> si [the giants] heten si gezücket
> dem milten künege Artûs
> ze Karidôl vor sînem hûs.
> des was michel klage dâ. (57, 16 ff.)

12. In LD as soon as Violet has told her adventure they take horse "without more talking," and ride away together (721 ff.).

In BI, on the other hand, Robert and the dwarf discover an abundant supply of provisions in the giants' cave, which had been obtained by ravaging the land round about,—thirty loaves of bread, white cloths, glasses, fowls all ready to eat, plenty of good wine, etc., and both rejoicing announce their good fortune. Soon the cloth is spread, and BI sits down opposite the two young ladies. The excellent way in which Robert, "qui s'entremet de tos mestiers," performs his duties, aided by the dwarf, is dilated upon. When they have eaten at their pleasure, the provisions are put away, and they again set out on their journey. Further details concerning Robert and his care of the horses.

Car. without delay puts the stag on his shoulders, and he and the maiden (who carries his spear) return to the pavilion. The dwarf marvels greatly when he sees them. Then they eat together "Di quella cierbia ch' era grossa e bella" (ii, 38, 4). The dwarf (who is "grazioso e sagio") also inquires in a fitting way who is the father of the maiden. She tells him all, and he does her great honor. Seeing Car.'s bravery, he serves him "piú che inprima di coragio." After a night of uninterrupted rest the party of four start off for the desolate city.

In Wig. the messenger does not, even after this victory, think the hero fit to cope with the enchanter. but Car. begs permission to ride with her that day, and promises never to do anything opposed to her wish. The dwarf speaks in favor of Wig.

13. LD goes with Violet to her home and tells her father what has happened. The earl offers him his daughter to wife, together with fifteen castles on the spot and all his possessions after he is dead; but LD declines: he must first do his duty. The earl, however, gives him rich meed for his valor, — a shield, fine armor, and a noble steed, — and the three take their departure.

As will be remembered, *Clarie* is taken home later by the Sire des Aies.

In Car. nothing more is said of the maiden. They all go directly to the desolate city.

In Wig. the second giant is forced to give his oath to take her back to Karidôl and deliver her over to Arthur and Ginovêre (who, by the way, is not mentioned in the other poems). He at once sets out, complaining "âne mâze" for his dead companion. All at Arthur's court rejoice when they come.

14. LD sends the giants' heads to Arthur "wiþ moche gle and game," and his fame becomes great at court (cf. Wig. above).

VI. THE SPARROW-HAWK ADVENTURE.

(LD, 751-1056; BI, 1483-1850; Wig., 64, 5-87, 21.)

1. *The Induction.* As LD and Elene are riding along they see a castle. LD remarks its beauty, and Elene tells him at once who owns it and how the owner "for love of his lemman" (769) has proclaimed the gift of a gerfalcon to any one who shall produce a fairer than she. If the applicant fails, he must fight with the lord. If he is defeated, his head is cut off and set up on a shaft whence it can be seen all the country round. On each *carnell* one or two heads are already to be seen. LD says he will challenge the knight and propose Elene for the prize of beauty. The dwarf advises him to be wary, for the knight is full of guile. They stay all night where they are. In the morning LD rides with the dwarf to the palace. *Giffroun* (for such is the knight's name), having risen early "to honoure swete Jhesus," sees LD, equipped with the armor Sir Antore had given him, come pricking "as prince in pride." Without more ado he rides to him and calls out with a loud voice to find out whether he is coming for good or ill. LD declares he has a fairer woman in the town than the knight's leman, and he intends to bear off the gerfalcon. The knight gently inquires how they are to settle the matter. LD replies that both women must be set in the midst of the market in *Cardevile* city, adding that if his leman loses he is ready to fight. Giffroun agrees to have the meeting at undern, and they hold up their gloves in compact. LD rides home in haste and bids Elene "buske and make her boun." Again the dwarf tells him his action is folly; but to no avail. Elene arrays herself in a robe of samite "to do Libeaus profite," in "kercheves whit: araide wiþ gold wire" (894), a gray velvet mantle about her neck, and a circlet of precious stones and gold on her head. LD puts her on her good palfrey, and all three ride to the market.

In BI the induction is entirely different. BI and his party issue at evening from a leafy wood and see a magnificent castle before them. Hélie (as usual) calls BI's attention to it. They stop at first to admire, but soon hasten on to reach it. On their way they meet a very beautiful young woman clothed in a splendid silk gown adorned with ermine, etc. No one ever saw a more beautiful woman. She has a broad forehead, face clear and white as the lily, black, arched, well formed eyebrows, a complexion like the rose in summer, shapely mouth, little teeth, fair hair like fine gold, *vairs* eyes, white hands, slender figure. She appears to be in great grief, wringing her hands and tearing her hair. She calls to Bl, who goes at once to her and inquires the cause of her sorrow. She tells how her lover has been killed that day and how she herself is ready to die of sorrow; how the chevalier of the castle owns a very valuable sparrow-hawk (kept in a plain by the monastery on a perch all of gold) which is promised to the most beautiful woman ; how her lover aspired to win it for her, but was killed by the chevalier. Bl offers to obtain the bird for her and avenge her lover's death. She rejoices and invokes God's protection on him. Her name is *Margerie*. She guides him past the bridge to the court.

In Wig. they travel on over mounts and vales until they see a maiden riding alone towards them. (Here a digression of nearly 40 lines ; the author wishes great happiness to women.) She is in great sorrow. She rides a fine horse, whose mane reaches to its knees and is blood-red. Her equipment is of gold and precious stones. She wears a dress of *blialt* and has a cap of red *siglat* in which is a swan-white feather. Her hair, golden and wavy, reaches to the saddle, and she wears a broad hat with peacock feathers. She calls out:

> 'owê mir armen wîbe. wê!
> daz leit daz klage ich iemer mê.' (66, 1–2.)

Wig. obtains his companion's permission to ride to the stranger, yet

> si vorhte sîner kintheit:
> dâ von was ir sîn arbeit
> und sîn rîten mit ir leit. (66, 37 ff.)

The stranger is very beautiful — no one like her in the land. If she is so handsome when in such great trouble, "owê, wem was si gelich : ê si daz leit gewünne " (67, 9–10). Any fool could tell she is of king's kin. It can be seen from her rich clothes that she has never known poverty. Wig. offers her his aid, but she says it will be of no use. About three miles or better from there is one who is called the King of Ireland. He has the most beautiful horse ever seen, and a wonderful parrot kept in a cage of gold, which cost more than 1000 pounds. There are precious stones galore about it. The horse is white as a swan. His left ear and mane are red cinnabar-colored; the right ear is coal-black. A black stripe runs along the back to the long, yellow tail. The horse had been placed in the midst of a crowd of women, to the most beautiful of whom it was to be given. She had been the choice of the knights; but when she went to take the horse, a great red knight drew the horse forcibly away and gave it to his loved one. This saddened the other knights; but none dared fight him, and the maiden rode away. The parrot complained bitterly when the Red Knight took it. The knights were to remain there until morning and then disperse. Wig. offers to fight for her, although the maiden tells him there is no hope of success. A child need not expect to win the bird from such a bold warrior; but finally they all ride on together, and Wig. with many a good story tries to drive away her sadness. Soon they hear the sound of the great tournament. Wig. asks where the Red Knight is, and his companion points out a rich red and blue samite tent. They are received gladly by her cousin, the daughter of the King of Persia, who sits in her pavilion, while an attendant reads to her of the Trojan war and of Æneas and Dido. Wig., suitably attired, takes the maid by the hand, and rides to the tent of the Red Knight, whom he finds lying on a richly covered bed with his *amie*. The parrot, when it sees her, bids her welcome, says it is hers by right, and has been taken away by force. This comforts Wig. The knight asks him what he wants. He demands the return of the horse and tells the knight he will fight with him for it in the morning. The latter laughs: he has never been beaten. He tells Wig. to come after mass and summon all the knights and ladies. He reminds him, however, that he has not full strength.

> der sinne sit ir gar ein kint
> iuwer kraft diu ist ein wint
> wider einen starken man. (78, 9 ff.)

But Wig. trusts in God and rides away with his lady. The news of the coming fight is spread about, and all pray for good luck to Wig. The evening is spent in festivities. In the morning the Queen of Persia and many other women arm him and conduct him to mass.

After many blessings Wig. springs on his horse. The queen gives him his shield, and the maid his spear, and he goes to the encounter with the Red Knight.

2. *The Castle* is simply described in LD as being "stout and stark," " in a park," " rially adijt," " ywalled wiþ ston," " wiþ carneles stiffe and stoute " (757).

In BI it is named *Bel Leu* (1488). It is surrounded by a river full of fish, much used for carrying merchandise and provided with plenty of mills, etc. On one side are vineyards of great extent. The castle is enclosed by deep ditches, surmounted by high walls.

3. *The Attitude of the On-lookers.* In LD the only remark made by observers as they pass is:

> Her comeþ a lady gay
> And semelich on to se.

LD wears the new armor given him by Sir Antore.

In BI they are all in a state of indignation at the chevalier for his treatment of Margerie's lover. When BI and his party come to the castle they are followed by a great crowd, "chevalier, borjois et serjant" (1645). Women and maidens leave their labors and ask about the new aspirant for the sparrow-hawk. Many answer: "We do not know; but look at his battered helmet and shield, and his hauberk *descloé;* he must be a good and tried knight." Then inquiries are made about the maidens, "qui tant sont beles" (1661). Margerie is at once recognized as the one whose lover had been killed the day before. Thus they ride to the place beside the orchard where the bird is kept.

4. *Before the Fight.* LD and Elene wait for the arrival of Giffroun. The gerfalcon is not exposed, but is brought by one of the two squires who accompany the knight. Giffroun is followed by his beautiful leman. The two women are placed on chairs in the *cheping,* and all decide that Elene is not comparable to her rival. Giffroun therefore claims the prize; but LD declares he must fight for it, and the struggle begins.

BI calls aloud to Margerie to take the hawk from its perch, for her beauty merits it. Just then the lord of the castle approaches, goes straight to Margerie, and in a very loud voice tells her not to take the hawk. BI comes up and demands why she should not have it. The lord replies that his own love is more beautiful and he will prove it by fight.

5. *The Knight* is called by Elene at the very beginning *Giffroun*, and the dwarf adds the appellation *le fludus*, by which he is afterwards known. It is said of him:

> He bar þe scheld of goules,
> Of silver þre white oules,
> Of gold was þe bordure.
> Of þe selve colours
> And of non oþer floures
> Was lingell and trappure. (913 ff.)

In BI we learn *after the fight* that the knight's name is *Giflet li fius Do*. He rides "un bel ceval de moult grant pris." His shield is of silver, adorned, like the rest of his equipment, with red roses.

In Wig. he has red hair and a red beard (a digression to discuss their significance). He is called *Hojir* of *Mannesvelt*, and is well known in Spain for his bravery although he is a *Sahse*. (Digression on how to win renown.) All his armor is also red, and on his shield Death is painted in very horrible guise.

6. *The Lady of the Castle* in LD attracts people from far and wide to see her beauty, which is described in all its details to the length of twenty-four lines. She rides "proud in pride," clothed in "purpel pall." No name is given her.

In BI she is called *Rose Espanie*. She rides a short palfrey, and is really not beautiful, though she appears to be so to her lover.

> La laide fait bele sanbler,
> Tant set de guille et d'encanter! (1719-20.)

7. *The Fight.* In LD the two ride at each other and fight with such vigor that

> Har schaftes breke asonder;
> Har dentes ferde as þonder,
> þat comeþ out of þe skie. (979 ff.)

Then follows a unique stanza:

> Þo gan Giffroun to speke:
> 'Bring a schaft, þat nell nouȝt breke,
> A schaft wiþ a cornall!
> Þis ȝinge, ferly frek
> Sit in his sadell steke
> As ston in castell wall.
> I schall do him stoupe
> Over his horses croupe
> And ȝeve him evell fall,
> Þauȝ he wer wiȝt werrour
> As Alisaunder oþer Arthour,
> Launcelot oþer Percevall!' (985 ff.)

LD, however, smites Giffroun with such force that the latter's shield falls from his grasp. All the onlookers laugh and wonder. Again Giffroun attacks him "as man þat wold awede" (1014); but LD casts down both him and his steed, so that the former's back cracks, and men on all sides hear the sound.

In BI the account is quite different. After a fierce struggle, "andui s'abatent des cevals" (1750). Neither being wounded, they jump up quickly and fight with "les brans vienois." Finally BI gives Giflet so severe a blow that he falls " tos estordis" on the spot, and his face strikes on a stone. BI pulls off his helmet. Not being able to get up, Giflet exclaims: "Conquis m'avés, ne l' puis soufrir!" (1778).

In Wig. the Red Knight comes preceded by boys calling "wichâ, herre, wiche" (80, 16). They are used to his winning. Many spears are lost in a short time. Finally a strong one is given Wig., and he turns to the warrior as Gawein had taught him and knocks him off his horse. Wig. dismounts, and they fight on foot. The Red Knight fights with such vigor that Wig. is hard pressed, and all the ladies are in great sorrow for his sake. The maid offers up a prayer for him; hearing which, he fights with renewed energy. The blood flows fast, but finally Wig. is victorious and wins the prizes. Amidst great tumult and rejoicing the Queen of Persia leads him to her tent, and he is followed by knights without number.

8. *The Result.* In LD all agree that the hero has won the ger-

falcon. They bear it to him and go, "lasse and more," with him to the town. Giffroun is borne home on his shield, and we hear no more of him.

When BI has his opponent down, he makes him promise to go to Arthur. When Giflet gets up, they embrace, and Giflet leads BI and the others to the castle, where they are well received and spend the night in pleasure.

Hojir also has to promise to go to Arthur and wait until Wig. comes. He is to say, if any one asks who has sent him, "daz hât der rîter mit dem rade" (82, 39). But Hojir wants to know Wig.'s real name, and learns it. He wishes Wig. success, expresses the hope of seeing him again, and departs for Britain.

9. In the morning BI and his party are about to set out, when BI inquires of Margerie what she desires to do. She replies that she wishes to go home to Scotland to her father, King *Agolans*. Hearing this, BI calls Giflet aside and insists on her having a knight to accompany her. He agrees readily. Hélie now recognizes in her an old friend, presents her with her little dog, and, after a moving scene, bids her farewell. Margerie departs with her hawk and her dog, both of which are very dear to her.

In Wig. it is midday before the fight ends, and as Wig. does not wish to remain until the next day, he and his party take an appropriate farewell. The Queen of Persia wishes him to go with her, but he refuses. Nothing is forgotten which can minister to their comfort. Wig. and the young lady for whom he has fought ride together, after them the other maid and the two dwarfs. When about to separate the lady begs him to go home with her that she may repay him for his noble services. He feels he must go on to Korntîn, but prays that God may protect and bless her. When she sees that her prayers are in vain, she is in much greater sorrow than before. She tells him she does not wish to take the prizes he has won for her : he should give them to his companion. This suggestion he follows.

10. LD, having got possession of the hawk, sends it to Arthur by a knight, *Claudas*, together with a written account of how it was won. Arthur is so delighted that he sends to *Cardevile*

An hundred pound honest
Of florins wiþ þe best. (1045-46.)

Then LD holds a feast, which lasts forty days, "wiþ lordes of renoun" (1050), and at the end of six weeks (!) he and the maid take their departure for Sinadoun.

VII. THE DISPUTE ABOUT THE DOG.

(LD, 1057-1296; BI, 1260-1482; Wig., 60, 20-64, 4.)

In BI and Wig. this adventure follows directly the one with the giants.

1. *The Induction.* In LD the dwarf recognizes the sound of horns which are, he says, those of Sir Otes de Lile. While they ride on talking,

>Þey siȝe a rach come flinge
>Overþwert þe way. (1070-1.)

Elene expresses a wish to have it.

>'Ne siȝ. I never no juell
>So likinge to my pay.
>God wold, þat I him auȝte!' (1079 ff.)

There remains nothing for LD to do but to catch it and give it to her. This done, they ride forth

>And telde, how kniȝtes fauȝt
>For ladies briȝt and schene. (1085-6.)

Before they have gone a mile, they see a hind pursued by two greyhounds. LD and his company stop under a linden to watch the result.

When BI is riding along by a forest ("une aventure va contant," 1263), he sees a stag with sixteen antlers pass ("langue traite, vait effrées," 1267). After it come leaping *bracet* of different colors, followed by one apart from the rest. This one, having a thorn in its foot, stops "en mi la voie" near Hélie. She, seeing its beauty, alights, seizes the dog, and mounts again, declaring she will carry it off to her lady.

In Wig., immediately after the departure of the giant to Arthur's court, while the dispute as to Wig.'s ability to fight the enchanter is still in progress, a beautiful little dog appears. The maid desires it, and Wig., glad to be able to do something to please her, catches it and lays it in her lap. They ride on "mit grôzen fröuden."

2. *The Dog.* In LD they all agree they never saw one so beautiful.

> He was of all colours,
> Þat men may sen of flours
> Betwene midsomer and may. (1075 ff.)

In BI it is white with black ears. On its right flank it has a black spot. It is small,—a little larger than an *ermient*,—no one ever saw a dog more beautiful.

In Wig. the dog is entirely white, "daz niht schœners mohte sîn" (60, 25). One ear is *val*, the other red as blood.[1]

3. *The Owner.* The dwarf in LD says that the owner's name is *Sir Otes de Lile.*

> ' Þat served my lady while
> In her semily sale.
> Whan sche was take wiþ gile,
> He fliȝ for greet perile
> West into Wirhale.' (1064 ff.)

He is clothed in *inde*, and rides a bay steed. The notes of his bugle reveal his station. On being called a *cherl* by LD, he retorts that his father was an earl, and his mother the Countess of Carlisle.

In BI he is a hunter who comes pricking up, followed by his dogs. He holds a horn, and has a lance in his hand.

> Corte cote avoit d'un burel;
> Le cors ot avenant et bel.
> D'une houses estoit hosés;
> Estrangement estoit hastés. (1297 ff.)

Later he is said to be a chevalier of high rank, who has had a castle built there for convenience in hunting.

In Wig. he is a large man with coal-black hair,—

> ieslich lok bewunden wol
> mit siden und mit golde,
> gezieret als er wolde. (61, 4 ff.)

---

[1] Compare the Red Knight's horse, p. 27, above.

He rides a good black horse.

> von bluomen fuort er einen huot.
> mit grüenem tymit was er gekleit. (61, 8-9.)

He carries in his hand a club well wound with strips.

4. *His Request*. As LD and Elene are under the linden, the knight rides up and blows his bugle. He asks courteously for the *rach :* he has had it seven years. LD bluntly refuses : he has himself given it to his companion, and no gift of his shall be taken back. The knight's threats have no effect. He rides home and tells his followers he has been shamed by one of Arthur's knights. They all swear the offender shall be taken

> þauȝ he wer grimmer gome
> þan Launcelet du Lake! (1145-6.)

They leap upon their steeds and soon come upon LD riding slowly on a hill.

The hunter sees Hélie putting the dog under her mantle and begs her to let it go. She, however, repeatedly refuses to give it up. The owner appeals to BI, who advises Hélie to return it; but the latter is obstinate and will not. Though unwilling to have her keep the dog, BI can do nothing but support her since she is determined. The owner goes away muttering vengeful threats. His servants come to meet him as he approaches his castle. He orders them to bring his steed and his arms in haste. They equip him suitably, and he spurs off to recover the dog.

In Wig. the owner, seeing his little dog in the lady's possession, is very angry, tells her it is his, and inquires who gave it to her. When he learns it is Wig., he turns to him, asks how he dared do such a thing, and threatens violence. Wig. replies that such talk only suits a woman. Whatever happens to him, he will not give up the dog "durch bœse rede noch durch drô" (62, 3). The knight turns his horse and rides off over the broad field to the forest to get his armor. The rest ride on happier than ever.

> mit manegem guoten mære
> vertriben si die selben zît. (62, 19-20.)

The knight returns on the gallop.

5. *The Fight.* When LD sees the field full of men, he forecasts trouble, and has Elene ride into the forest. They shoot at him "wiþ bowes and wiþ arblaste" (1174) and make wide wounds; but he lets his steed run and bears them all down, so that they think:

> 'þis is the fend Satan,
> þat mankende will forfare.' (1181-2.)

He is soon beset again, "as deer is in a nette," by a new group of twelve, with the lord himself at their head. There is a fierce struggle. Sparks spring from shield and helmet. LD slays three; four flee; the lord and his four sons remain. Against these five LD fights on, but he is hard pressed. His sword breaks at the hilt. A fierce blow nearly strikes him from his saddle. His foes are ready to despatch him; but he recovers, seizes his axe, and cuts off the heads of three steeds. The lord in terror flees; but LD overtakes him under a chestnut tree and makes him promise to go to Arthur.

In BI the hunter, now armed, comes up *alone* to the group and in a loud voice again demands the dog. Then follows a great struggle. Finally both are thrown from their horses and fight together on the ground. The hunter finally loses his sword; BI prevents his getting it again, and makes him vow to go to Arthur. Somehow or other he knows BI's name. BI inquires his name in return, and finds it to be *L'Orguillous de la Lande*. They take leave of each other. Hélie keeps the dog.

When Wig. sees the knight approaching, he tightens his horse's girth, and then spurs to meet him with such force that he drives his spear through the knight, whose shaft breaks without harming Wig. They tie his horse and relieve the knight of his equipment, thus depriving him of his honor. (Such was the custom in those times — digression of 35 lines.) There is, of course, no sending to Arthur. The combats in Wig. are not detailed.

6. In LD we have a unique scene. LD goes home with the conquered lord to the latter's castle, fifteen knights conducting Elene thither. There she tells of LD's brave deeds, and the lord rejoices in such a knight. LD remains there a fortnight to let

his wounds heal; and then the lord sets off to gladden Arthur's heart by telling him more of the prowess of the new knight of the Round Table.

VIII. AT THE ILE D'OR.

(LD, 1297-1548; BI, 1851-2470; Car., ii, 9-19.)

1. According to LD, the hero has ridden many a mile and seen terrible adventures in Ireland and Wales, when on a beautiful June day he sees a fair city by a river's side.

BI, on the evening of the same day on which he leaves Margerie, comes to a beautiful castle.

In Car. the first adventure is with the enchantress.

2. *The City.* Four lines suffice to describe it in LD.

> A fair cite
> Wiþ paleis proud in pride
> And castelles hiӡ and wide
> And ӡates greet plente. (1311 ff.)

Two pages are required in BI. The city is surrounded by an arm of the sea. Nothing can equal the beauty of the white marble walls. They are so high that

> Nus hom ne pooit engien faire
> Qui peüst à crenals tocier. (1876-7.)

There are two towers of red marble, and a wonderful palace ("cil qui le fist sot d'encanter"). The stone resembles crystal; the vault above and the pavement below are both covered with silver, while a shining carbuncle at the top sheds light on the whole. Twenty towers support the castle; they are all of one color. Much merchandise is carried to and fro from the city, which is therefore very rich.

In Car. we hear only of a noble castle in a valley between two mountains.

3. *The Lady of the Castle* in LD is

> a lady of pris,
> Roddy as rose on rise. (1321-2.)

In BI she is said to know the seven arts, much astrology, methods of enchantment, etc.: "Onques nus hom ne vit si bele" (1916).

She is her father's only heir, and still unmarried. She is "la pucele as blances mains."
In Car. the castle belongs to a duchess,

> Giovane e bella e fresca di natura,
> Che molta giente avea a pericol messa,
> Perch' era d' arte maestra sicura. (ii, 9, 2 ff.)

In LD the account is given by Elene ; in BI and Car., by the authors.

4. In BI the feature of the heads on poles is introduced here. Cf. LD, 778 ff.

5. *Induction to the Fight.* While still a good way off, Elene tells LD how a horrible giant "hath beleide about" the beautiful lady in the castle. LD determines to fight.

> 'I have y-sein,' he says, 'gret okes
> Falle for windes strokes
>   And smale stonde full stille.' (1351 ff.)

So they ride to the city. The giant sees LD ("upon a bregge of tre") and calls to him to turn back; but he retorts that when Arthur made him a knight he vowed never to turn back, and advises the "devell in blak" to make ready.

In BI a knight has awaited adventure summer and winter in a pavilion at the head of a bridge. When he sees BI coming, he goes to meet him and tells him that he cannot pass without fighting. Hélie now (!) declares that such is the regular custom, and that if he is killed, his head will be placed with the one hundred and forty-three already set up here on stakes. If any one defends himself here against all comers for seven years, he shall have the lady of the castle to wife. The present knight has only two years more to serve. BI begs to be allowed to pass, for he is on a mission from Arthur and does not wish to stop. Seeing that he cannot avoid a fight, he takes his lance and makes ready.

6. *The Hero's Opponent* in LD is a giant who is described as follows :

> He is as black as pich ;
> Nowher ber is non swich
>   Of dedes sterne and stoute.

He is þritty fote of lenghe
And miche more of strenghe,
Þan oþer knijtes five:

. . . . . .

He bereþ on everich browe
As bristelles of a sowe,
  His heed greet as an hive;
His armes þe lenghe of an elle;
His fistes beþ full felle,
Dintes wiþ to drive. (1327-44.)

He is later described as being

Beld as wilde bore.
His scheld was blak as pich
Lingell, armes, trappure swich;
Þre maumettes þer inne wore,
Of gold gailich y-geld. (1362 ff.)

He believes on Termagaunt.

In BI he is a knight who is hated by the lady of the castle and all her following.

Il estoit fels de cuer et mals,
Et trop tirans et desloyals. (2019-20.)

His shield and other equipment bear the sign of the "blances mains."

7. *The Fight.* In LD both break their shafts, but at once draw their swords. LD knocks the giant's shield to the ground. The latter dashes out the brains of LD's horse. LD, without delay, seizes an axe which hangs at his saddle-bow and cuts off the head of the giant's horse. They fight from prime to evensong. Then LD thirsts and begs for permission to drink from the river. Maugis (for such is the giant's name) grants this, but while LD is lying on the bank drinking through his helmet, the giant treacherously strikes him into the river. LD, however, gets out, says he is twice as light as before, and that he will reward Maugis for this baptism. The fight is renewed. Maugis cuts LD's shield in two; but LD runs and gets one Maugis has previously been obliged to drop, and they continue the fight on the river's side until dark. Then LD cuts off Maugis's

arm, and the giant runs away. LD follows, splits the giant's back in two, and finally strikes off his head.

The fight in BI is very unlike this. They are at first more than an acre apart. Then they rush at each other at full speed, and engage in fierce conflict. They are both thrown down with their horses. When they recover from the shock, they catch sight of each other, draw their swords, and begin again. Helmets smash, hauberks break, sparks fly. At last BI knocks off the knight's helmet, and splits his head from brains to teeth.

8. *The Attitude of the Crowd.* In LD lords and ladies turn out "to se þat selly siȝt" (1386) and pray God "loude and still" to help the Christian knight. After the fight is over LD bears the giant's head into the town, and the people come to meet him "with a fair procession." The lady of the castle welcomes him and conducts him to a chamber, where she

> dede of all his wede
> And cloþed him in pell. (1496–7.)

In BI old and young, of every condition, go to the fight, except the mistress of the castle, who with her ladies watches it from the windows of the tower. They one and all hate the knight and desire his death. During the fight the people get down on their knees and promise God "aumonnes et vels pentéis" (2142) if their lord be killed. He thinks they pray for him. Never was so great joy as when he is slain. They present themselves to BI, tell him he has slain the best chevalier that ever mounted a steed, that they and the kingdom are his, and that he has also won the most beautiful woman in the world. They lead him to the castle, where he is well received "à crois et à procession" (2192). The barons rejoice, conduct him to the palace, and there remove his armor.

9. *The Lady of the Castle* is called in LD *la dame d'amour*, and it is emphasized that she is an enchantress "þat moch of sorcery can" (1532).

> For his fair lady
> Couþe more of sorcery,
> Þen oþer swiche five.
> Sche made him melodie
> Of all maner menstralsy
> Þat any man miȝte descrive.

> When he siȝ her face,
> Him þouȝte, þat he was
> In paradis a live.
> Wiþ fantasme and fairie
> Þus sche blered his iȝe,
> Þat evell mot sche þrive! (1513 ff.)

In BI she is described in 35 lines of most extravagant adulation. Certainly "Onques nus hom ne vit tant bele" (2236). Her knowledge of sorcery is evident from the tricks later played on BI.

10. *La dame d'amour* receives LD with gratitude for saving her from the giant, leads him to a chamber, and offers to give over her city and castle to him and be his wife. He gives in to her fascination and remains with her.

In BI she enters laughing, throws her arms about BI's neck, declares that he has conquered her, and she will not part from him. She wishes to give him her lands and her love. They sit down on a seat with a covering of brown Thessaly silk and pledge affection. Many valiant chevaliers are in the castle. The lady says she will assemble her barons and on the eighth day take him as her husband. When evening comes, they wash and sit down to meat together, and are honorably waited on by all the attendants. Old and young rejoice.

11. *The Night at the Ile d'Or* is not found in LD. In BI, after supper, the hero's bed is prepared for him. (It takes nine lines to describe its beauty.) After all the servants have retired, the lady appears to him in the night with a splendid mantle thrown loosely about her, revealing all her charms. He is rejoiced to see her, and they embrace. She confesses her great love for him; but when he wishes to enjoy more, she draws back, declares that only when married will she give herself up to him, and leaves him alone. When she is gone, he is distracted with love, but finally falls asleep and dreams all the night that he holds her in his arms. At dawn he awakes and takes his departure.

12. Thus in BI at this time he only remains one night, while in LD he is said to have stayed "twelf monþe and more" (1507).

13. In both cases his departure is occasioned by a rebuke from the messenger.

Elene meets LD one day by chance beside the castle tower. She tells him that his action is dishonorable and that he is "fals of fay" to King Arthur. LD's heart almost breaks for sorrow and shame. At once he steals away "at a posterne unsteke" (1540), gets his steed and armor, and leaves the place.

After supper, Hélie, realizing BI's great temptations, calls him aside, reminds him that all the barons have been sent for, and begs him not to do a deed of *vilonie* and forget her lady in distress. He declares his willingness to go, and she plans the escape. With Robert's assistance she will arrange to have the horses at the door leading to the chapel at daybreak. BI is to come there and tell the porter he wishes to go to church. She will have his armor and steed ready. BI praises her arrangements, and they separate. In the morning they depart together in great joy.

14. Hélie is urged to spend the night at the castle; but she refuses all solicitation, and goes to the town to make ready unobserved for the early start.

No mention whatever is made of Elene after the fight, until it is told how she rebukes LD more than a year after.

15. In LD it is said that the hero on leaving the castle makes *Gifflet* the steward of the *dame d'amour* his squire.

16. In Car. there is no opposing giant or knight, no fight, no staring populace, no offer of marriage, no love lost, no prompting to depart, no desire to return. The account is as follows:

It is the custom of the castle that whenever a knight comes there bearing armor he shall spend the night with the lady of the castle. After supper she calls Car. to her and says to him:

> 'Ora m' ascolta, cavalier pregiato,
> Vo' che prendi di me gioia e disire:
> I' vo' che dormi co meco ne' letto;
> Di mi arai gran gioia e gran diletto.'   (ii, 12, 5 ff.)

He is quite willing. The lady, however, adds this condition: when she calls him to her he must not come, when she tells him not to come then must he come. He must always do the opposite of what she says. He promises; but when in the night she calls him to her, he does not hesitate, but starts up to obey the summons. When he is about to cross the threshold the lady roars loudly. It sounds like the sea tossed about in a tempest. Car. stops in great fear. He sees no longer house or walls, but instead a great river. Four giants appear on the bank, who suspend him over the water just high enough for his feet to touch it, and he remains dangling there until day breaks the spell. The dwarf rises and finds Car. up. He tells him the horses are ready and they should depart. Car. says he is very willing, for he has spent an unhappy night. The omniscient dwarf assures him that many others have had a similar experience.

Perch' ell è d' arte maestra saciente. (ii, 19, 8.)

With this should be compared the description in BI of the first night BI spends at the castle after his return (see p. 55).

IX. THE ADVENTURE WITH LAMPART.

(LD, 1549-1860; BI, 2471-2829; Wig., 102, 21-106, 30 (cf. 96, 2 ff.).)

1. *Induction.* (*a*) In LD they ride fast for three days (on bay and brown steeds) before they reach the city Sinadoun.

In the evening of the day on which BI and his party leave the Ile d'Or, they see the castle which is called *Galigan*.

In Wig. this adventure is the first after Wig. leaves the court.

(*b*) In LD they come to a

<blockquote>
castell hiȝ and wide
And paleis proud in pride,
Work of fair fasoune.   (1555 ff.)
</blockquote>

In BI this castle is described at length with its bridge, its towers, its high walls, the large number of houses in the town, the wood near by, the fertile lands about, etc.

(*c*) LD's attention is attracted by a custom "þat he siȝ do in toune." The citizens are gathering "gore and fen" which had been cast out. He asks Elene what it means. She replies that no knight ever gets *ostell* there for fear of the steward *Sir Lambard*, but advises LD to try. He will first be asked to joust, and, if he loses, the steward's trumpets will be blown, and then maidens and boys will gather and throw *fen* on him, so that he will be forever shamed, and Arthur lose his honor. LD decides to go

> To do Arthur profit
> And make þat lady quit. (1600–1.) (How?)

He calls Gifflet to accompany him.

BI inquires if they are to rest at the castle. Hélie's reply (40 lines long) informs him that the citizens never entertain any one. All reception is given by the lord of the castle, *Lampart*, and he gives lodging to no armed man without first jousting with him. If the stranger overcomes the lord, he is received with honor; if not, he is sent on foot into the city, and all the people shame him by throwing upon him a mixture of mud, ashes, and the like. She therefore tries to dissuade him from going (cf. LD). He bids her not to fear. God can aid him, and he will fight with the chevalier.

2. *The Crowd*. In LD nothing is said of the on-lookers until the fight is in progress. They then comment on LD's bravery, and when he makes Lampart rock in his saddle

> As a child doþ in a cradell,
> Wiþ oute main and miʒt.
> Ech man tok oþer be þe lappe
> And louʒe and gonne her hondes clappe
> Baroun, borgais and kniʒt. (1712 ff.)

In BI, as they ride along the public streets to the castle, the people follow them, laughing, point them out to one another, get stuff ready to throw at them, and plan amongst themselves the best way of preparing for their sport. Robert calls his master's attention to them.

3. LD and Gifflet ride to the gate and ask for lodging. The porter (!) inquires who their governor is. They reply King Arthur. The porter goes to his lord and announces that two knights of the Round Table have come, one of whom is armed in rose-red armor with three lions of gold. The lord is glad, and sends word for LD to get ready to joust. The porter returns quickly and tells them first to equip themselves and then ride into the field to await his lord. They do this

And beldly þer abide,
As bestes brou3t to bay. (1652–3.)

Lambard's shield is of fine azure, with three black boars' heads therein,

þe bordure of ermine,
Nas non so queinte of gin
From Carlile into Kent,
And of þe same painture
Was lingell and trappure. (1660 ff.)

He has two squires, who bear two shafts. He rides to the field as light as a leopard.

In BI they go straight to the lord of the castle, whom they find in joy over his chess, for he has mated a chevalier. He rises, and stands in his "robe d'eskerlate" and other fine apparel, while BI, who remains on horseback (as at Arthur's court), salutes him. Lambard is willing to lodge him on the regular conditions, and leads him to the place where they are to joust. A carpet is spread out, and Lambard sits down on the image of a leopard portrayed in it. He is soon armed and mounted. It is as much as two valets can do to carry his lance.

4. *The Fight.* When LD sees his opponent, he rides to him and begins the fight. Both break their shafts. Lambard calls in great vexation for another. Finally LD knocks Lambard's shield from him, breaks his shaft, hits him in the *lainer* of his helmet with such force

þat pisaine, ventaile and gorgere
Fli3e forþ wiþ þe helm in fer. (1708–9.)

Another helmet and shaft are brought him; but again his shaft breaks, and he falls backward from his steed. He is sore ashamed, and gives in when LD inquires if he wants more.

In BI they run at each other from a distance, break their lances, the splinters going as high as one could throw. Each calls for a new lance. Robert selects the best, runs with it to his lord, and begs him, for the love of God, not to forget "les laides torces, ne les pos" (2646), for the streets are full of people who await his overthrow (cf. LD). BI replies that he must not be dismayed: God will aid him. At last Lampart is knocked from his saddle. He rises

Studies on the Libeaus Desconus. 45

quickly, goes to BI, and admits that BI has won his lodging. BI dismounts; valets remove his armor, and afterwards that of Lampart.

5. *After the Fight.* In LD Lambard declares LD must be of Gawein's kin, and he is welcome if he will fight for the knight's lady. LD replies that that is what Arthur bade him do, but he knows not

> Wherfore ne why,
> He who her doþ þat vilany,
> Ne what is her dolour.   (1744 ff.)

Elene is brought in by ten knights and tells of LD's bravery on the way. They sit down to supper with great glee. The two knights talk of adventures, and LD learns about the lady of Sinadoun. He is told that two clerks of necromancy, *Maboun* and *Irain*, keep her confined in a castle which they prevent any one from entering. The lady is often heard to cry out; but no one can see her. Her foes have sworn her death unless she gives herself over to them. She is the heiress of all the dukedom, and is meek and debonair. LD swears that "þourȝ help of swete Jhesus" he will win her and hew off the sorcerers' heads by the chin. They continue their revelry. Many barons and citizens come to hear of the fight, and find LD and the knight talking "of kniȝtes stout and stiþe" (1836). In the morning LD is provided with fresh arms "of the best" and starts off.

After the fight Hélie and Lampart go aside. The latter is the seneschal of Hélie's mistress. Hélie tells him of her journey to Arthur's court, and they rejoice at the outcome. Lampart goes to BI and praises him for his bravery. Then they sit down to supper. Directly after, they go to bed. In the morning they again hear mass, offer up prayers, partake of dinner, have the horses saddled, and depart.

6. In LD, Lambard accompanies the hero to the gate of the castle, but none are willing to go farther, except Gifflet, whose offer is refused.

> To Jhesu þan þey cride,
> To sende hem tidinges glad
> Of hem, þat longe had
> Destroied her welþes wide.   (1857 ff.)

Lampart goes with BI also. BI and Robert ride ahead. Hélie, Lampart, and the dwarf follow *consillant*. BI looks about and sees them thus engaged.

>N'est mervelle se paor a. (2747.)

In the evening they pass a forest and then come to the desolate city (*Cité Gaste*). The towers, palaces, etc., are described (2755 ff.). There the company stops. Lampart and Hélie weep. They arm BI, and when he goes, Robert swoons. "Jamais ne l'cuident revéoir" (2821). See X, 1 (p. 47, below).

7. As has been seen (p. 15 above), part of the adventure with the steward has been transferred in Wig. to the fight with the first knight, and is therefore not repeated at this point in the poem.

The beginning of an episode foreign to our cycle (and therefore not regarded in the present analysis) intervenes in Wig. between the sparrow-hawk contest and the fight with the steward. The latter runs in Wig. as follows. After the sparrow-hawk adventure has been successfully accomplished and Wig. and the messenger are riding along together, the latter informs our hero that they are near the city of her mistress, tells him of the enchanter and the way the distress was brought about, and how Wig. is to undertake the adventure. They soon come before a beautiful city and see a knight riding out armed. Wig. asks who he is, and the messenger tells him:

>des libes ist er gar ein helt,
>unde ist truhsæze hie.
>riterschaft die minneter ie. (103, 22 ff.)

She advises him to avoid a fight; but he scorns the idea. The two knights come together on the heath. They both fight so well,

>daz niemen kunde wizzen, wer
>daz sine baz hiet vertân. (104, 3-4.)

The *truchsess* goes up to him, bids Wig. welcome, and, seeing the messenger who had been sent out from the distressed city, greets her gladly. They all ride together to the castle, where the messenger and the dwarf tell of Wig.'s bravery, and exhibit the prizes he has won. There is great rejoicing. Wig. is presented to the lady (Larie) and her mother, and from this point the narrative in Wig. differs from all the other versions.

X. THE RESCUE OF THE ENCHANTED LADY.

(LD, 1861-2196; BI, 2830-3427; Car., ii, 40-66.)

1. In LD and BI whatever information is given to the young hero before he enters the city is given by Lampart, in Car. by the dwarf. (There is no character like Lampart in Car.)

In LD very little is told (see p. 45, ix, above.) There are only 18 lines in LD corresponding to 100 in BI. In the latter Lampart takes up 40 lines (2773-2814) in telling BI what he is to expect to see, what he ought to do, and what he should leave undone. In this speech he describes the desolation of the city, the palace with the thousand windows in each of which is a *jogleor*, their instruments, torches, and salutation. He adds a warning not to enter the chamber, but to await adventure in the middle of the hall.[1] (Cf. Car., p. 48, below.)

When Car. comes to the city, the dwarf says to him : " Now you will need to prove your valor and be a hero, for this is the city." Car. replies : " Che dite voi? I' non vegio niente " (ii, 40, 7). The dwarf then points out to him some large stones in a mound and tells him those were formerly towers and palaces. The change was brought about by magic. The paths in the middle were the streets along which the people were accustomed to go night and day. Car. looks towards what was formerly the gate of the city, and sees dragons and serpents coming towards him. He calls aloud in fear and begins to flee ; but the dwarf calms him and assures him he shall go among lions and all sorts of wild beasts, and not be harmed. The dragons are the transformed barons of the land ; the lions, the knights; the bears, the judges ; the boars, the notaries ; the stags, leopards, and goats, the common people ; the hares, rabbits, and fawns, little children ; and the beautiful white animals are all women and fair damsels. The dwarf tells him he must pass by these trans-

---

[1] On this point cf. Paris, *Rom.*, XV, 17, note 1.

formed people and go on into the palace with its old towers "fatte con valore," and that from the open place there he must cry out in a loud voice: "Issue forth, traitor, thou who holdest this city in evil torment." Then shall appear an armed knight on a steed, who will ride fiercely at Car., and wish to strike him with a sword. Car. must be "ardito e posente." This is the magician who keeps the city and its inhabitants in this condition because the princess will not love him. He will appear as a great giant. If he flees, Car. must not enter at the same door he goes in at, nor go into the palace; since, if he does so, he will be struck down into the fire. If Car. knocks him to the earth, under no circumstances must he leave him alive. He must kill him immediately, then seek his girdle and break whatever he finds at once. When afterwards he shall see the great serpent in the square, he must go and kiss it on the mouth. The dwarf then commends him to God. He himself cannot go on the enchanted ground, else he also shall become a beast.

2. LD rides right into the palace, hears "trompes, hornes, schalmeis" (1864) before the high dais, and sees a fire "stark and store" in the middle of the hall. He goes on, leading (!) his horse, sees no other persons but minstrels making glee. He goes on farther, seeking some one to fight with, sees pillars of jasper and crystal "y-flourished wiþ amall," brass doors, glass windows "wrouȝt wiþ imagerie" (1899), and the whole beautiful painted hall. He sits on the dais; all the minstrels disappear; the torches go out; the doors and windows rattle; the stones of the wall fall; the dais begins to shake; the earth quakes; the hall-roof *unlocks*, "and þe faunsere ek: as it wolde asonder" (1920). He sits there in dismay.

BI has to cross a bridge over a stream which flows before the city. (The city is described in 16 lines.) He marks himself with the sign of a cross and enters by a gate which he finds broken down. He traverses the wide streets with the marble windows (the pillars are all fallen), and does not stop until he comes to the hall. There he sees the *jogleors* in the windows, each with a torch before him. They are playing on all sorts of instruments. When they see him, they salute him as the chevalier

> 'Qui est venus la dame aidier,
> De la maisnie Artur le roi.' (2880-1.)

BI is in great terror, but curses them, as Lampart had instructed him. He rides on into the hall without stopping. A *jogleor* closes the door behind him. The hall is brilliantly lighted by the torches. In the centre is a large table resting on seven *dormans*. He stops in the middle of the hall, leans on his lance, and there awaits adventure.

With the prayer "Idio m' aiuti," Car. passes the gate. When he enters, there is at once set up a great noise from the lions, serpents, and other beasts.

> Tutti s' apresentaron dov' egli era;
> E rimiravan lui e suo destiere
> E pare' che 'l vedeser volentiere. (ii, 52, 6 ff.)

His terrified horse has to be urged on by hard spurring. He soon reaches the square, and sees an immense beast.

> E 'n sua senbianza era molto piaciente,
> Con tre catene a collo d' ariento,
> E facie gran tenpesta e gran lamento. (ii, 54, 6 ff.)

It rises on its tail, starts toward Car., and finally says, "Baron, fa che sia ardito e dotto" (55, 8). Car. answers nothing, but calls aloud for the magician.

3. While LD is sitting on the dais, he hears horses neigh (!) and his spirits revive. He soon sees two armed men with trappings of purple *inde* and "gold garlands gay" (1932). One of them tells LD he has to be "queinte of ginne" to win the lady "pat is so precious." LD declares himself ready, leaps into his saddle, seizes his lance, and rides to meet his foe. Maboun's shaft breaks. LD bears him down over his horse's tail and nearly kills him. Irain, seeing this, comes on fresh to the fight. LD leaves Maboun, meets Irain, and tears off the latter's hauberk. They both break their lances, and fight with their swords. Maboun gets up to help his companion. Irain, encouraged, wounds the neck of LD's steed. LD, however, cuts in two Irain's thigh, and despite the latter's charm he falls down, "pat sory sire." LD alights to fight again with Maboun. Sparks fly from their helmets; but at last Maboun breaks LD's sword. With his sword gone and his horse lamed, LD fears he shall lose his fame. However, he runs to Irain, seizes the

latter's sword, and again attacks Maboun with such vigor that he smites off his left arm bearing the shield. Maboun offers to yield and give up the maiden if his life be spared. He had poisoned the swords, and fears death; but LD only desists when Maboun's head is off. He then runs to kill Irain, but the latter is nowhere to be found. This makes him sigh sorely, for he dreads sorcery.

While BI is on horseback leaning on his lance in the middle of the hall, he sees issue from a dark room a chevalier who rushes at him. They fight fiercely; both are thrown from their horses; often they are brought to their knees; but at last the chevalier retreats hurriedly to his room. BI follows; but just as he is about to cross the threshold he sees great axes ready to fall, remembers Lampart's injunctions, and saves his life. He is unable to find his horse, it is so dark. He calls upon God. The torches are again lit. The minstrels again play. BI's fear is dispelled. He catches his horse, seizes his lance, mounts, and returns gladly to the centre of the hall. Then there issues from the room another chevalier "grans et corsus." His steed has eyes like crystal, a horn in its forehead, and emits fire from its mouth. The chevalier, clad entirely in black armor, rides towards BI at full speed. The stone pavement nearly gives way. BI commends himself to God and spurs to meet his adversary. After both are unhorsed, they fight a fierce fight on foot with their swords until BI kills the giant. The body at once decays, and from it rises a horrible stench. BI touches it to see if there is still life in it; but he finds it quite dead and the face already horribly disfigured. He crosses himself and goes for his horse.

When Car. calls aloud in the hall, an armed knight issues from a palace of shining marble, draws his sword, and comes spurring at Car., who throws his spear at him. The giant is wounded and retreats through the door of the palace. Car. not following him, he reappears through another door, and tries to strike Car. with a small axe; but Car. throws his other spear at him unerringly. It passes through the shield into his cuirass, and he falls dead. Car. severs his head from his body, searches his girdle, and finds a rich shining gold ring, which he at once breaks. As soon as it is broken, all the beasts of the city rush suddenly about the dead body and show it no mercy. "Non è niuno che abi pietade" (ii, 60, 6). Car. now mounts his horse, and goes to the place where the great serpent is.

4. As LD sits lamenting the escape of Irain, a window in the stone wall opens, and a serpent with a woman's face appears. Her body and wings shine brightly. Her tail is *unmete*, her paws "grim and grete." LD sweats from terror as she draws near. " Er Libeaus hit wiste" (!) the serpent kisses him and coils about his neck. Immediately (!) the tail and wings fall off, and the fairest woman he has ever seen stands naked before him.

In BI, after the fight the minstrels rush off with a terrific uproar; the torches go out; BI cannot stand at first, but at last makes his way to the table, leans against it, and prays to God for aid. He regrets his rude departure from "la damoisele as blances mains," and determines to go to seek her if he can get out, and never to leave her again. Thus meditating, he is aware of a serpent coming from a closet, so bright she illumines the whole castle. Her eyes are as two carbuncles. In her tail are three knots. She seems to be gilded underneath. BI puts his hand to his sword. The serpent bows her head and makes signs of humility, and he puts it back. He repents; but again the serpent shows signs of friendship. He remains still, marvelling at her beautiful mouth. She fascinates him by her look, darts to him, kisses him on the mouth, and turns away. BI is about to strike; but her humble bows keep him from it. She returns to her closet, and shuts the door behind her.

In Car., when the serpent sees Car. return to her she rises from her position and throws herself "a salto a salto" towards him.

> Come l' aguglia quando va a ferire,
> Così fa quella biscia allo ver dire. (ii, 61, 7-8.)

Car. is not eager to approach, and his horse is much afraid; but at last he summons up courage, remembers the words of the dwarf, and with his drawn sword in his right hand "il cavalier sovrano" draws near the serpent, who is standing "umile e piano," and kisses her on the mouth. Then comes the glorious transformation.

> De! odi quie una nuova novella:
> Chè come quella serpe fu basciata
> Ella sì diventò una donzella
> Legiadra e adorna e tutta angielicata;

> De paradiso uscita pare ella,
> D' ongni bellezza ell' era adornata;
> E draghi e leoni e serpenti
> Diventar come prima, ch' eran gienti. (ii, 64.)

It sounds like a thunderbolt leaving heaven when the lady turns into her former shape, for then are the powers of magic overcome.

5. In LD the princess at once tells the hero that he must be of Gawein's kin, for only by kissing Gawein or one of his race could she be freed. She says she will give him fifty and five castles, and be his wife, if it be Arthur's will. LD is very glad; but leaps on his horse at once and leaves the lady alone — fearing Irain, who is not dead. He rides to the palace and tells what has taken place. The steward sends handsome robes, kerchiefs, garlands, etc. They conduct her home and put on her head a crown of gold and stones with great rejoicing. All the lords do her homage.

While BI is quietly ruminating over the "fier baiser," he hears a voice from above, which tells him that he is the son of Gawein and the *Fée Blancemal*,[1] and that his right name is *Giglain*. Being very tired, he falls asleep on the table, with his head on his shield. When he awakes, it is broad daylight, and there stands beside him a more beautiful woman than any other *except* "celi as blances mains." Her dress is described to the length of 25 lines. She takes nearly 100 more to tell him the situation. She is the daughter of the good King *Gringars*, three months after whose death she and the city were enchanted by *Mabon* and *Eurain*. She offers him her land, *Gales*, for him to rule, and begs to become his wife. He says that he is very willing, but that Arthur's permission must first be obtained. Hélie, Lampart, Robert, and the dwarf come to them with great joy. They remove BI's armor, and find him badly wounded. Every care is taken of him, and he is conducted to a superb apartment in which nothing is lacking.

In Car. the disenchanted princess first gives thanks to Christ the Saviour, and then, holding out her arms to Car., says to him:

> 'Tu sarai l' amor mio fino.' (ii, 65, 8.)

---

[1] This is, according to Foerster, the correct form in the manuscript. See *Hist. Litt.*, XXX, 176, note.

Their joy surpasses description. The dwarf, knowing what has happened, hurries with his companion into the city, where a great feast is held.

XI. THE CONCLUSION.

(LD, 2197-2232; BI, 3428-6122; Car., ii, 67-72.)

Since the hero has attained the object with which he set out from Arthur's court, it is now fitting that he should hasten home to announce the happy accomplishment of his mission. The English poet, therefore, takes but 36 lines in which to complete the story. In these we are told summarily that, after seven days' stay with Lambard, LD and the rescued princess go to Arthur, who receives them gladly and gives the lady to LD to wife. The bridal ("which no tale tells of") is of the best. The feast lasts 40 days. Arthur with many knights conducts them home, and they live together for many years, "wiþ moche gle and game" (2228).

In Car. also it requires but six stanzas to finish the poem. The news of the liberated city goes throughout all the land, even to Arthur. Car. is unwilling to return until he has avenged his father; but when Arthur learns who he really is, he sends ambassadors to make peace and beg him to come to court. Car. stops the war he is waging and returns with the ambassadors. His mother is sent for and comes eagerly to court. Calvano and his brother get on their knees before Car., and ask pardon for murdering his father. Car. pardons them. The king makes him his counsellor and one of his knights, and gives him the rescued princess to wife. They turn back to the city with the mother, and

> con giente assai, baroni, e donzelli. (ii, 71, 8.)

The conclusion reads thus:

> E po' furon più savi che Merlino,
> Secondo che raconti la scrittura,
> E 'n poco tenpo gli naque un banbino,
> Miglior di lui non portò armadura.
> Lo re Artù amava il paladino,
> E fue de' cavalier della ventura
> Il più prod' uomo e 'l più forte di corte,
> Tutti vi guardi Idio dalla ria morte. (ii, 72.)

A striking contrast presents itself when we look at the French story. It is now not much more than half finished. The poem is continued for 2700 lines more, and the author follows Bl through a series of adventures of a very different kind from those in which he has already figured. It will not be necessary to do more than give a brief summary of the rest of the poem, as it has no parallel elsewhere, being purely the invention of Renaud de Beaujeu.

XII. CONTINUATION OF BI.

When they hear of their lady's rescue, the barons and dignitaries of her land gather to the desolate city. The archbishop and clergy perform religious ceremonies to cleanse the city of sorcery. The princess tells her lords she wishes to marry Giglain. A large deputation wait on the latter and ask him to accept her as his wife; but he declares he must first have Arthur's consent. All the city is restored. The princess, *Blonde Esmerée*, gets ready to leave with a great retinue. Giglain is cured of his wounds in a fortnight, but is harassed by thoughts of the lady "as blances mains." He dreams continually of her as he saw her last during the night. He feels himself dying of love for her, and laments his rudeness in leaving her so abruptly. He asks advice of Robert, who counsels him to slip off secretly to the Ile d'Or. On the fourth day after, the queen is ready to start off with 100 knights in her company. They await Bl, who finally comes up armed. They wonder at this; but he tells them he is called elsewhere; they must go on without him; he will follow as soon as he can. The queen is exceeding sad, but must submit. Bl rides eagerly to the Ile d'Or. Outside the castle he meets a great company. His loved one is among them, and he draws aside to talk with her. He pours out his love; but she is indignant at his former conduct, and leaves him alone in his despair. Robert gets lodging for them both at the place where they had stayed before, and tries to cheer his lord; but Giglain is in imminent danger of death because of his unrequited love. Then comes a young lady bearing a message from the *fée* inviting him to her presence. He declares himself healed, and goes with the messenger to the palace, passing through an orchard of surpassing beauty. Giglain is pardoned by the *fée*, who tries unsuccessfully to conceal her love.

Studies on the Libeaus Desconus.

That night he is given a room next hers, and the door is left open; but she warns him not to stir from his bed. The open door, however, is too much to be resisted. He finally decides to go to her; but just when he thinks himself in her room, he finds himself instead on a plank over a tempestuous stream. It is so narrow he cannot go ahead or retreat, and in his terror he calls aloud for help. The servants rush in with candles, and find him hanging from the sparrow-hawk's perch. He goes to bed much ashamed; but when the servants are asleep he tries again. This time he fancies the ceiling is falling on him, and he again calls for aid. The servants find him with his pillow over his head. He gives himself up to his shame and remorse. All at once a maiden appears, and summons him to the presence of the *fée*. At first he fears he dreams; but, being reassured, he goes with her to a chamber which seems to him like paradise. His loved one no longer has scruples, and the two give themselves up to each other. Giglain tells her laughingly of his former terror, and she explains how she happened to know magic. She knew he would return to her. She had guided his whole life, had prompted Hélie to seek aid at Arthur's court, had aided him in all his adventures, and had revealed to him his name. As long as he will follow her counsel he shall want nothing; but if he depart from it, he shall lose her. In the morning she summons her barons and commends Giglain to them as their lord.

Meanwhile the queen has reached Arthur's court (having on the way met those whom Giglain had sent to the king), where she is welcomed. She tells of the bravery of Giglain, whom she declares to be the son of Gawein, and begs that he be given her for a husband. Arthur rejoices, and proclaims a great tourney in *Valledon*, by which he hopes to lure Giglain to court. News of it comes to the Ile d'Or, and our hero hears it gladly. The *fée* declares he must not go: if he does, he will never return to her. He protests his love, but is determined to go, and tells Robert to make ready. She, knowing that he is lost to her, transports him during the night to the woods, and when he awakes he finds everything ready and Robert beside him. He fears that through his folly his loved one is lost to him, but decides to go on to Valledon. There then follows a long-winded description of the tournament, covering many pages. Of course Giglain is victorious in every encounter, and we can give no answer to the question of the author: "Que vos iroie je contant?" (5953) except to say that he has done his duty too well. Then follow scenes between Giglain and Arthur, Giglain and those he had before conquered, Giglain and the queen, etc. The hero agrees, at Arthur's request, to marry the queen, and with a great company they set out for Sinadoun, where they are received with great rejoicing. Giglain marries Blonde Esmerée and is crowned king.

> Puis fu rois de moult grant memore,
> Si com raconte li istore. (6101–2.)

Renals de Biauju, the author, now finishes with another expression of his love, and prays his loved one, for God's sake, not to forget him. If she shows him "biau sanblant," he says he will bring (in a new romance) Giglain back to his true love. If not, he will never speak of him again.

> Si ert Giglains en tel esmai,
> Que jamais n'avera s'amie. (6116–7.)

WHEREIN THE POEMS AGREE.

Having thus given a detailed comparison of the different features of the four poems, it is not necessary to repeat at length all the disagreements between LD and BI. There are at least 150 significant points in which the two poems differ. It is well, however, to call attention to points in which LD agrees with Car. as opposed to BI; for, inasmuch as we cannot admit any connection between the English and the Italian poems, agreements between them as opposed to the French poem are of no little importance.[1] These are, then, as follows:

AGREEMENTS OF LD AND CAR. AS OPPOSED TO BI.

1. The introductions are the same in general features. A young boy is brought up alone in a forest by his mother, and is strictly kept aloof from all men. He discovers by accident the existence of other human beings, and is unwilling to remain longer living in his isolation.

---

[1] For the relations of this comparison to the work previously done by Kölbing, Paris, Mennung, and Kaluza, see above, p. 4, n. 1.

Studies on the Libeaus Desconus.

He finds his way to Arthur's court, and asks to be made a knight.— In BI nothing at all is told of his early history: he comes unexpectedly and suddenly to court, and, before he will dismount, demands that Arthur grant the first request he shall make.

2. The king at once openly asks his name. — In BI it is not until they have been for some time seated at the feast that Arthur sends Bediver secretly to inquire who his guest is.

3. In Car. and LD it is not until after the welcome is extended to the stranger that they go to meat. — In BI they are at the table when he rides up.

4. The dwarf protests against the sending of the young knight.— In BI he says nothing while at court.

5. The king receives the protests with: "This knight, or none!" — In BI he says he cannot help sending the young man: he would if he could.

6. The lady and the dwarf remain until the young knight is ready to accompany them. — In BI they ride off, and have gone some distance before he overtakes them.

7. There is no hint in LD or Car. of Robert, who is one of the most important characters in BI.

8. Although the messenger is angry, she never refuses the boy's services. — In BI she is constantly begging him to return. He rides with her against her will.

9. In LD and Car. the hero hears the maiden in distress calling on the Virgin Mary. There are no definite words of the lament in BI. Cf.

        'O Vergine gloriosa
    Guardami, madre, di crudele afanno,
    Che io non muoia cotanto penosa
    Nè mia verginità non ronpa panno.' (ii, 28, 1-4.)

with
    'Nou help, Marie milde,
    For love of þy childe,
    þat I be nou3t for3ite!'
    Quoþ Libeaus: 'Be seint Jame!
    To save his maide fro schame
    Hit wer a fair aprise.' (634 ff.)

10. The hero starts off alone to the adventure with the giants. — In BI he has to wait until his horse is brought by Robert, and until

the whole company get ready to join him. Robert serves as a guide and discovers the giant for him.

11. The giant by the fire uses as a weapon the spit he is roasting with. — In BI he uses a club.

12. The maiden is the daughter of a knight near by. — In BI her father is not mentioned, though her brother is.

13. She had been carried off by *two* giants. — In BI one alone takes her and brings her to his companion in the wood.

14. The enchantress plays but a small part in LD and Car., compared with the part she plays in BI. She has no love for the young hero; and he neither returns to her nor desires to return. The extent of the episode of the enchantress in BI, and the different treatment, have been recognized by all investigators as points of great importance.

15. When the hero is about to enter the enchanted city there is no sad farewell with his companions. — In BI there is much weeping. Robert even falls in a swoon to the ground.

16. The transformation of the enchanted lady takes place at once after the kiss is given. — In BI she returns to the closet whence she had issued, closes the door behind her, and does not return until the knight is awake from his sleep and it is broad daylight.

17. In Car. and LD the point just mentioned (16) is the real culmination of the story. — In BI the story is now not much more than half finished. Long descriptions of the return visit to the Ile d'Or and the great tournament remain to be given. There is no trace of these in LD or Car.

18. The young knight marries the disenchanted lady gladly. He has no desire for any one else. — In BI he does indeed, after a time, marry her at the request of the king; but the enchantress still remains his true love, to whom he is to return if the supplementary poem is ever written.

19. In Car. and two MSS. of LD (Ashmole and Naples) the boy's mother appears again at the end of the story.

AGREEMENTS OF LD, CAR., AND WIG., AS OPPOSED TO BI.

The agreements between LD and Wig. as opposed to BI, are also highly significant. Some of them occur in features (e.g. the adventure with the dog) which are not found in Car. at all. For the whole matter, see the chapter on *Wigalois*, pp. 208 ff., below. At this stage of the argument it is important to indicate that while there is really no point in which all three poems, BI, Car., and Wig., agree as opposed to LD, there are several in which LD, Car., and Wig. agree as opposed to BI. These are the following: (1.) All three tell of the youth of the hero, and explain why he comes to court.[1] (2.) He is humble and courteous in his demeanor while there. (3.) The king at once inquires his name. (4.) He asks to be made a knight. (5.) The table is made ready after he comes. (6.) He starts off *alone* to undertake the fight with the giants. (7.) There is no Robert, no return visit to the Ile d'Or, etc. BI has a host of details and other new features found nowhere else.

Moreover, this list would be largely extended if all the adventures were found in all of the poems: Car. has some which Wig. has not, and Wig. has some not in Car.

RELATION OF LD TO BI.

Such considerations as these have convinced Paris, and those who accept his views, that the English *Libeaus Desconus* is not based on the poem of Renaud de Beaujeu, but that the two go back to a common original; yet, as we have seen, Kaluza and many other scholars are not affected by them. I shall now adduce certain additional arguments, which it is hoped may assist to demonstrate the soundness of Paris's position.

I. *Proper Names.* Of the 177 proper names in BI 28 only occur in LD;[2] i.e. there are 149 names in BI which are not found in LD.

---

[1] True, Kaluza holds (*Introd.*, pp. lx, cxxxiii) that the introductory strophes in LD did not originally belong there, merely because they differ slightly in metre from the rest of the poem, with one exception where the same metre is again used; but, as Kaluza admits, this change in form is not unexampled in English poetry, and it may be due merely to the caprice of the poet. Moreover, as Paris points out (*Rom.*, XX, 299), this introduction is in all the MSS., recalls the essential features of the opening of the *Carduino*, and (cf. pp. 191, 192) is exactly the account given of the birth of our hero (?) in one continuation of the *Perceval*. These considerations far outweigh any conclusions drawn only from a capricious change of metre.

[2] According to Kaluza's index, there are in all 51 proper names in LD, but several of those in LD which are not in BI are merely saints' names used in

Of these 149, some 140 are also missing in both Car. and
Wig. Of course the author of LD might conceivably, if he were
making over Renaud's poem, have omitted all these names intentionally. But, in this case, it would be strange that Wirnt, whose
relations with Renaud's poem, whatever they may be, are not the
same as those of the English author, and who, in any case, was in no
kind of communication with LD, should have no name in that part
of Wig. which is based on the same story as LD which is not in the
English poem. And the complication of chances rises into impossi-
bility when one observes that Car., standing in a very different relation to Renaud's poem from both LD and Wig., and by no possibility
derived from Renaud, also omits the 140 names in question. It is
surely more reasonable to suppose that the names omitted in LD
were, at least in great part, not in the original of LD nor in that of
BI than to assume such an accidental coincidence of omission in LD,
Wig., Car.,— three poems written in different languages, at different
times, and in different countries.

II. *Borrowings of BI from Erec.* Under this head, I do not
intend to consider borrowings of "saga-material," of which several
probable instances have been pointed out by Mennung,[1] but borrowings in the matter of phraseology, and even of long descriptions.
Such borrowings have not, so far as I know, been hitherto noticed,[2]
and their importance for the decision of the question at issue is
obvious.

A few of the most striking parallels may be given first. In each
case the BI passage is in the left-hand column.[3]

---

adjurations, of which the English poet is fond, e.g. Denis, Edward, Gile, Jame,
John, Michell; and others are insignificant, e.g. Bedlem, June, Kent, Satan, Termagaunt, Wirhale. For a list of the proper names in BI, see the appendix to
this volume.

[1] *Der Bel Inconnu*, pp. 16, 49. Cf. Paris, *Rom.* XX, 299–300. These instances
will all be discussed later (see below, pp. 133, 134). For a consideration of the
way in which Renaud has modified some of the narrative features of his original
in his desire to imitate the *Erec*, see below, pp. 106 ff. This last consideration
will be found to add strength to the argument from phraseology, etc.

[2] Paris, *Rom.*, XX, 300, n. 4, says that Renaud "avait beaucoup lu Chrétien."

[3] Some of the most significant parallels will be found in the next chapter (pp.
112 ff.; see, e.g., pp. 130–1). In the passages from BI the edition of Hippeau
has been followed, and no attempt has been made to correct his frequently absurd

SIMILAR PASSAGES IN BI AND EREC.

1.

Tant durement le tire et sace,
Que l'elme del cief li esrace.
Cil n'a pooir de relever;
Que que il doie li grever,
Li convient dire et consentir:
'Conquis m'avés!'
(1773 ff.; cf. 1160.)

Et sache et tire si que toz
Les laz de son hiaume a deroz
. . . . . .
Ne n'a pooir de relever.
Que que il li doie grever,
Li covient dire et otroiier:
'Conquis m'avez.'
(6003-10; cf. 5041-2.)
Cf.
Erec par le hiaume le sache,
A force del chief li arrache.
(985-6.)

2.

La dame par le main le guie
Sor une kuite de brun pale
Qu'aportée fu de Tesale,
Iluec se sont andoi asis.
(2256 ff.)

An une chanbre fu assise
Dessor une coute de paille,
Qu'aportee fu de Tessaille.
(2406 ff.)

---

spelling and grammar. Foerster's excellent edition of *Erec* has been used for the extracts from that poem. On the one hand, then, the passages are taken from a very inexact transcript of a single MS., on the other from a text edited from several MSS. If we had the exact MS. of *Erec* which Renaud used, the parallels would doubtless show even greater similarity than appears here. We may note that there is also a text of *Erec* in the codex in the library of the Duc d'Aumale which contains the unique text of BI. Of the text of BI Foerster says (*Zt. f. rom. Phil.*, II, 78): "Der Hippeau'sche Text kann nur im uneigentlichen Sinne als eine Ausgabe des im Aumalecodex geschriebenen Textes angesehen werden. Nicht nur dass hunderte von Zeilen nicht allein dem Wortlaut, sondern auch dem Sinne nach geändert sind, so sind etwa 80 Zeilen ausgelassen, 9 neue Verse statt der bestehenden, die 11. offenbar nicht gefielen, und 10 neue Verse statt der in der Hs. fehlenden von ihm selbst geschmiedet, ohne dass etwas von all dem auch nur mit einem Sterbenswörtchen angedeutet würde." Cf. also the words of Mussafia, who in his review of BI has pointed out some necessary corrections in the text (*Jahrb. f. rom. u. engl. Lit.*, IV, 419 ff.). A good edition would in all probability only make the parallels closer. It is evident further that the text of *Erec* may be of importance in determining that of BI, or *vice versa*.

Un tapit a fait aporter.
Quant à terre fu estendus,
Si est tost cele part venus;
Et puis est se Lanpars asis
Sor l'image d'un lupart bis,
Que el tapis estoit portraite.
De lui armer forment s'afaite.
Cauces de fer li font caucier
Qui moult faisoient à prisier.
  (2595 ff.)

Es vos son ceval c'on amaine;
Il i sailli de terre plaine.
La pucele l'escu li tent,
Et il par le grince le prent.
Au col le mist, puis prist sa lance.
  (1037 ff.)

Lors s'entrevienent anbedui
Des lances de totes leur forces;
Ne leur valurent ii escorces
Li escus qui as cols lor pendent,
Li cuir ronpent et les ais fendent,
Les mailles ronpent des haubers,
Par les cors se metent les fers;
Si durement se sont feru
Que andoi se sont abatu;
Ne furent pas a mort blecié;
Isnement se sont redrecié.
Cascuns a sa lance à lui traite,
Il n'i ot cele qui fust fraite;
El pavement les ont jetées;
Del fuerre traient les espées;
Grans cols se fierent des brans nus,
Sor les elmes, sor les escus.
  (2992 ff.)

3.
Et fist un tapit de Limoges
Devant lui a la terre estandre.
  . . . . . .
Erec s'assist de l'autre part
Dessus l'image d'un liepart,
Qui el tapit estoit portreite.
Por armer s'atorne et afeite:
Premieremant si fist lacier
Unes chauces de blanc acier.
  (2628-38.)

4.
Puis comande qu'an li amaint
Son cheval, et l'an li amainne.
Sus est sailliz de terre plainne.
La pucele aporte l'escu
Et la lance qui roide fu,
L'escu li baille, et il le prant,
Par la guige a son col le pant.
  (718 ff.)

5.
As fers des lances s'antranvïent
Anbedui de totes lor forces.
Ne lor valurent deus escorces
Li escu qui as cos lor pandent.
Li cuir ronpent et les es fandent,
Et des haubers ronpent les mailles.
Anbedui jusque as antrailles
Se sont des gleives anferré,
Et li destrier sont aterré;
Car mout ierent li baron fort.
Ne furent pas navré a mort,
Mes duremant furent blecié.
Isnelemant sont redrecié,
S'ont es aus lor lances retreites;
Ne furent maumises ne freites.
Anmi le chanp les ont gitees.
Del fuerre traient les espees,
  . . . . . .
Si granz cos sor les hiaumes fierent
  . . . . . .
Les escuz fandent et esclicent.
  (3774-97.)

6.

Et quant il le chevalier voit,
A haute vois lors li escrie :
'Vasal, vasal, or est folie
De mon cien qu'en faites porter !
Or le vos estuet conperer.'
(1388 ff.)
Cf.
Folie fu del gué passer ;
Je vos l'ferai cier compérer.
(395-6.)
and
Le m'avés fait cier conperer.
(4309 ; cf. 1384, 1349.)

Einçois qu'Erec veü l'eüst,
Si s'escria : ' Vassaus, vassaus !
Fos estes . . .
Vos conparroiz ancui mout chier
Vostre folie, par ma teste !'
(5906-5913.)
Cf.
Folie t'a amené ça . . .
Moult le t'estuet conparer chier.
(848-50.)
Also
' Vassaus,' fet il, 'folie feites.'
(4027 ; see 4015, 4418, 4428, 4818.)

7.

Moult orent andui beles armes
Les escu prendent as enarmes ;
Cevals poingnent por tost aler, . . .
Fendent escus, faussent haubers, . . .
Des lances les esclisses volent ; . . .
Des tronçons donent grans colées ;
Après revienent as espées.
Si s'en vont eus entre férir.
Lors oïssiés elmes tentir, . . .
Moult fiert bien cascuns de l'espée ;
Moult est dure d'els la mellée ;
Moult sont vasal, fier caple font,
Lor elme tot embaré sont
Et lor escu tot decopé.
Si furent andui moult lassé, . . .
Li ceval se vont esloignant . . .
A la terre caient andui :
Moult prioit Deu cascuns por lui.
(1400-29.)

Et les escuz [pranent] par les enarmes.
Andui orent mout beles armes.
(2195-6.)
Por assanbler les chevaus poingnent,
. . . . . .
Les lances esclicent et froissent, . . .
Contre terre anbedui se ruient,
Li cheval par le chanp s'an fuient . . .
Des tranchanz granz cos s'antre-
donent,
Li hiaume quassent et resonent.
Fiers est li chaples des espees :
Mout s'antredonent granz colees, . . .
Tranchent escuz, faussent haubers . . .
Li chaples dure longuemant :
Tant se fierent menuëmant
Que tot se lassent et recroient.
Andeus les puceles ploroient :
Chascuns voit la soe plorer,
A Deu ses mains tandre et orer.
(866-92.)

8.

Mais grant dol fait la damoisele.
Ses puins tort, ses cevels decire
Cele qui a et dol et ire, . . .

La pucele aloit detirant
Ses mains, et ses crins descirant.
(4331-2.)

Cil demanda à la pucele :
'Por coi plorés, amie bele,
S'il vos plait, je le veul savoir.'
(1538-49.)

Si li a demandé et dit :
'Dites moi, bele amie chiere,
Por quoi plorez an tel meniere ?
De quoi avez ire ne duel ?
Certes je le savrai mon vuel.'
(2514 ff. ; cf. 1960.)

9.

Cele qui l'esprevier ara
Et à la perce le prendra,
Si ara los de la plus bele,
Et si convient à la pucele
Qui vaura aveir l'esprevier,
Que maint o soi i chevalier,
Por desrainier qu'ele est plus bele
Que nule dame, ne pucele.
(1574 ff.)[1]

Qui l'esprevier voudra avoir,
Avoir li covandra amie
Bele et sage sanz vilenie.
S'il i a chevalier si os
Qui vuelle le pris et le los
De la plus bele desresnier,
S'amie fera l'esprevier
Devant toz a la perche prandre.
(570 ff.)

10.

Ensi vers le castel s'en vont ;
Passent les lices et le pont.
(1640-1.)

Einsi vers le chastel s'an vont,
Passent les lices et le pont.
(5493-4.)

11.

'Venés avant, ma douce amie,
Prendre à la perce l'esprevier.
Par vos le veul je desrainier.
Car vos le devés moult avoir,
Tant avés biauté et savoir,
Ensement et pris et valor.'
(1685 ff.)

'Bele,' fet il, 'avant venez !
L'oisel a la perche prenez ;
Car bien est droiz que vos l'aiiez.
. . . . . .
Del desresnier tres bien me vant, . . .
Que a vos ne s'an prant nes une, . . .
Ne de biauté ne de valor.'
(827-35.)

12.

Armés sor un ceval ferrant.
(1695.)

Armé sor un cheval ferrant.
(1122.)

13.

Vostre estre et vostre non me dites.
(1782.)

Vostre estre et vostre non me dites.
(3862.)

---

[1] The difference in these two passages is due to the fact that in one case Margerie needs a knight to support her, while Erec must get an *amie* before he can enter the tournament.

14.

l'aventure,
Qui tant est perilleuse et dure!
(3195-6.)
s'aventure,
Qui moult estoit greves et dure.
(1953-4.)
Cf. 4816-7: aventure: dure.

l'avanture
Qui tant est perilleuse et dure.
(5431-2.)

15.

Des fueres traient les espées,
Dont il se donnent grans colées.
Les escus treient et esclissent,
Haumes effondrent et debrissent,
Les haubers rompent et desmaillent ;
Des espées souvent s'asaillent ;
Sor les elmes tels cols feroient
Que estinceles en voloient.
(2132 ff.)
Cf.
Escus fendent, hiaumes esclicent,
Elmes esfondrent et deslicent.
(5599-5600.)
Et cil trait del fuere s'espée.
(3148.)

Del fuerre traient les espees,
. . . . . .
Si granz cos sor les hiaumes fierent
Qu'estanceles ardanz an issent,
Quant les espees ressortissent.
Les escuz fandent et esclicent,
Lor haubers faussent et deslicent.
(3790-8.)
Cf.
Del fuerre a fors l'espee treite.
(3054; cf. 4668.)

16.

Tot cil qui cele joste virent
Moult durement s'en esbahirent.
(2126-7.)

Tuit cil qui ceste joste virent
A mervoilles s'an esbaïrent.
(2211-2.)

17.

Et la dame s'i est asise, . . .
Li Desconneüs siet lès li,
Et Helie tot autresi.
(2281-4.)

Il se sont assis tuit troi,
Erec et ses ostes lez soi,
Et la pucele d'autre part.
(481 ff.)

18.

Et deriere ot ses crins jetés ;
D'un fil d'or les ot galonés.
De roses avoit 1 capel
Moult avenant et gent et bel
D'un afremail son col frema.
(2229 ff.)
F

Les deus puceles d'un fil d'or
Li ont galoné son crin sor ;
Mes plus estoit luisanz li crins
Que li fis d'or qui mout est fins,
Un cercelet ovré a flors
. . . . . .

Les crins ot blons et reluisans,
Comme fin or reflanboians.
D'un fil d'arge fu galonnée.
(1530 ff.)
Or fu tant avenant et bele
Que nus hom son per ne trovast,
En tout le mont, tant le cerkast.
(5078 ff.)
Si l'avait bien nature ouvrée.
(2206.)

Deus fermaillez d'or neelez
An une cople anscelez
Li mist au col une pucele.
Or fu tant avenanz et bele
Que ne cuit pas qu'an nule terre,
Tant seüst l'an cerchier ne querre,
Fust sa paroille recovree;
Tant l'avoit bien Nature ovree.
(1655-72.)

19.

Plus de c. mars d'argent valoit.
(2350.)

Qui plus de çant mars d'arjant vaut.
(1636.)
Cf.
Plus de cent mars dargent ualoit.
(Förster's note to 2380, l. 28.)

20.

al main que l'aube creva.
Isnelement et tost leva:
. . . .
Venus s'en est à la capele.
(2449-53.)
Cf.
Au main quant li aube est crevée,
Si se leve Blonde Esmerée.
(6065-6.)

L'andemain lués que l'aube crieve
Isnelemant et tost se lieve,
. . . .
Au mostier vont.
(697-700.)
Cf.
L'andemain lués que il ajorne,
Erec se lieve, si s'atorne.
(4279-80.)

21.

Lances reprendent por joster
Et laissent tost cevals aler;
Et puis durement s'entrevienent,
Les lances alongées tienent;
Si se fierent de tel angoisse
Que l'une lance l'autre froisse.
(2630 ff.)
For the rhyme, (par tel) angoisse:
froisse, see also BI, 4551-2; 5529-
30: and *Erec*, 3611-2.

Chascuns au plus tost que il pot
A sa lance retreite a lui,
Si s'antrevienent anbedui,
Et revienent a droite joste.
Li uns ancontre l'autre joste,
Si se fierent par tel angoisse
Que l'une et l'autre lance froisse.
(5950 ff.)

22.

Lors furent vallet apresté
Qui maintenant l'ont desarmé.
(2678-9.)

Lors furent vaslet apresté,
Qui le corurent desarmer.
(1242-3; cf. 4283.)

Cf.
Vallet le corent desarmer.
(91.)

De sus la boucle, à l'or clarie,
Là si feru del fer trençant,
Que l'escu li perce devant.
La lance fu et roide et fors ;
Et il l'enpaint par cel esfors.
(2663 ff.)
Cf.
Lances orent roides et fors ;
Si se fierent par tels esfors
De sor les boucles des escus, . . .
En fist cascuns passer le fer.
(5623 ff. ; cf. 5651-2.)
Lances orent roides et fors ;
Si s'entrefierent par esfors.
(2116-7.)[1]

Or li portés moult grant honor.
(2700.)

Les armes font avant porter
Por le Desconnéu armer.
A bones coroies de cer
Li lacent les cauces de fer ;
Le hauberc li ont el dos mis,
Le hiaume après el cief asis.
Et quant il l'orent bien armé.
(2765 ff.)
Cf.
Il vest l'auberc, l'elme laça,
Et Helie li çaint l'espée.
(1030-1.)

23.

[Les lances] s'an furent plus roides
et forz.
Sor les escuz par tel esforz
S'antrefierent des fers tranchanz
Que par mi les escuz luisanz
Passe de chascune une toise.
(5943 ff.)
Cf.
Que li escu percent (869) ; lance
roide et fort (3686).
For rhyme, forz : par tel esforz, see
also 5015-6.

24.

Si li portez mout grant enor.
(472.)

25.

Les armes quiert et l'an li baille.
. . . . . .
Lace li les chauces de fer
Et queust a corroie de cer.
Hauberc li vest de buene maille,
Et si li lace la vantaille.
Le hiaume brun li met el chief :
Mout l'arme bien de chief an chief.
Au costé l'espee li çaint.
(708-17.)
Cf.
La pucele meïsmes l'arme.
(709.)

---

[1] Much stress cannot be laid on agreements in descriptions of fights. Cf. *Raoul de Cambrai*, ed. Meyer and Longnon (*Soc. des Anciens Textes Français*), 1882, pp. lxii ff.

26.

Trestos à Diu les commanda,	'Et ce que je vos voi plorer,
Et il i recommandent lui.	Me fet grant mal et grant enui.'
Mais moult lor torne à grant anui,	A Deu les comande, et il lui.
Que il le ont véu aler,	Departi sont a mout grant painne.
Si commencièrent à plorer.	Erec s'en va.
Jamais ne l'cuident revéoir;	(2762 ff.)
Or le gard Dius par son pooir!	Que ja mes reveoir nes cuident.
Lanpars ploroit et la pucele;	(4293.)
Robert ciet pasmés à la terre.	Cf.
De l'autre part plorait li nains,	[Les janz replorent d'autre part.]
. . . . . .	Dames et chevalier ploroient,
D'estrange guise grant dol fait;	Por lui mout grant duel demenoient.
Et le Desconnéus s'en vait!	N'i a un seul qui duel n'an face.
(2816-28.)	Maint s'an i pasment an la place.
	(2744 ff.)
	Cf.
	Enide a mout grant enui torne.
	(5676.)

27.

Sor les elmes, sor les escus,	Que de rien ne s'antrespargnierent.
Ont grans cols et pesans ferus,	Si granz cos sor les hiaumes fierent.
De nule rien ne s'espargnoient.	(3793-4.)
(2920 ff.)	

28.

Moult fu la damoisele gente; . . .	Mout estoit la pucele jante,
Onques nus hom ne vit tant bele.	Car tote i ot mise s'antante
Le front ot large et cler le vis,	Nature qui feite l'avoit.
Et blanc come est la flor de lis.	. . . . . .
(1519-24.)	De cesti tesmoingne Nature
Cf.	Qu'onques si bele criature
une dame	Ne fu veüe an tot le monde.
Tant bele, c'onques nule fame	. . . . . .
Ne fu de sa biauté formée;	Plus ot, que n'est la flors de lis,
Tant estoit fresse et alosée,	Cler et blanc le front et le vis,
Tant le sot bien nature ovrer,	Sor la blanchor par grant mervoille
C'onques si bele n'ot el mont,	D'une color fresche et vermoille
De bouce, d'iols, de vis, de front,	Que Nature li ot donee,
. . . . . .	. . . . . .
De sa biauté est grans mervelle.	Onques Deus ne sot feire miauz
. . . . . .	Le nes, la boche, ne les iauz.

Issi l'avoit nature faite,
Par grant estude l'ot portraite.
(3235-52.)
and
Mout i ot gente damoisèle ;
La color ot fresse et novièle.
(855-6.)

    li miudres chevaliers
Li plus vaillans et li plus fiers
De la mainie Artur le roi.
Nesun millor ne sai que toi,
Fors que tes père Dans Gauvains,
Qui est de totes bontés plains.
(3330 ff.)
Cf.
Car millor ne savons el mont.
(3494.)

De robe porpre estoit vestue,
Onques miudre ne fu véue ;
Moult estoit riches ses mantials,
II sebelins ot as tasials ;
La pene fu et bone et fine ;
Et si estoit de blance ermine.
Les ataces qui furent mises
Furent faites de maintes guises ;
. . . . . .
De cel drap dont li mentials fu,
Fu li blials qu'ele ot vestu ;
Moult estoit ciers et bien ovrés ;
D'une ermine fu tos forrés.
Plus de v onces d'or, sans faille,
Avoit en tor le kieuetaille.
As puins en ot plus de IIII onces,
Par tot avoit asés jaconces,
Et autres pierres de vertu,
Qui furent deseur l'or batu.
(3253-74.)
Cf.
La pene d'edres fu bendée,
D'ermine de gris geronée ;

Que diroie de sa biauté?
(411-37.)
Cf. fresche et novele, 620, 1586,
1607, 2153, 2198.

29.
    il est chevaliers si buens
Que l'an ne puet mellor trover,
. . . . . .
Ne cuit que soit ses parauz nus.
(6300-5.)
Car n'avoit an tote sa cort
Mellor chevalier ne plus preu
Fors Gauvain son tres chier neveu ;
A celui ne se prenoit nus.
(2286 ff.)

30.
Mout fu buens li mantiaus et fins :
Au col avoit deus sebelins,
Es tassiaus ot d'or plus d'une once ;
D'une part ot une jagonce,
. . . . . .
La pane fu de blanc ermine ;
Onques plus bele ne plus fine
Ne fu veüe ne trovee.
La porpre fu mout bien ovree
A croisetes totes diverses,
. . . . . .
Les ataches li sont bailliees,
Beles et bien aparelliees.
(1609-26.)
Et le bliaut qui jusqu'as manches
Fu forrez d'erminetes blanches.
As poinz et a la cheveçaille
Avoit sans nule devinaille
Plus de demi marc d'or batu ;
Et pierres de mout grant vertu.
(1595 fl.)
Cf.
Que vos diroie del mantel?

Li sebelins moult bons estoit ; Mout fu riches et buens et biaus :
En nul païs millor n'avoit. Quatre pierres ot es tassiaus.
(1515 ff. ; cf. 2225-6, 2376-81.) (6804 ff.)

31.

L'uns acole l'autre et enbrace ; Li rois les acole et salue,
N'i a celui joie ne face. Et la reïne doucemant
. . . . . Les beise et acole aussimant ;
Quant entreconjoï se furent, N'i a nul qui joie ne face.
Por Giglain desarmer corurent, Iluec meïsmes an la place
Si le desarment en la place Li ont ses armes desvestues ;
Et Robers son elme deslace. Et quant ses plaies ont veües,
Quant de tot fu il desarmés Si retorne la joie an ire.
Si l'ont rait et plaié trové.
. . . .
Et quant ses plaies ont lavées, Quant ses plaies orent lavees,
Si les ont tantost rebendées. Ressuiiees et rebandees,
Puis le mainent en une cambre. Li rois lui et Enide an mainne
(3400-18.) An la soc tante demainne.
  (4208-32.)

32.

Giglains en la cité sejorne ; Demorer quinze jorz toz plains,
Tot fu garis en la quinzaine. Tant qu'il soit toz gariz et sains.
(3643-4.) (4235-6.)
  Cf.
  A lui garir mistrent tel painne
  Les puceles qu' einçois quinzainne
  Ne santi il mal ne dolor.
  (5217 ff.)

33.

Dame, ne puet estre autrement. Sire, ne puet estre autremant.
Je m'en vois : à Diu vos commant. Je m'an vois ; a Deu vos comant.
(3858-9.) (2737-8.)
  Cf.
  Bien voi qu'aler nos i estuet,
  Des qu'autremant estre ne puet.
  (5477-8.)

34.

Que il sont el castel venu. Tant qu'il vindrent a un chastel
. . . .
Si chevaliers, ses demoiseles, De chevaliers et de puceles ;
Dont il en i avoit de beles. Car mout an i avoit de beles.
(4015-9.) (345-50.)

35.

Laiens moult bon ostel avés.
(4033.)
La nuit, sont à l'ostel venu ;
Liément ils i sont recéu.
Li ostes moult bel les reçut.
(4040 ff.)

Car buen ostel et bel avez.
(3200.)
Tost furent a l'ostel venu,
A joie furent receü,
Li ostes mout bel les reçut.
(3203 ff.)

36.

Une robe aporte moult bele,
Partie de deus dras divers,
De soie, d'un osterin pers,
. . . . . .
L'autre d'ermine bon et fin,
Ki estoit d'un rice osterin ;
Et li vairs el diaspe estoit.
(4144-53.)
Parée fu de dras de soie
De mult cier pris. Que vos diroie ?
Mais moult en i ot de divers,
Bofus, tois, osterines, pers.
(4658 ff.)

Ot Guivrez fet deus robes feire,
L'une d'ermine et l'autre veire,
De deus dras de soie divers.
L'une fu d'un osterin pers,
Et l'autre d'un bofu roiié,
. . . . . .
Enide ot la robe d'ermine
Et l'osterin, qui mout chiers fu,
Erec le ver et le bofu.
(5225-34.)

37.

En tot le mont n'ot sa parelle,
Tant estoit bele, à grant mervelle.
(4267-8.)
Cf.
Onques nus hom n'ot sa parelle
(: mervelle.)
(4790-1.)

Qui tant par est bele a mervoille
Qu'an ne puet trover sa paroille ?
(535-6.)

38.

Là faisoit on metre les tables,
Car il estoit tans de souper.
(4378-9 ; cf. 5937-42.)

Fist el palés metre les tables
Et fist le mangier aprester ;
Car tans estoit ja de soper.
(4774 ff. ; cf. 4260-1.)

39.

Por laver font l'iaugue crier ;
Si se sont au mangier asis.
Pain et vin ont à table mis,
De tot quanques mestier lor fu
Ont tot à lor voloir éu.

L'eve lor done an deus bacins.
Tables et napes, pains et vins
Tost fu aparelliez et mis,
Si se sont au soper assis.
Trestot quan que mestiers lor fu

Quant mangié orent à loisir,   Ont a lor volanté eü.
A grant aise et à lor plaisir.   Quant a lor eise orent sopé
Se sont des tables levés tuit.   Et des tables furent le é.
  (4380 ff.)   (495 ff.)
Cf.   Cf.
Quant mangié orent, à loisir.   Quant orent mangie a plaisir.
  (2291 : also 938, 941.)   (note to l. 6943 ; cf. 3181.)

40.

'Je m'en vais, à Diu vos commant.'   'A Deu,' fet il, 'vos comant gié.'
Giglains respont: 'Dame, et je vos!'   Erec respont: 'Sire et je vos.'
Ensi departirent andos.   Einsi departent antr'aus dos.
  (4418 ff.)   (3436 ff. ; cf. 5868–9.)

41.

Ensi le destraint et justise.   Einsi se justise et destraint.
  (4457.)   (3735.)
Amors le destraint et justise.
  (4894.)

42.

Après s'est ens el lit couciés,   Erec an l'un couchier se vet;
Moult fu dolens et esmaiés ;   An l'autre est Enide couchiee,
Ne puet dormir, ne reposer,   Mout dolante et mout correciee;
Viller l'estuet et retorner.   Onques la nuit ne prist somoil:
  .   .   .   .
Onques la nuit n'a pris somel.   Tote la nuit vellier l'estuet.
  (4425–36.)   (3442–55.)

43.

Tant fu bien fait et tant fu bials,   Par verité dire vos os
Qu'en tot le mont, ne en la mer,   Qu'an tot le monde n'a meniere
Jà nus hom ne poroit trover   De peisson ne de beste fiere
Poisson, beste, n'oisel volant   Ne d'ome ne d'oisel volage,
Ne fust ouvrés el pavement.   Que chascuns lonc sa propre image
  (4675 ff.)   N'i fust ovrez et antailliez.
                                                   (6876 ff.)
                                                   Cf.
                                              Ne soz ciel n'a oisel volant.
                                                 (5755.)

44.

Et Giglains quant il fu el lit,   la joie et le delit
Desor ara de son delit.   Qui fu an la chanbre et el lit.
Ensanble li amant se jurent.   (2071–2.)

Quant il furent ensenble et jurent,
Molt docement andoi s'enbracent ;
Les levres des bouces s'enlacent ;
Li uns à l'autre son droit rent ;
Fors de baiser n'orent content ;
Et cascuns en voloit plus faire
De baiser dont son cuer esclaire.
As baisers qu'il firent d'amors
Del cuer se traient les dolors.
Et si les aboivrent de joie.
Amors les mainne bone voie,
Les oils tornent à esgarder ;
Les bras metent à acoler,
Le cuers s'atornent al voloir.
L'uns velt de l'autre près manoir ;
Por l'amor qu'entr'els II estoit
Veut l'uns ço que l'autres voloit.
Je ne sai s'il le fist s'amie,
Car n'i fu pas, ne l'en vi mie ;
Mais non de pucele perdi
La dame dalès son ami.
Cele nuit restoré se sont
De quanques il demoré ont.
    (4704 ff.)
Cf.
Il avoit joie en sa baillie ;
Entre ses bras avoit sa mie
Que il souvent acole et baise ;
Moult estoit à joie et à aise.
    (4772 ff.)
Giglains se couce lès sa drue.
Dalès li se jut tote nuit,
Si orent moult de lor deduit.
    (5294 ff.)
Son pis sor le sien retenoit
Nu à nu, que rien ni avoit.
    (2413-4.)
Dalès li se jut tote nuit,
Si orent moult de lor deduit.
    (5295-6.)
La nuit jurent à grant deduit.
    (5943.)

[Or ot sa joie et son deduit,
Ansanble gisent par la nuit.]
    (5239-40.)
La ou il jurent an un lit,
Ou orent eü maint delit.
Boche a boche antre braz gisoient,
Come cil qui mout s'antramoient.
    (2475 ff.)
Lor droit randent a chascun manbre.
Li oel d'esgarder se refont,
Cil qui d'amors la voie font
Et lor message au cuer anvoient ;
Que mout lor plest quan que il voient.
Après le message des iauz
Vient la douçors, qui mout vaut miauz,
Des beisiers qui amor atraient.
Andui cele douçor essaient,
Et lor cuers dedanz an aboivrent
Si qu'a grant painne s'an desoivrent ;
De beisier fu li premiers jeus.
Et l'amors, qui est antr'aus deus,
Fist la pucele plus hardie
De rien ne s'est acoardie ;
Tot sofri, que que li grevast.
Einçois qu'ele se relevast,
Ot perdu le non de pucele ;
Au matin fu dame novele.
    (2090 ff.)
Cele nuit ont bien restoré
Ce que il ont tant demoré.
    (2087-8.)
Cf.
Or fu acolee et beisiee,
Or fu de toz biens aeisiee,
Or ot grant joie et grant delit ;
Que nu n a sont an un lit
Et li uns l'autre acole et beise ;
N'est riens nule qui tant lor pleise.
    (5245 ff. ; cf. 1424.)
De li fist s'amie et sa drue.
Tot mist son cuer et s'antandue

	An li acoler et beisier. (2439 ff.) An un lit certes nu a nu. (3399.)

45.

Quant il l'enprist à souvenir, De rire ne se puet tenir. Quant la dame en rire le vit, Se li a tot maintenant dit: ·Dites le moi, fait ele, amis, Por quel cose vos avés ris. Ri avés, je ne sais por coi: Biaus ciers amis, dites le moi. Moi ne l'devés vos celer mie.' Cil li respont: 'ma douce amie.' (4780 ff.)	Quant il l'an prist a sovenir, De plorer ne se pot tenir. (2483-4.) Que si formant plorer la vit, Si li a demandé et dit: ' Dites moi, bele amie chiere, Por quoi plorez an tel meniere? De quoi avez ire ne duel? Certes je le savrai mon vuel. Dites le moi, ma douce amie, Et gardez, nel me celez mie.'[1] (2513 ff.; cf. also 2742, 3552.)

46.

Et quant l'a véu la roïne, Si le salue et si l'encline. (5095-6.)	La u Yders vit la reïne, Jusque devant ses piez l'ancline, Saluëe l'a tot premiers. (1183 ff.)

47.

De s'amie ot tot son voloir Tot ço que il voloit avoir. (5235-6.)	Or ot totes ses volantez. (5241.)

48.

Quant Giglains au matin s'esvelle, De ce qu'il vit ot grant mervelle. (5303-4.)	s'esvella Et de ce mout se mervella Que si formant plorer la vit. (2511 ff.)

49.

Au main quant l'aube fu crevée, Li saint sonnent au grant mostier; Tuit sont levé li chevalier. Giglains s'est levés et s'amie; Au mostier de Sainte-Marie	L'andemain lués que l'aube crieve Isnelemant et tost se lieve, Et ses ostes ansanble o lui Au mostier vont orer andui Et firent de Saint Esperite

---

[1] The only real difference between the two passages lies in the fact that Renaud makes an inquiry after the cause of laughter, instead of grief, as in *Erec*.

S'en alerent andoi orer;
La dame fist messe canter.
Quant la messe cantée fu
Si se sont el palais venu.
(4932 ff.)
Cf.
Quant li saint sonent au mostier,
A messe vont li chevalier.
(5945-6.)

Messe chanter a un hermite . . .
Quant il orent la messe oïe, . . .
Si s'an repeirent a l'ostel.
(697-706.)
Cf.
Ja estoit la messe sonee
Si s'an vont a la mestre eglise
Oïr la messe et le servise;
A l'eveschié s'an vont orer.
(6888 ff.)
and
Quant tote la messe oïe orent,
Si sont el palés retorné.
(6918-9; cf. 2385-6.)

50.

Quant armé furent li baron
En la plaingne sous Valedon,
La véissiés tant elme cler
Et tante ensaigne venteler,
Et tans destriers, bauchant et bai,
Plus nombreus que dire ne sai,
Et tans escu reflanboier,
Et tante guimple desploier,
Sor elmes tantes connissances,
Tant blanc hauber et tantes lances,
Paintes à or et à ason,
Fremir tant vermel siglaton
Et tant pingnon et tante mance
Et çainte tante espée blance,
Et tant brocher ceval de pris.
(5498 ff.)

Li tornois assanble et ajoste
Desoz Tenebroc an la plaingne.
La ot tante vermoille ansaingne . . .
Et tante guinple et tante manche, . . .
Tant i ot lances aportees
D'arjant et de sinople taintes:
D'or et d'azur an i ot maintes;
. . . . .
Tant blazon et tant hauberc blanc,
Tante espee a senestre flanc,
Tanz buens escuz fres et noviaus, . . .
Tant buen cheval bauçant et sor,
Fauves et blans et noirs et bes.
(2136-57.)
Cf.
Sor chevaus bes, sors et bauçanz.
(2344.)

51.

Onques cele de Cornouaille
Del grant Morholt, ne de Tristant,
. . . . .
Ne fu tels bataille véue.
(3010-5.)

Onques, ce cuit, tel joie n'ot,
La ou Tristanz le fier Morhot
. . . . .
vainqui.
(1247 ff.)

52.

Dorenavant vos veul conter
Briement, sans trop longue raison,

Mes je vos an dirai la some
Briémant et sanz longue parole

Comment de Galles li baron
Et li evesque et li abé
Et tot li prince, et li casé,
Vinrent, quant sorent la novele
Qu'estorse fu la damoisele,
Et qu'ensi est cose avenue.
Puis n'i ot nule retenue,
Que tot ne venissent à cort,
Por la grant joie qui lor sort.
Tot li palais vint cele part,
Petis et grans, moult lor est tart,
Qu' il aient lor dame véue
Moult i est grans lies méue.
Arcevesque, évesque et abé
Et tot li autre clerc letré,
S'est venu à porcession,
Et canterent à moult haut ton ;
Et portent crois et encensiers,
. . . . . .
A casses, à tot les cors sains.
(3429-50.)

Novele par le païs vole
Qu'einsi est la chose avenue.
Puis n'i ot nule retenue,
Que tuit ne venissent a cort.
Trestoz li pueples i acort.
(6174 ff.)
Liez est li rois et sa janz liee :
N'i a un seul cui mout ne siee
Et mout ne pleise ceste chose.
(6165 ff. ; cf. 6364-71.)
Maintenant sont avant venu
Tuit li prelat, juene et chenu ;
Car a la cort avoit assez
Venuz evesques et abez.
(6861 ff.)
Ancontr' aus s'an ist tote fors . . .
La processions del mostier.
Croiz et textes et ancansier
Et chasses a toz les cors sainz,
. . . . . .
Ne de chanter n'i ot po fet.
Onques ansanble ne vit nus
Tant rois, tant contes ne tant dus
Ne tant barons a une messe.
(6899-6909.)
Cf.
    moi fu tart
Que ça m'amenast avuec lui.
(6284-5.)

53.

Trestout ensanble à la rescousse
Sor lui cascuns sa lance estrousse.
Cil se tient bien qu'il ne caï.
(5537 ff.)

Quant Erec point a la rescosse,
Sor un des lor sa lance estrosse.
(2241-2.)
Mes bien se tint qu'il ne cheï.
(3825.)

54.

Et fiert si Keu le senescal,
Qui venus estoit asanbler,
L'escu li fist au bras hurter,
Et les estriers li fist laissier,
Si qu'envers l'abat del destrier.
(5574 ff.)

Keus li seneschaus.
(1091.)
Si bien le fiert que il abat
Et lui et le destrier tot plat.
(3035-6.)
L'escu giete jus et la lance,

Celui laisse et autre i abat
A terre del cheval tot plat.
(5909–10.)

Chevaliers prent, cevals gaaigne.
(5763.)

A vii^{xx} chevaliers mult pros.
Les regnes prendent par le nos.
(5869–70.)

Vers le cief dou rent a véu
Erec, un moult bon chevalier,
Sor un cheval fort et legier.
Por joster avoit l'escu pris,
Et la lance sor fautre mis.
Giglains encontre lui s'adrece,
L'anste brandist, l'escu enbrece,
Des esperons au cheval donne ;
Li uns envers l'autre esperonne.
Moult très durement se requierent ;
Par si grant vertu s'entrefierent,
Que li escu percent et croissent,
Et les lances brisent et froissent.
(5675 ff.)
Cf.
Lances briser et escus fendre.
(5858.)

De totes parts fremist li rans ;
Moult par i ert la noise grans,
Des cols et des lances li frois.
(5897 ff.)

Li un keurent por les fors prendre ;
Li autre keurent por desfendre.
(5891–2.)

Si se leisse cheoir a terre.
(3069–70.)

55.
Chevaliers prant, chevaus gaaingne.
(2228 ; cf. 2222.)

56.
Qui mout estoit vaillanz et preuz.
Les resnes pranent par les neuz.
(2193–4.)

57.
Erec sist sor un cheval blanc,
Toz seus s'an vint au chief del ranc
Por joster, se il trueve a cui.
De l'autre part anconlre lui
Point li Orguelleus de la Lande
. . . . . .
Chevaliers fu de grant proesce.
Li uns contre l'autre s'adresce.
(2171–86.)
Erec l'escu formant anbrace.
(2878.)
Erec cele part esperone,
Des esperons au cheval done.
(205–6.)
As fers des lances se requierent,
Par si grant vertu s'antreficrent
Que li escu percent et croissent,
Les lances esclicent et froissent.
(867 ff.)
Cf.
Lances brisent et escu troent.
(2163.)

58.
D'anbes deus parz fremist li rans,
An l'estor lieve li escrois,
Des lances est mout granz li frois.
(2160 ff.)

59.
Li un corent por les foiz prandre
Et li autre por le defandre.
(2169–70.)

60.

A son ceval lasque le frain,
Si le fiert. si de grant ravine,
En l'escu deseur la potrine.
. . . . . .
Si le fiert si, sor le mamele,
Ne l'pot tenir potrails ne sele,
Que ne l'abatist del destrier,
Et ne le fist tost trebucier.
(5776–86.)
Cf.
Si le fiert si en l'escu haut,
Qu'estriers ne sele ne li vaut,
Que del destrier ne l'abatist.
(5849 ff.)
Feru l'a par si grant puissance,
Droit en mi le pis, de la lance,
Que nule riens ne l'pot tenir,
Qu'à terre ne l'fesist venir.
(5704 ff.)

Aguissans point, baisse sa lance
Et fiert Flore, le duc de France,
En mi le pis, par tel aïr,
Que del destrier le fist partir.
(5871 ff.)

Si saillirent atant les vespres.
(5930.)

Moult bien le refaisoit Giglains;
Maint chevalier prist à ses mains.
(5911–2.)
Bien l'avait fait Giglains devan
Mais or le fist il assés mieus.
Car ainc on ne vit as plus pre
Chevalier qui mius le fesist.
(5954 ff.)

Que tuit li portent garantie
Qu'il avoit vencu le tornoi.
(5926–7; cf. also 5966, 5972–3.)

Et sist sor un cheval d'Irlande,
Qui le porte de grant ravine.
Sor l'escu devant la peitrine
Le fiert Erec de tel vertu
Que del destrier l'a abatu.
(2176 ff.)
Si bien le fiert sor la memele
Que vuidier li covint la sele.
(2243–4.)
Çangle ne resnes ne peitraus
Ne porent le roi retenir,
Ne l'estuisse a terre venir.
Einsi vola jus del destrier,
N'i guerpi sele ne estrier.
(2204 ff.)
Cf.
Andui poingnent, si s'antrevienent,
Les lances esloigniees tienent; . . .
Sor l'escu fiert par tel aïr, . . .
Anmi le piz le fausse et ront, . . .
Et cil cheï.
(2861–73.)

61.
Les vespres salirent a tant.
(2252.)
62.
Si bien le fist Erec le jor
Que li miaudre fu de l'estor;
Mes mout le fist miauz l'andemain.
Tant prist chevaliers de sa main.
(2253–6.)
Car n'avoit an tote sa cort
Mellor chevalier ne plus preu.
(2286–7.)
63.
Trestuit d'anbes deus parz disoient
Qu'il avoit le tornoi veincu.
(2260–1.)

Quant entre conjoï se furent,
Por aler à la cort se murent
. . . . .
A son ostel trovent Artus.
Quant il les vit, si lieve sus,
Giglan com vit, va le baisier
Et de ses deus bras l'enbracier.
Lors véissiés grant joie faire,
Les chevaliers vers Giglan traire
Et saluer et conjoïr. .
(5975-87.)

Plus bele avoir vos ne poés ;
Et si est de moult grant parage ;
Ne por biauté, ne por lignage,
Ne le devés vos laissier mie,
. . . . . .
Il vit la dame bele et sage.
(6040-9.)

Ne fus nus hom plus bien venus
N'à plus grant joie receús
Com Giglains fu en cele terre.
(6089 ff.)

Tant ont chevaucié par les plains,
Et tant ont lor cemin tenu,
Qu'il sont à Valedon venu.
(5978 ff.)
Cf.
Or cevaucent plains et boscages,
Et landes, et vals, et rivages ;
Tant ont coru par les contrées
Et tant erré par lor jornées,
Et tant lor droite voie tinrent,
Qu'al castel des Puceles vinrent.
(5355 ff.)
Quatre jornées, voire plus,
Avoit chevauché la roïne.
(4966-7.)

64.
Quant bien et bel atorné furent,
Por aler a la cort s'esmurent.
A cort vienent : li rois les voit
. . . . . .
Si beise Erec et puis Guivret,
Enide au col ses deus braz met,
Si la rebeise et fet grant joie.
. . . . . .
Chascuns del conjoïr se painne.
(6457-70 ; cf. 6454.)

65.
La pucele est et bele et sage,
Et si est mout de haut parage.
(1277-8.)
Ne por biauté ne por lignage
Ne doi je pas le mariage
De la pucele refuser.
(1565 ff.)

66.
Onques nus rois an son reaume
Ne fu plus lieemant veüz,
N'a greignor joie receüz.
(2398 ff.)

67.
Le bois trespassent et la plainne.
Tote la droite voie tindrent
Tant que a Caradigan vindrent.
(1086 ff.)
Cf.
Tant trespassent puis et pandanz,
Forez et plaingnes et rivieres
Quatre granz jornees plenieres
Qu'a Carnant vindrent au quint jor.
(2312 ff.)
and
Tant ont erré et chevauchié
Qu'il vindrent . . .
(3667-8.)

Et chevauchierent bos et plains.
(2468.)
Tant ont cevauché et erré,
Que il sont à Londres venu.
(6006-7.)

68.

Que tant com la hanste li dure,   Erec tant con hante li dure
L'abati à la terre dure.   Le trebuche a la terre dure.
(5553-4.)   (2189-90.)

69.

Or veul je votre non savoir.   Mes vostre non savoir desir.
(1469.)   'Sire,' fet il, 'vostre pleisir.
'Sire,' fait il, 'tot vraiement   Quant vos mon non savoir volez
Vos en dirai la verité.   Ne vos doit pas estre celez.
Jà mos ne vos en ert celé.   Cadoc de Tabriol ai non.'
Je sui,' fait il, 'sire des Aies.'   (4511 ff.)
(1190 ff.)   Cf.
Cf.   'Mes dites moi, nel me celez,
Se li demanda...   Par quel non estes apelez?'
Et conment a non, que li die   Et cil respont: 'Jel te dirai,
Qui est, ne dont ne li coilt mie.   Ja mon non ne te celerai.
(870-4.)   Erec ai non.'
Hélin a non.   (1055-61; cf. also 2699, 4075,
(1195; cf. 1472; cf. also 3922,   4152, 5050, 6257.)
4742, 4788.)

70.

Et rivieres et praeries,   De forez et de praeries,
Et si est grans gaagneries,   De vingnes, de gaeigneries,
D'autre part les vignes estoient.   De rivieres et de vergiers.
(1495 ff.; cf. 3544-5.)   (2319 ff.)

71.

Il ne remaint arme el castel,   An tot le chastel n'a remés
Li villart et li jovencel.   Home ne fame, droit ne tort,
(2086-7.)   Grant ne petit, foible ne fort,
Trestot s'en vont, petit et grant,   Qui aler puisse, qui n'i voise,
Ni a remés keu ne serjant.   (5698 ff.)
(2363-4.)   Il n'i remaint juenes ne viauz.
    (2688: cf. 4870.)

72.

Qui bien soc prendre mon consel,   Qui as estoiles se consoille
Et à la lune et au solel.   Et a la lune et au soloil.
(4851-2.)   An autre leu ne prant consoil.
   (6782 ff.)

73.

Et portent ostoirs et faucons   Espreviers et faucons de mues
Et ostoirs et bons espreviers.   Et li autre aportoient fors
(3809-10.)   Terciaus, ostors muëz et fors.
Espreviers portent et faucons,   (352 ff.; cf. also 5362-3.)
Ostoirs, tercets, esmerillons.
(3906-7.)

74.

Li castels fu clos de fossés   une haute tor,
Grans et parfons, et loncs et lés;   Qui close estoit de mur an tor
Sor les fossés hals murs avoit,   Et de fossé le et parfont.
Dont li castels tos clos estoit.   (3671 ff.)
(1499 ff.; cf. 2830 ff.)

75.

Ceste ne trove sa parelle,   Auoit une escharbocle dor
Tant estoit bele à grant mervelle.   Assises furent par menuoille
Sa biauté tel clarté jeta.   Nus ne uit onques sa paroille
(2198 ff.)   Chascune tel clarte gitoit
Une escarboucle sus luissoit,   De nuiz con se il iorz estoit
Plus que solaus resplendissoit,   Au matin grant li solauz luist
Et par nuit rent si grant clarté   Si grant clarte randoit par nuit.
Com se ce fust en tens d'esté.   (p. 88, ll. 16 ff.)
(1897 ff.)   Cf.
Qui jetoit une tel clarté   D'escharboncles anluminees; ...
Com i cierge bien enbrasé.   Nule riens n'est clartez de lune
Tot le palais enluminoit,   A la clarté que toz li mandre
Une si grant clarté jetoit.   Des escharboncles pooit randre.
Hom ne vit onques sa parelle.   Por la clarté qu'eles randoient,
(3103 ff.)   Tuit cil qui el palés estoient ...
   (6842-8; cf. 429-34, 6844-5.)

76.

Tant estoit biaus à demesure   Et fu tant biaus qu'an nule terre
Qu'en tot le mont, tant com il dure,   N'estovoit plus bel de lui querre.
Ne trovast on un chevalier   Mout estoit biaus et preuz et janz.
Ne qui tant fesist à proisier: (87 ff.)

Sages et pros et cortois fu.
    (4301 ff.)
Cf.
Moult estoit bials à demesure.
    (3892; cf. 3649.)

Haumes laciés, haubers vestus.
    (5371.)

    les cevals poingnent,
Et por joster si s'entreloingnent,
   .   .   .   .   .
Si s'entrevont entreferir,
Que les escus se font croissir,
   .   .   .   .   .
Andui s'abatent des cevals.
Ne furent navré ne blecié;
Isnelement sont redrecié,
   .   .   .   .   .
... tronçons des espées,
S'entre donnent moult grans colées.
En tos sanblans bien se requierent,
Sor les elmes sovent se fierent.
    (1743-60.)
Cf.
    si s'eslongent,
Por tost aler lor cevals poingent.
Molt aloient tost li ceval.
Si s'entrefierent li vasal
Des lances grans cols à devise.
    (2618 ff.)
Sor les escus haut se requierent
De lances tels cols sentrefierent,
Que des cevals s'entr'abatirent.
    (2915 ff.)
Il ne fu navrés ne bleciés.
Isnelement est redreciés.
    (2670-1.)

Lors s'entrevinrent fierement,
Sor les escus se vont ferir,
   .   .   .   .   .

Cf.
Car mout es biaus a desmesure.
    (5520; cf. 1484.)
Mout est preuz et sage et cortoise.
    (3642.)
77.
Hiaumes laciez, haubers vestuz.
    (4965.)
78.
Cil plus d'un arpant s'antresloi-
    ngnent,
Por assanbler les chevaus poingnent,
As fers des lances se requierent,
Par si grant vertu s'antrefierent
Que li escu percent et croissent,
   .   .   .   .   .
Contre terre anbedui se ruient,
Li cheval par le chanp s'an fuient.
Cil resont tost an piez sailli,
   .   .   .   .   .
Des tranchanz granz cos s'antre-
    donent.
Li hiaume quassent et resonent,
Fiers est li chaples des espees:
Mout s'antredonent granz colees.
    (865 ff.)
Cf.
Ne furent pas navré a mort,
Mes duremant furent blecié.
Isnelemant sont redrecié.
    (3784 ff.)

79.
Andui poingnent, si s'antrevienent,
   .   .   .   .   .
Sor l'escu fiert par tel aïr,

Le Biaus Desconnéus fiert lui ;
L'escu perce, l'auberc desront,
Dedens le cors le fer repont.
Mort le trebuce del ceval.
  (1082-97.)
Cf.
Et cil r'a si très-bien feru
Helin de Graies, par vertu,
De sa lance, ens el pis devant
L'auberc li ront et vait faussant ;
. . . . . .
Del bon ceval le fist caïr.
  (1109-14.)

Devant le roi en vint tot dreit . . .
Le roi salua maintenant,
Et puis les autres ensement.
  (75-8.)
Cf.
Li un les autres saluerent.
  (5098 ; cf. also 3276, 3511, 3854,
    4162, 4167, etc.)

Ne porïons vile trover,
Ne maison, en ceste contrée,
Environ nos, d'une jornée.
  (596 ff.)

Robers i vint isnelement,
Ki le desarma en la place ;
L'elme fors de cief li esrace,
Puis li a desceinte l'espée,
Quant ot la teste desarmée,
L'auberc li traist, de blance maille,
Quant deslacié ot la ventaille.
  (804 ff.)

Qu'il li pardoinst à ceste fois.
  (839.)

De l'un chief an l'autre le fant ;
Ne li haubers ne le defant :
Anmi le piz le fausse et ront,
Et de la lance li repont
Pié et demi dedanz le cors.
Au retreire a son cop estors,
Et cil cheï. Morir l'estut.
  (2861-73.)

80.

Jusque devant le roi s'an vindrent,
Si le saluent maintenant,
Et la reïne einsemant.
  (6596 ff.)
Cf.
Li un les autres saluërent.
  (2354 ; cf. also 5533, 5548, 6231,
    6373, etc.)

81.

             une jornee tot an tor
N'avoit chastel, vile ne tor,
Ne meison . . .
  (3137 ff.)

82.

Li escuiiers Erec desconbre
De son hiaume, si li deslace
La vantaille devant la face.
  (3170 ff.)
Hauberc li vest de buene maille,
Et si li lace la vantaille.
Le hiaume brun li met el chief . . .
Au costé l'espec li çaint.[1]
  (713-17.)

83.

Ceste foiz vos iert pardonee.
  (2854.)

---

[1] Positive statement (arming) instead of negative (disarming).

84.

Seur destriers sors, bais et bauçans,
O v^c chevaliers armés.
(5455–6.)
Cf.
Et avoit en sa conpaignie
v^c chevaliers de maisnie.
(5446–7.)

Chevaliers i ot bien cinc çanz
Sor chevaus bes, sors et bauçanz.
(2343–4.)

85.

Quant venus fu tos li barnés,
Qui à la cort fu asamblés,
Grans fu la cors qui fu mandée,
Quant i fu la cors asamblée.
Là véisiés grant joie faire,
As jogléors vièles traire,
Harpes soner et estriver,
As cantéors cançons canter.
(17 ff.)

Furent assanblé li baron.
(6365.)
Granz fu l'assanblee et la presse.
(6369.)
Einsi jusqu'a la cort l'an mainnent
Et de joie feire se painnent
Si con li cuer les an semonent.
Rotes, harpes, vïeles sonent.
(6379 ff.)

86.

Ainc Elaine . . .
N'Isex la blonde, ne Bliblis,
Ne Lavine de Lombardie,
. . . . . .
N'orent pas de biauté la disme.
(4258–64.)
Onques n'ot de biauté le quart
Nule dame qui dont fust née.
(5084–5; cf. other references to
Yseut (4336), and Yseuls la
bele (5492).)

Plus bele que ne fu Helainne.
(6344.)
Onques Lavine de Laurante,
Qui tant par fu et bele et jante,
N'ot mie de biauté le quart.
(5891 ff.)
Iseuz la blonde.
(424.)
Cf.
une dame si bele
Qui Iseuz sanblast estre s'ancele.
(4943–4.)

87.

Les escrins carcent as somiers,
Et rices cofres, rices males,
Moult jetent grant avoir de Gales,
Hanas, copes d'or et d'argent,
Et moult rice autre garnement.
(3811 ff.)

Les somiers que il lor menoient,
L'or et l'arjant et les besanz
Et toz les autres garnemanz
Qui estoient dedanz les males,
An son reaume d'Outre-Gales.
(1870 ff.)

88.

Si bele riens ne fu veüe.
. . . . . .
Si l'avait bien nature ouvrée,
Et tel biauté li ot donnée,
Que plus bel vis, ne plus bel front,
N'avoit feme qui fust el mont,
Plus estoit blance d'une flor
Et d'une vermelle color
Estoit sa face enluminée.
(2198-2212.)
Cf.
Mains ot blances com flors de lis.
(2219.)

De cesti tesmoingne Nature
Qu'onques si bele criature
Ne fu veüe an tot le monde.
. . . . . .
Plus ot, que n'est la flors de lis,
Cler et blanc le front et le vis.
Sor la blanchor par grant mervoille
D'une color fresche et vermoille,
Que Nature li ot donee,
Estoit sa face anluminee.
(421-32 [1]; cf. 2414-15.)

89.

Ja nus hom ne demant plus bièle,
Se ele n'eüst tel paor.
(702-3.)

Et s'il ne fust granz a enui,
Soz ciel n'eüst plus bel de lui.
(5901-2.)

The following parallels are given, not because it is supposed they have any significance in themselves, but merely for completeness. They are therefore numbered separately.

1.

Qui moult legiers et fors estoit.
De relever moult s'esforçoit.
(1434-5.)
(The next lines rhyme relever: grever.)

Ne se santent de rien grevé,
Isnelemant sont relevé;
Car fort estoient et legier.
(5959 ff.)

2.

Esloignent plus d'un arpent.
(2088.)

Cil plus d'un arpent s'antresloi-
ngnent.
(865; cf. 4040.)

3.

Car Dius nos puet moult bien aider.
(2532.)
Dius nos en puet moult bien aidier.
(2653; cf. 310.)

Mes Deus li povra bien eidier.
(3428; cf. 663, 3567, 5525, 5935.)

---

[1] Part of this passage is cited before (p. 68).

4.

Si s'entreviennent anbedui.
(5622.)

Si s'antrevienent anbedui.
(3012, 5952.)

5.

Iluec ot mainte joste faite,
Maint cop féru d'espée traite.
(5668–9.)

Mes Erec tint l'espee treite,
Une anvaïe li a feite.
(4465–6.)
l'espee treite : feite.
(3855–6.)

6.

'Alés, dist il, mi escuier,
Amenés moi mon bon destrier
Et mes armes ; si m'armerai,
Gardés que n'i faites delai.'
Cil les vont querre isnelement,
Les aportent hastivement.
(1367 ff.)

Ses chevaus comande anseler
Et fet ses armes aporter.
Vaslet corent, si li aportent.
(4281 ff.)

7.

Cele respont : 'Dol doi avoir :
Ne je jamais joie n'aurai.
. . . . .
    de dol morrai ;
Li cuers me crieve de dolor.
Lasse! comment vivrai mais jor?'
(1550–58.)

An sospirant li dist : 'Biaus sire,
N'est mervoille se je faz duel ;
Que morte seroie mon vuel.
Je n'aim ma vie ne ne pris.'
(4338 ff.)

8.

Puis li demande qu'ele a fait.
(2688.)

Si li demande qu'ele fet.
(4172.)

9.

Moult est bons et ciers ses cevals,
. . . . . .
N'ainc hom ne vit si bien movant.
(2967–71.)

Cheval ot buen et bien movant.
(2960.)

10.

Gauvains lès lui séoir le fist.
(102.)
Dalès lui l'a sor l'erbe asise.
(869.)

Et delez lui a destre assise.
(1762.)
Li rois les fet lez lui seoir.
(6462 ; cf. also 1305, 3313, 6834.)

11.

Li vis, qu'il ot bien fait et cler,
Li devint moult pales et tains :
Moult estoit febles et atains.
   (3995 ff.)
Cf.
Qui moult estoit pales et vains.
   (3563.)
Tos en devint pales et vains.
   (3651.)
Car il le vit et pale et taint.
   (4131.)

Le cors bien fet et le vis cler.
   (2492.)
Toz li devint pales et blans
Li vis con se ele fust morte.
   (3720-1.)
Car mout estoit et pale et tainte :
atainte.
   (5243-4.)
Cf.
je le vi si pale et taint.
   (4183.)

12.

Par le frain son roncin tenoit.
   (5311.)

Einz tint par les frains an sa main
Les chevaus. (3101-2.)

13.

Et fiert Mordret sor l'elme cler,
Si que tot le fist estonner.
   (5637-8.)

Tel cop a delivre li done
Sor le hiaume, que tot l'estone.
   (973-4.)

14.

Après vos à la cort irai,
Si tost comme je le porrai,
Le roi Artur. Me salués
Et vostre congié me donés.
   (3852 ff.)

Si je m'an vois, je revandrai
Quant Deu pleira et je porrai.
Toz et totes vos comant gié
A Deu, si me donez congié.
   (2757 ff.)

15.

Adont s'asisent au soper.
Moult sont bien servi à devise
Et si ont mès de mainte guise.
   (2711 ff.)

Si se sont au soper assis.
   (498.)
De mes divers sont tuit servi.
   (6939.)

16.

Esprevier bien mué et bel.
. . . . . .
Sor I perce tote d'or.
   (1569-72.)

   cist oisiaus
Qui tant par est muëz et biaus.
   (807-8.)
Iert sor une perche d'arjant
Uns espreviers mout biaus assis.
   (566-7.)

17.

Quant Lanpars l'ot, grant joie en a. Gauvains l'ot, acoler le va.
Vers lui maintenant s'en ala   . . . . . .
Maintenant le va acoler.   De joie l'acole et anbrace.
(2702 ff.)   (4155-8.)

18.

Ses escus en argent estoit.   Tanz buens escuz . . .
Roses vermelles i avoit   D'arjant et de sinople biaus.
De sinople les roses sont.   (2153-4.)
(1696 ff.)

19.

Del venéor a la foi prise.   Lors an a Erec la foi prise.
Une autre cose li devise.   Tuit sont venu a la devise.
(1465-6.)   (1069-70.)

20.

Erec i estoit, li fius Lac;   Li seconz Erec li fiz Lac,
Com s'i fu Lasselos dou Lac.   Et li tierz Lanceloz del Lac.
(39-40.)   (1693-4.)

21.

Come rose ot vis coloré,   Mout remire son chief le blont,
Le iouls ot vairs, bouce riant,   Ses iauz rianz et son cler front,
Les mains blances, cors avenant;   Le nes et la face et la boche.
Bel cief avoit, si estoit blonde.   (1491 ff.)
(148 ff.)

22.

En son cief ot un cercle d'or.   Un hiaume a cercle d'or listé.
(145.)   (2658.)

23.

Son escu a pris et sa lance.   Son escu a pris et sa lance.
(681.)   (4302.)
      Son escu prent,   La lance et l'escu prist aprés.
Et après, sa lance ensement.   (3963; cf. 2857, 3593, 4744.)
(387-8.)
Son escu prist isnelement;
Et puis après reprist sa lance.
(1396-7.)

24.

Tot maintenant i fait aler
III des moult haus, à lui parler.
(3502-3.)

Maintenant murent li message:
Li baron, qui l'alerent querre,
Li plus haut home de sa terre.
(6514 ff.)

25.

Quant la dame el palais entra.
(5093.)
Cf.
. Si se sont el palais venu.
(4940.)

Quant eles vindrent el palés.
(6831.)
Cf.
Si vienent el palés.
(5311; cf. 5559, 6811, 6826.)

26.

Qui ne fust à fin or portraite.
Moult estoit la roube bien faite.
(5061-2.)

Ceste oevre fu el drap portreite,
De quoi la robe Erec fu feite.
(6791-2.)

27.

Se tu ne l' fais, à ceste espée
Auras jà la teste copée.
(1173-4.)
Cf.
Jà li eust la teste copée.
. . . . . .
Moult doucement merci li crie.
(1446-50; cf. 1168.)

La teste li eüst coupee
Se il n'eüst merci criëe.
(991-2.)

28.

Cil des Aies prison fiance
Qu'il en ira, sans demorance,
Droit à la cort Artu le roi.
(1175 ff.)
Cf.
Et si fiancerés prison,
Que vos irés, sans oquison,
Ens en la cort Artu le roi.
(1783 ff.; cf. 477-9.)

Donc alez tost sanz demorer
A mon seignor, le roi Artu.
(4526-7.)
Cf.
Fiancier t'an estuet prison,
Et sanz nul respit or androit
Iras a ma dame tot droit.
(1028 ff.)
Sanz achoison.
(3472.)

Au secors faire veul aler.
(208.)
Secors, qu'ele en a grant mestier.
(175.)
Ce sanble mestier ait d'aïe.
(628, 645.)
Or m'a vostre secors mestier.
(552.)

29.
Cele part vuel aler le cors,
Si savrai quel besoing ele a.
(4320-1.)
[Ele a] mestier d'aïe et de secors.
(4319.)
Et de secors mestier avoit.
(4314.)
Cf.
Mestier d'aïe, 3909; secors mestier, 3913; grant mestier, 3932.

Moult le faisoit bien en l'estor
(: le jor).
(5551-2.)
Cf.
Si bien le fait.
(5646.)

30.
Si bien le fist Erec le jor
Que li miaudre fu de l'estor.
(2253-4.)

Là ot vuidée mainte sele
Et maint chevalier abatu.
(5558-9.)

31.
Tant prist chevaliers de sa main
Et tant i fist seles vuidier.
(2256-7.)

Sonnent flahutes et buissines.
(5883.)

32.
Sonent timbre, sonent tabor,
. . . . . .
Et buisines et chalemel.
(2052-4.)
Cf.
Cil flaüte, cil chalemele.
(2046.)

Giglains qui fiert le Sagremor
. . . . . .
Qu'il l'abati.
(5905-8.)

33.
La fu abatuz Sagremors.
(2238.)

Le rois lor dist : . . .
'Biaus niés,' fait-il.
(6022-4.)

34.
'Biaus niés Gauvains,' ce dist li rois.
(4077.)

35.

Cele nuit à grant joie furent	A grant joie ...
A Londres la cité.	Vindrent a Nantes la cité.
(6063-4.)	(6582-4.)

36.

Si com raconte li istore.	si con l'estoire reconte.
(6102.)	(3590.)
	Cf.
	Lisant trovomes an l'estoire.
	(6736; cf. 6742.)

37.

Guerpir lor estuet les cevals,	Guerpir lor estuet les estriers,
A la terre caient andui.	Contre terre anbedui se ruient.
(1427-8.)	(872-3.)
Cf.	Cf.
Les arçons li a fait guerpir;	Le cheval guerpir li estuet.
Li estrier ne l' porent tenir.	(3066.)
(439-40.)	Que les estriers eüst guerpiz.
	(3604.)

38.

En lor mains tiennent les espées,	Fiers est li chaples des espees:
Dont il se donnent grans colées.	Mout s'antredonent granz colees.
(451-2.)	(881-2.)
Cf.	
S'entre donnent moult grans colées.	
(1758.)	
Là ot feru de grans colées	
De roides lances et d'espées.	
Moult par estoit li caples grans.	
(5651 ff.)	
Cf. also 465-6, 1409-10 5902, 5720-1, 5860; for fier caple font, see 1417; cf. 5653, 5614, 5754, 5895.	

39.

Et vint tot droit à son seignor,	A son seignor vint, si l'esvoille.
Et cil maintenant l'esvilla.	(3468.)
(967-71.)	

40.

Quant li rois entent la parole,
Moult en fu liés ; la dame acole.
(5137–8.)

Li rois de joie saut an piez.
'Certes,' fet il, ' mout an sui liez.'
(4197–8.)
Li rois les acole et salue.
(4208.)

41.

Au Desconnéu font le lit.
Onques nus home plus bel vit.
De kuïtes pointes et moles
Que feroie longes paroles?
(2343 ff.)

Li lit furent aparellié
De blans dras et de coutes moles.
A tant faillirent les paroles.
(692 ff. ; cf. 3275.)

42.

N'avoit vestu fors sa cemise,
. . . . . .
Moult estoit la cemise blanche.
Mais encor est la cars moult plus,
Que la cemise de desus!
(2383–8.)

sa fille qui fu vestue
D'une chemise . . .
Un blanc chainse ot vestu dessus ;
N'avoit robe ne mains ne plus.
. . . . . .
Mes dessoz estoit biaus li cors.
(402–10.)

43.

Li doi vallet l'en ont mené
En sa loge, l'ont desarmé,
Puis l'ont coucié en un biel lit.
Mais moult i ot poi de délit.
Bliobliéris est plaiés.
(513 ff.)

Son seignor desarme et desvest, . . .
Fist un lit feire, haut et lonc ; . . .
S'ont Erec couchié et covert.
. . . . . .
Car bleciez estes et plaiiez.
(5132–51.)
Cf.
Vaslet corurent plus de vint
Por lui desarmer.
(1298–9.)

44.

moult li escrie :
Que por Diu laist que ne l'ocie.
(469–70.)

et cil li prie
Por Deu merci qu'il ne l'ocie.
(3840–1.)
Cf.
Merci! Ne m'ocirre tu pas.
(994.)

45.

Et blances napes et hanas, . . .
De bon vin ont trové asés.
(891–4.)
Les napes ont sor l'erbe mises.
(921.)

Buen vin ai et fromages gras,
Blanche toaille et biaus henas.
(3153–4.)
Puis a devant aus estandue
La toaille sor l'erbe drue.
(3173–4.)

A number of parallels will now be given to show that the two poems have the same stock of phrases in common.

1.

Chevaliers, borjois et sergant;
Dames et puceles.
(1645–6.)
Les dames et li chevalier,
Et li clerc et li escuier.
(2086–7.)
Dames, chevaliers, ne puceles.
(3904.)
Li duc, li prince et li baron.
(3527.)
Contes et dus, princes casés.
(3975.)
As dus, as contes, as marcis.
(4942.)
Maint roi, et maint duc et maint conte.
(5091.)
De ducs, de contes et de rois.
(5592; cf. also 5512.)

Dames, chevalier et borjois.
(4741.)
Chevalier, dames et puceles.
(5541.)
Dames et chevaliers.
(2745.)
Clers et chevaliers et puceles.
(2334.)
De chevaliers et de borjois.
(2389.)
De chevaliers et de serjanz.
(2464.)
Ou roi ou duc ou conte.
(6933.)
Assez i ot contes et dus.
(1963.)
Tant rois, tant contes ne tant dus
Ne tant barons.
(6908–9; cf. also 2653, 2722, 4958, 5096, 6949.)

2.

Sa lance a el fautre mise.
(357.)
Et la lance sor fautre mis.
(5679.)

Chascuns sa lance sor le fautre.
(2928; cf. 4441, 5768.)

3.

Ne vos en esmaiés de rien.
(3798; cf. 3739, 3743, 4064, 4071, 4732.)

Ne soiiez de rien esmaiiee.
(4920; cf. 951, 3413, 4871, 5183, 5529, 5839, 5854.)

4.

En haut s'escrie.   An haut s'escrie.
(243; cf. 1389, 1723, 2878, 4486.)   (4611; cf. 4677, 4841.)

5.

tot à devis.   tot a devise.
(374, 556.)   (2717.)
à lor devise.   a lor devise.
(734.)   (2940.)
à ma devise.   a ma devise.
(1621; cf. 576, 2675, 914, 2622,   (528; cf. 2021, 5289, 5324.)
2712, 2617, 4095.)

6.

à estros: vos.   a estros: vos.
(398; cf. 998, 2776, 3723,   (668.)
3941, 4362.)

7.

Sans nule faille: bataille.   Sanz nule faille: bataille.
(413, 1053, 1999.)   (262, 1159.)
Sans faille: bataille.   Sanz faille.
(367, 384, 888, 1117, 1166, 1354,   (1031, 5858.)
1586, 1600, 1669, 2062, 2091.)
Sans faille.
(1439, 1659, 3703, 3873, 4448,
5264, 5395, 6060; cf. 4856.)

8.

Mo(u)lt do(u)cement.   Mout doucemant.
(402, 836, 1168, 1450, 2359, 2418,   (905, 912, 4375, 6408, 6592; cf.
3511, 4708; cf. 2410, 4761.)   1761.)

9.

Gente de cors et de vis bièle (bele).   Jante de cors et de vis bele.
(136, 4608; cf. 156.)   (5884.)

10.

Moult bele et gente.   Mout bele et jante.
(970, 1507, 1674, 1702, 1922,   (810, 1419, 6617; cf. 34, 58,
2403, 4237.)   1784, 3234, 5892.)

11.

bon et bel.   bon et bel.
(1888, 2835.)   (613, 1276, 1334, 1585, 1914,
     5319, 6774, 6805.)

12.

bien et bel.
(943, 1802, 1962.)

bien et bel.
(463, 522, 2225, 2612, 6457, 6606, 6868.)

13.

Moult pros et sage.
(3474; cf. 612, 1001, 5036, 6026.)

Mout preuz, mout sage.
(1354; cf. 89, 3642.)

14.

Qui moult fu sages et cortois.
(4842.)
Sages et pros et cortois fu.
(4305; cf. 3204, 3474, 5407, 5816.)

Mout est preuz et sage et cortoise.
(3642; cf. 687, 1354, 2276.)

15.

Tant estoit biaus et bien apris.
(4279; cf. 155, 613, 2282, 4140, 5030.)

Ele estoit bele et bien aprise.
(1677; cf. 5302.)

16.

Moult bele.
(27, 96, 162, 1512, 4377, 4633, 5451.)
Moult bon.
(2967, 5064, 5114, 5416.)

Mout bele.
(398, 2807, 5498.)
Mout bon.
(1530, 3830.)

17.

de moult grant pris.
(825, 1700; cf. 419, 2260.)

de mout grant pris.
(2239; cf. 2297, 4641, 4912, 5480.)

18.

vaillans et preus.
(525, 2047; cf. 28, 68, 962, 3367.)

vaillanz et preuz.
(1189, 1354, 2193, 6435; cf. 54, 316, 1051, 1219.)

19.

Gauvains li cortois.
(93.)
moult cortois.
(5445.)

Gauvains li cortois.
(6827.)
mout cortois.
(128, 3226, 3315; cf. 2276, 4067, 4078.)

20.

Moult rices.
(1862, 2895, 3367, 3532, 4841, 5628.)
Moult ric(h)ement.
(3600, 5409.)

Mout riches.
(1274, 1334, 2641, 3608, 6805.)
Mout richemant.
(2809.)

21.

Debonaire et franc.
(3470, 3721, 4354; cf. 492, 4312.)

Deboneire et franc.
(378, 5060; cf. 1485, 1632, 4103, 6230, 6652.)

22.

Chevalier adreit.
(76; cf. 4037.)

Chevalier adroit.
(150, 5717; cf. 748, 769.)

23.

Ma douce amie.
(1685, 3847, 4789; cf. 1327.)
Ma doce dame.
(3376.)

Ma douce amie.
(1403, 1441, 1837, 2519, 4568.)
Ma douce dame.
(1579.)

24.

Biaus dous amis.
(1463; cf. 2297.)
Biaus amis.
(2410, 2419, 3774, 4893, 4903, 4908; cf. 3778.)

Biaus douz amis.
(4252, 5449, 5469, 6497.)
Biaus amis.
(5608.)

25.

Avenant et bel.
(1298, 2232, 2486, 4338, 5078; cf. 142.)

Avenant et bele.
(1668, 6275; cf. 1581, 6345.)

26.

bien acesmé.
(2904, 5835.)

bien acesmez.
(3577.)

27.

Par tel vertu.
(788; cf. 1110.)
de grant vertu.
(2121, 2910; cf. 4751, 5839.)

Par tel vertu.
(3603; cf. 4219.)
de grant vertu.
(1731.)

28.

à eslès.
(5554.)

a eslés.[1]
(2158; cf. 4873, 6832.)

---

[1] The difference in accent is due to the difference in the editing.

29.

Onques nus hom ne vit tant (si) bele.
(1522, 1916, 1860, 2236; cf. 1282.)
Onques nus home plus bel (ne) vit.
(2344, 4680.)
Onques si bele de veüe Ne vit nus.
(2752-3.)
Plus bel ne veirés vos jamais.
(2348, 1902.)
Si bele riens ne fu veüe.
(1514, 138; cf. 3254, 5068.)
Onques si bele ne fu née.
(1738; cf. 663.)
Plus bele feme ne fu née.
(2362.)
Millor chevalier ne vit nus.
(335.)
Jà millor de lui ne verrés.
(554; cf. 5422, 5473, 5808.)
Millor de vous certes ne sai.
(2254; cf. 2699, 5457.)
Plus bele de li je ne sai.
(1731; cf. 99 ff.)
Ainc hom ne vit nule millor.
(1904; cf. 1518, 3119, 3197.)
Ainc nus hom ne vit son parel.
(2039.)
De plus bele parler n'oïstes.
(1530; cf. 702.)
Onques si bele n'ot el mont.
(2222, 3243; cf. 4302 ff., 5053.)
Onques si bele n'ot sous nue.
(2224.)
Millor rien n'ot ne rois, ne quens.
(1508; cf. 148, 4192 ff., 4159, 4170, 43.)
Tot cil qui l' voient redisoient
Que si biel homme ne savoient.
(99-100.)

Onques si bele criature
Ne fu veüe an tot le monde.
(422-3.)
tant bel home onques ne vi.
(3227.)
Onques plus bele ne plus fine
Ne fu veüe ne trovee.
(1616-7.)
onques mes tant bele ne vi.
(4721.)
onques mes veü n'avoit.
(444.)
Le mellor chevalier por voir,
Que il cuidast onques veoir.
(4121-2.)
Le miaudre hom qui onques fust nez.
(2601.)
Onques si bele ne conui.
(1204.)
Onques ne fu de mere nez
Miaudre chevaliers de cestui.
(3652-3; cf. 3235.)
Onques mellor n'ot cuens ne rois.
(1388, 2620.)
Li miaudre qu'an porra savoir.
(569; cf. also 435, 1255, 3110 ff., 4121-2, 5713.)
Tuit soloient dire l'autre an
Qu'an tot le mont ne savoit l'an
Mellor chevalier ne plus preu.
(2549 ff.)

30.

Et cil volentiers otria.
(599.)
Et cil moult volentiers l'otroie.
(2588.)
Volentiers is very common in both poems.

Et cil volantiers li otroient
(2958.)

31.

à grans esfors.
(5709; cf. 5844.)

grant esforz.
(3836.)

32.

aler à l'encontre.
(1543, 2516; cf. 1366, 5094.)

aler a l'ancontre.
(209. 1174, 4987, 4992, 6905; cf. 3968, 5548.)

33.

Venir tot droit.
(75, 967, 1128, 1722, 2955, 3069. 3458, 3841, 4202, 6001.)

Venir tot (tuit) droit.
(116, 3032, 4593; cf. 207, 347.)

34.

Congié prandre.
(269. 1352, 1475, 1849, 2353, 2360, 3612. 3769.)
Congié demander.
(2335, 3570, 3762, 3961, 4310.)
Congié doner.
(3855.)

Congié prandre.
(3292, 3435, 3516, 6397, 6405.)
Congié demander.
(2301, 3294-5.)
Congié doner.
(2921, 3309; cf. 2273, 2279, 2295.)

35.

Vos en dirai la verité.
(1191; cf. 5959.)

La verité vos an dirai.
(2541, 5388; cf. 6033, 6051, 6115, 6139, 6247, 6260, 6292, 6764, 6876.)

36.

Je l' dirai;
De rien, nule rien, mentirai.
(875-6; cf. 29, 878, 1976, 3949, 4630, 5262.)

je vos dirai,
Si que de rien ne mantirai.
(6315-6; cf. 6740, 6767.)

37.

Por voir.
(877, 1618, 2566, 4908, 5000, 5326, 6087; cf. 888, 1226.)

Por voir.
(1043.)

38.

Sans mentir.
(2009, 3350.)
Sans mentir et sans decevoir.
(3355; cf. 2176, 4682.)

Sanz mantir.
(967, 1390.)
Sanz mantir et sanz decevoir.
(6790; cf. 1777.)

39.

à grant mervelle.
(3710, 3717, 4300.)

a grant mervoille.
(5508.)

40.

moult grant peril.
(6038.)

mout a esté an grant peril.
(1146; cf. 4348.)

41.

N'est merveille si je me plain.
(250.)
N'est mervelle se paor a.
(2747; cf. 4482.)

N'est mervoille se je faz duel.
(4339; cf. 4990.)
N'est pas mervoille s'il s'esmaie.
(4974; cf. 1755, 4854, 6023.)

42.

Qui onques n'ot ire ne duel.
(52; cf. 1540.)
Moult font grant dol.
(549; cf. 1538, 3869, 5153.)
Molt demenoit grant dolor.
(704.)
Qui a dol moult grant.
(1546; cf. 179-80, 861-2, 3492, 4818.)

Qui onques n'ot ire ne duel.
(1960.)
Qui mout an avoit grant duel fet.
(4581; cf. 2751, 3809, 4733, 4945, 5829, 6527.)
mout grant duel demenoient.
(2746; cf. 2673, 4289.)
ai mout grant duel.
(2735; cf. 2460, 2485, 3318, 4250, 4688, 4856.)

43.

Moult dolant.
(546, 1198, 3873; cf. 2059, 3870.)
Moult angoissiés.
(4104; cf. 4795.)
Dolans et coreciés.
(5352.)

Mout dolante.
(2779, 4400; cf. 5130, 5512, 5877.)
Mout angoisseus.
(2696, 6422.)
Dolante et correciee.
(194.)

44.

au plus tost que vos por(i)és.
(3767, 4867; cf. 422, 426, 4307, 3852.)

Au plus tost qu'il porra.
(2285; cf. 3701, 5561.)

45.

Robers [li escuiiers] fu moult de bel Li escuiiers devant aus sert,
servise. Qui son servise pas ne pert.
(918.) (3179–80.)
Devant le roi fait son servise. Li serjanz fu de bel servise.
(62.) (3165; cf. 1896, 2010, 5213,
Moult les savaient bel servir. 6191, 6390–1, 6567.)
(933; cf. 67, 931, 1802.)

46.

Es-vos venant les chevaliers Quant il virent un chevalier
Tos trois armés sor lor destriers. Venir armé sor un destrier.
(543–4.) (139–40.)
Ci voi venir III chevaliers Et s'estoient armé tuit troi.
Trestos armés sor lor destriers. (2799; cf. 1107.)
(978–9.)
Quant voient le chevalier
Venu sor son destrier armé.
(2877–8; cf. 366, 953 ff., 2504,
2965–6, 5380, 5421, 5804.)

47.

en nule guise. an nule guise.
(462, 4172, 5120.) (1576, 3344, 4256, 4497, 6062.)

48.

ploroient de pitié. de pitié ploroient.
(1850.) (1471; cf. 1465.)
de joie plorer. de joie plorer.
(868.) (683, 4473, 6892.)

49.

venir as fenestres. venir as fenestres.
(2098.) (1142; cf. 1522.)

50.

arierc se trait. arrieres se tret.
(2936.) (4111; cf. 3835.)

51.

grant aléure. grant aleüre.
(2886.) (254, 2768, 2774, 2900, 3959,
4188, 4674, 4934.)

52.

Cil le vit venir. Cil le voit venir.
(2911; cf. 3142, 3837, 4256, (2859; cf. 3572, 4205.)
5524, 5699, 5735.)

53.

A son cief a son escu mis. A son chief a mis son escu.
(3229; cf. 5307.) (3096.)

54.

Puis a mis la main à l'espée. Lors met a l'espee la main.
(5787, 445, 3129.) (4033.)

55.

mien enscient. mien esciant.
(3678.) (855, 4318, 4530, 5910.)

56.

aportèrent or et argent. porter arjant et or.
(3625-6; cf. 4656.) (2714.)

57.

Ne sait que face. ne set que face.
(4026.) (3064.)

58.

moult li plot. Mout li plot.
(4373.) (1676; cf. 3290, 6283.)

59.

u mors u pris. ou morz ou pris.
(575; cf. 999.) (4971, 5040, 2834.)

60.

sor son ceval isnel. Sor un cheval . . . isnel.
(5377.) (3573; cf. 2197.)

61.

bel et cler. clercs et beles.
(5401.) (618, 6853.)

62.

à mult grant conpaigne. a mout riche conpaingne.
(5419; cf. 5481.) (1940.)

ses escus d'asur estoit.
(73.)
Un chevalier i ai véu
Qui porte un escu d'azon.
(5818-9.)

Hardis estoit comme lupars.
(5458.)

Isnelement leva.
(203, 2450, etc.)

l'espee d'acier.
(5715.)

C. chevaliers.
(5378, 5730, 5739, 5792.)

Iluec le guerredon li rent.
(4736; cf. 4748.)

aler c(h)evauçant.
(691, 1264, 5735.)

Es vos poi(n)gnant.
(1293, 1099, 1120.)
Par la forest s'en vait poi(n)gnant.
(1385: cf. 275, 769, 1127, 1365, 1381.)

moult durement le vait férir.
(447; cf. 5710.)
Moult très durement se requierent;
Par si grant vertu s'entrefierent.
(5684-5.)
L'escu le fait del col voler.
(432.)

63.
uns chevaliers armez
D'unes armes d'azur et d'or.
(584-5; cf. 2142 ff.)

64.
Orent sanblance de liepart.
(6728.)

65.
Levez isnelemant.
(3470.)

66.
espié d'acier.
(3585.)

67.
çant chevaliers.
(1942.)

68.
je randrai le guerredon.
(632; cf. 4566, 4569.)

69.
aler chevauchant.
(2801, 5768-9.)

70.
Ez vos poignant.
(3589.)
Parmi la forest a droiture
S'en vet poignant grant aleüre
(3619-20; cf. 106, 4308.)

71.
L'uns anvaïst l'autre et requiert:
Erec si duremant le fiert
Que li escuz del col li vole.
(3013 ff.)
(For the rhyme, le requiert: le
fiert, see 953-4.)

(For *durement*, see 1141, 1424,
1431–3, 2632, 5821.)
(For the rhyme, le requiert: le
fiert, see 3023–4, 463–4; fierent:
requierent, 1139–40.)

72.

vos ne targerés gaire. Ne tarda gueires,
(3766.) (1915.)

73.

a or broudée. brosdé a or.
(5075.) (5881.)

74.

For expressions of *grant joie*, see grant joie.
272, 1179, 1480, 2462, 2466, (681, 1247, 1301, 1316. 1445,
2702, 3219, 3397, 4374, 4618, 1535, 1900, 2039, 2069, 2338,
4635, 5026, 5144, 5974, 5994, 2355, 2369, 2372, 2387, 2782,
6004, 6010. 4007, 4192, 4595, 6118, 6296,
 6334, 6352, 6356, 6469, 6582,
 6593, 6632, 6657, 6945.)

75.

For accounts of arming, see 260, Arming.
343, 387, 675, 1040, 1369, 1805, (2626, 2660, 3696, 4302, 4885,
1950, 1957, 2048, 2065, 2457, 4965, 5332, 5691.)
2610, 5343.
Disarming. Disarming.
(607, 805, 1161, 1440, 2679, (988, 1298, 3260, 4206, 4683,
3407, etc.) 5132, etc.)

76.

liés; joianz. joianz et liez.
(Cf. 482, 3909, 3921, 4175, (372, 685; cf. 3208, 3409, 3513,
4365, 4703, 5244.) 4198, 4560, 4723, 5061, 5238,
 5299, 6165, 6339, 6897.)

77.

Commendation to God. Commendation to God.
(2434, 3614, 3859, etc.) (271, 274, 1454, 1457, 2302,
 3423, 3928, 4303, 4374, 6403.)

78.

vermelles: à mervelles. vermoilles: a mervoilles.
(1706–7, 1881–2; cf. 2039–40, (5899–5900; cf. 429, 1755,
4299–4300.) 4334.)

79.

Ceval (destrier) Gascon.
(1080, 5758, 5856; cf. armés
sor le Gascont, 1699.)

Le bai de Gascoingne.
(2663.)

80.

Daybreak.
(1147, 1182, 2449, 3233, 4932, 5944, 6065.)

Daybreak.
(69, 1347, 3461, 3499, 4244, 4278, 5271.)

81.

L'uns acole l'autre et enbrace.
(1794.)
l'enbrace et acole.
(2682, etc.)

Li uns l'autre beise et acole.
(3920.)
l'acole et anbrace.
(4158, etc.)

82.

ferir tot à bandon.
(5584; cf. 5782.)

ferir tot a bandon.
(975; cf. 3022, 6687.)

83.

quites serra.
(2249.)

soiiez toz quites.
(5458.)

84.

Car tant en ai oï parler: aler.
(2493.)

J'an ai sovant oï parler: aler.
(5434.)

85.

Parmi la porte entrent errant.
(2546.)

Parmi la porte antre an la cort.
(383.)

86.

Les cevals fisent enseler.
(2726; cf. 1180, 6070.)

Ses chevaus comande anseler.
(1432, 4281; cf. 3489, 6440.)

87.

Quant il les vit, si ot vergoigne.
(4568; cf. 3930.)

Vergoingne an ot.
(447.)

88.

Moult fesistes grant mesprison
(3965.)

traïson Vers vos feroie et mesprison.
(5640; cf. 6098.)

89.

Puis resont à l'ostel venu.
(2719.)

Tost furent a l'ostel venu.
(3203.)

	90.
Ki ne fu ne fols, ni vilains.	Ele n'estoit mie vilainne.
(4360; cf. 154.)	(475.)
	91.
D'un drap de soie estoit vestue	De dras de soie . . .
(: veüe).	Que d'autre robe fust vestue (: veüe).
(1513-4.)	(1575-8.)
	92.
Quant l'aube esclarci.	Quant l'aube est esclarcie.
(3803.)	(1430.)
	93.
Moult forment crie et pleure.	Por quoi si formant plore et crie.
(629.)	(4336.)
	94.
Artus n'i vaut plus demorer.	Erec ne voloit pas antandre.
(5831.)	(2215.)
	95.
Li murs en furent rice et bel,	Qui close estoit de mur an tor.
Dont li castels tos clos estoit.	(3672.)
(1868-9.)	
	96.
Moult fu li castels bien asis.	un chastel Mout bien seant.
(1861.)	(345-6.)
	97.
Sor son puing porte l'esprevier.	Peissoit sor son poing l'esprevier.
(1815.)	(1308.)
	98.
un ceval d'Espaigne.	Un corant destrier d'Espaingne.
(5760.)	(2395.)
	99.
Que vos iroie je contant?	Por quoi vos feroie lonc conte?
(5953, 6095, 4337.)	(1084.)
Que feroie longes noveles?	
(6069, 3627.)	
	100.
I soient andoi couroné.	coroné seront andui.
(6057; cf. 6034, 6100.)	(6549.)

101.

Ci faut li roumans et define. Li contes fine ci a tant.
(6103.) (6958.)

These lists, though they contain a number of passages where the agreement is not very striking, or where the agreement is due to the existence in the poetic language of a considerable stock of current phrases, are yet sufficient to establish the fact of very extensive borrowing by Renaud from the *Erec*. The effect of this observation on the question of the relations between LD and BI is clear. LD shows no trace of these borrowings. It is inconceivable that the author of LD, if, as Kaluza thinks, he based his work on BI, should have eliminated all.

The arguments drawn from the comparison of proper names, and especially from these parallel passages, combined with the considerations previously adduced,[1] may fairly be held to demonstrate that the English poem is not derived from that of Renaud de Beaujeu.

CHANGES INTRODUCED BY RENAUD.

The establishment of this proposition makes much simpler the discussion of the remaining questions. Since it is now certain that many things in Renaud's poem are due to modifications introduced by him in an original which has perished, we may proceed to examine what these changes are, as well in details, as in general features.

Notable among the latter are: the omission of all account of the hero's youth; the added importance given to the stay at the Ile d'Or, and the return visit; the introduction of the squire Robert; and the account of the tournament.

It is almost certain that there was in the original Desconus story an introductory part, such as is found in all versions but BI, telling of the youth of the hero, his solitary life in the woods, and his going to Arthur's court. Why, then, did Renaud omit this? The reason seems to be that, as he was forming his poem on the model of *Erec*,[2]

---

[1] Another argument will be found below, pp. 120 f.; cf. also p. 150.

[2] It was natural for Renaud to turn to *Erec*, for this was the very poem from which borrowings had been made by the author of his original (see pp. 113, 133, 145, 152, below).

he decided to begin it in the same way. Chrétien opens his poem by giving us his name and telling us his desires in writing the story, which, he says,

> Tret d'un conte d'avanture
> Une mout bele conjointure. (13-14.)

He adds:

> Tant con Deus la grace l'an done . . .
> Des or comancerai l'estoire. (18-23.)

Renaud follows suit, and begins in the same way by telling of himself and his motives in writing the book :

> Por li veul un roumant estraire
> D'un moult biel conte d'aventure ; . . .
> Vos veul l'istoire commancier ;
> En poi d'eure puet Dius aidier. (4-8.)

Chrétien goes on directly to tell of Arthur and his court, and introduces us to the chief characters of his story without any previous explanations. In this point also Renaud wished to follow him, and therefore he had to omit everything which in his original preceded the boy's coming to court.

It may be, however, that Renaud was the more disposed to make this change because, as we shall see later, he to some extent identified himself with his hero, and so was not likely to make prominent the latter's wild life in the woods. In fact, the hero's youth is not emphasized in the way in which we should expect, and·as we find it emphasized in LD.

It is remarkable that Renaud nevertheless leaves clear traces that this introduction was an essential part of his original,[1] for the boy declares, when asked his name, that he knows nothing of his father, and that his mother called him only *Belfil*, just as LD's mother called him only by the same name, *Beaufis*. Moreover the words of the *fée* to BI also show that Renaud knew the introduction of the story. She tells BI that she had always known him to be a son of the valiant Gawein.

> Por ce vos amai je forment,
> Ciés vostre mère moult sovent

---

[1] Cf. Paris, *Rom.*, XV, 15, n. 3.

Aloie je por vos véir;
Mais nus ne m'en fesist issir.
Votre mère vos adoba
Au roi Artur vos envoia. (4877 ff.)

This clearly implies the solitary life of the mother, and states plainly that she had given him armor and sent him to Arthur (as in Car.).

The motives which Renaud avows in writing the book also help us to understand the changes he has made. He was not a poet by profession. This poem was probably the first he ever wrote, and it he began to write with a conscious purpose, — to evince his love to one whom he adored, and to show her what he could do ("Mostrer vuel que faire sai," 10). It was to be a means of pressing his suit. To attain his twofold purpose he therefore, it is evident, decided on two things. First, he would show his love by identifying his loved one with one of the characters of the story, whom he would describe as the most beautiful being in the world and the possessor of irresistible charms. Secondly, he would endeavor to write as good a poem as he could, that her respect for him and his powers might be heightened.[1]

There was but one character whom he could identify with his loved one, and that was the enchantress of the Ile d'Or. To bring about this end he has to change the whole ending of the story. He represents the young hero as in love with her, and her only. He goes on to free the enchanted princess, from a sense of duty, that he may not lose his honor. Hardly has he accomplished his end before he longs for her whom he has left. His only desire now is to return to her and obtain her forgiveness for his having gone away before. He feigns a reason for not accompanying the disenchanted princess, whose proffered hand he declares he cannot then accept. He travels back to the Ile d'Or, and when he gets an opportunity pours out his love with ardor to the *fée*. She, however, scornfully repulses him, for he has done her a wrong, albeit it was to maintain his honor. The young hero is so overwhelmed with grief that he is like to die, and his companion's comforting avails little. There is but one thing that saves his life: his loved one relents and bids him

---

[1] On the second point cf. Paris, *Rom.*, XV, 10.

come to her. She has only been testing him, and now that she sees his love is sincere, she gives herself up unreservedly to him, and his fidelity has its reward.

Here we can see Renaud expressing his hopes, and perhaps even alluding to his own experiences. He had offended his loved one, it may be, and had been repulsed; but his love had kept on increasing until his distress was too great to bear. He hoped that his *amie* was only testing him, and that the evidence he gave her in his poem of the ardor of his affections and the constancy of his devotion would secure for him the object of his hopes, and restore him to happiness.

But Renaud could not neglect entirely the original ending of the story. After a while he brings Bl back to Arthur, at whose request he marries the princess and goes home to live with her. Despite this apparent inconstancy, however, his heart is still fixed on the *fée*, and in the concluding lines of his poem Renaud, while reiterating the expression of his own affection, says that if his loved one will show him *biau sanblant*, he will, in a new story, bring Giglain back to his true love. If not, he will never speak of him again.

> Si ert Giglains en tel esmai,
> Que jamais n'avera s'amie. (6116-7.)

We must believe, as Paris says, that his "mult amée" remained relentless, for we do not know of any other poem on this subject by Renaud.

It is, then, because of this avowed affection that Renaud introduces at different places in his poem personal digressions of various kinds,[1] notably that very interesting passage where he speaks of his "mult amée," whom he would fain call his *amie* (1226-59).

Having thus made the *fée* the leading figure in his poem, with the exception only of the hero himself, and having identified her with his own loved one, Renaud does not surprise us when we see the incidents in which she plays a part increased in importance, and her marvellous beauty and skill dwelt upon at length. It is not surprising, further, that she should be the one to reveal to him his noble birth. It is but fitting that she should return his love and avow affection for him from the beginning of his career.

---
[1] "Ils rappellent les interruptions du même genre qui se trouvent dans *Partenopeus de Blois*." Paris, *Rom.*, XV, 10.

But the original Desconus poem must have been comparatively short, while *Erec*, which Renaud had chosen as a guide in matters of form and expression, was much longer. The story, then, had to be extended, and the means our poet took are well known to us. Had he followed his original, even expanding as much as he has done in the corresponding parts, his poem would have been shorter by at least the 2500 lines now taken up mainly by the account of the return visit to the Ile d'Or and the great tournament which was proclaimed to lure BI back to court.

The Squire Robert. It has always been one of the strongest arguments of Kölbing, Paris, and the others who have held that the English poem was not drawn from BI, that there is in the latter a squire who is the hero's constant attendant and helper from the time he leaves the court, while no such character is to be found in LD, Car., or Wig. Kaluza, however, still maintains that the author of LD leaves clear signs that he knew such a figure by the mention of *Gifflet*, the steward of the Ile d'Or, whom LD takes as his man when he leaves the castle.[1] It is then evidently Kaluza's opinion that the English poet made up his mind at the beginning that the character of Robert was unnecessary, and sedulously avoided mentioning him or making the slightest reference to his constant interference in the French story. This must have required strict attention from the author, and caused him no little trouble. The only reason for introducing the squire at the end would surely be because the poet found that some one was needed to do what Robert did in BI. Has Kaluza, however, even this justification for his theory?

If we follow Robert's doings in BI from the time when Gifflet enters the story in LD, we see that it is he who grows anxious at the way the people of Galigan treat his master as they ride along, and who calls the latter's attention to them. It is he who during the fight selects the best shaft he can get and bears it to his master, who has broken his own. It is he who begs him for the love of God not to forget " les laides torces, ne les pos," for the streets are full of people who await his overthrow. It is he who swoons from grief when BI enters the enchanted city and who greets him with joy after

---

[1] "Es ist dies offenbar eine reminiscenz an den knappen Robers des frz. gedichtes." Kaluza, *Lib. Desc.*, p. cxxxiv.

he is victorious in the encounter. It is he, moreover, who afterwards remains his faithful helper in every extremity, and who returns with him to the court of King Arthur. If now we turn to Gifflet, we see that he accompanies LD to Lambard's house, but says not a word and gives no help; and that he offers to go with LD to the enchanted city, but has his offer refused. Then he disappears from the narrative. His name is thus mentioned only three times, and he practically does nothing at all. If the author of LD had been sedulously keeping Robert out of his story, would he have introduced him just at the end without a reason? Robert is certainly an invention of Renaud's; and it seems to me far easier to suppose that he was developed out of Gifflet rather than that Gifflet was a useless "reminiscence" of him. It is easy to put a drop of ink into a glass of clear water and color the whole; but it is not easy to make the colored water clear again.

Further considerations seem to settle the matter. We shall later have occasion to discuss some possible relations between the Welsh *Peredur* and our cycle.[1] It is necessary at this point to anticipate that discussion so far as to remark that as Peredur was nearing the end of his journey, and as he was about to leave the scene of one of his adventures, he took with him a certain knight who offered to be his man. The latter did nothing of importance, and was soon lost sight of. May not this knight represent the original of Gifflet? Be it noted that Wig. has no character corresponding to Gifflet, the steward of the mistress of the Ile d'Or, because there is no account in it of a visit to the castle of the enchantress. We have, however, an example in the German poem of the same sort of thing, for our hero makes Adân his assistant when near the end of his adventures, even though he had got along without a helper up to that time.[2]

The Tournament. The only other important addition is the tournament, which is the means of getting BI back to court. Just as Erec, in the rapture of his delights with Enide, forgets his old-time pursuits until his companions mourn and he is stimulated to seek adventure again by their suggestion, so BI's abandoning himself to pleasure causes all his friends to grieve, and they suggest to Arthur

[1] See below, pp. 147 ff.
[2] We might ask also if the porter in Lambard's house in LD is a reminiscence of the porter of the city of the Ile d'Or in BI.

that a great tournament be proclaimed, in the hope of winning the young knight back to a chivalrous life.[1]

Aside from these important changes, which have been made by Renaud for reasons already examined, there are many smaller changes in which the influence of *Erec* is noticeable.

1. When Renaud introduces the dwarf, he provides him with a *corgie*, such as the dwarf has in *Erec*. The dwarf's smallness, which caused him shame, is also commented on, as in *Erec*. There is no parallel to these features in the other poems.[2]

2. When Hélie appeals to the king against the sending of BI, Arthur replies that he, as king, cannot break his promise.[3]

3. It seems probable that the speech of Bliobliéris in BI in which he asserts that he has kept his place for *more than seven years* and slain many a knight — a point in which, as will be seen (p. 226), Renaud clearly varies from his original — is a reminiscence of the passage in *Erec* in which Erec is told of the knight he is to meet in the adventure of *la joie de la cort*. Cf. BI, 417 ff.:

> Et je certes plus de VII ans
> Maintes gens i ai fais dolens,
> Et maint bon chevalier de pris
> I ai abatu et ocis.

with *Erec*, 5435 ff. :

> Et passé a set anz ou plus
> Que del chastel ne revint nus
> Qui l'avanture i alast querre;
> Si sont venu de mainte terre
> Chevalier fier et corageus. . . .
> L'avanture don nus n'estort,
> Qu'il n'i reçoive honte ou mort.

---

[1] Cf. the description of the tournament in *Durmart*, 6969-8738, with that in BI, 5498-5960. Cf. also the return of Fergus to take part in a tourney proclaimed by Arthur (*Fergus*, pp. 172 ff.). See the note in Jessie L. Weston's trans. of *Parzival*, London, 1894, I, 304.

[2] Cf. BI, 163 ff., with *Erec*, 143 ff., 161-2. There are verbal resemblances between the passages.

[3] Cf. "Rois sui: si ne dei pas mentir," BI, 241 (see also 217), with *Erec*, 1793: "Je sui rois, ne doi pas mantir." The phrase is, however, proverbial: cf., e.g., the prose *Tristan*, ed. Löseth, p. 215, and Chaucer, *Merch. T.*, 1067 ff.

4. Erec hears the cries of a woman in distress in a wood, and calls the attention of Enide, his companion, to the sound.[1]

> Tot maintenant Enide apele.
> 'Dame,' fet il, 'une pucele
> Va par cel bois formant criant.
> Ele a par le mien esciant
> Mestier d'aïe et de secors.
> Cele part vuel aler le cors,
> Si savrai quel besoing ele a.' (4315 ff.)

In like manner, when BI hears the young woman's cries, he arouses Hélie and exclaims:

> 'Ha! Pucèle, oés-vos crier? ...
> Ce semble mestier ait d'aïe,
> Por ce reclaime Diu et prie.
> Jo vel aler poi li aidier,
> Si je voi qu'ele en ait mestier,
> Haiderai li à mon pooir.' (637-49.)

5. The maiden who is freed from her trouble, in both poems,[2] offers to be the servant of her rescuer in the same words:

> Tos jors mais serai vostre ancèle. (BI, 865.)
> Toz jorz serai mes vostre ancele. (E., 4366.)

6. In Erec, as well as in BI, the hero has a fight with three warriors who come against him.[3] BI was evidently influenced by this episode in the following points:

---

[1] In this and the sparrow-hawk adventure (see No. 8, below), we must suppose that borrowings in these incidents were made by the author of the original of LD and BI; but there is no need to believe that these were of a verbal nature, as were those of Renaud from *Erec* (see pp. 133 ff., below).

[2] Cf. the following passages from the descriptions of the fight:

Mes Erec tint l'espee treite,	Car cil li cort atot l'espée,
Une anvaïe li a feite,	Si féri moult bien le jaiant;
Dont li jaianz fu mal serviz,	Un cop li donne moult pesant,
Si le fiert parmi la cerviz	Sus en la teste, en la cervèle,
Que tot jusqu'as arçons le fant.	De si ès dens met l'alimèle.
. . . . . .	Si li a tolue la vie . . .
Et li cors chiet toz estanduz. (E., 4465-71.)	Li jaians ciet sor l'erbe drue. (BI, 794-801.)

[3] Cf. Mennung, pp. 16, 49.

(*a*) Erec is warned by Enide of their approach, as is Bl by Robert. Cf.

> 'Biaus sire, ou pansez vos?
> Ci vienent poignant aprés vos
> Troi chevalier qui mout vos chacent.
> Peor ai que mal ne vos facent.' (E., 2845 ff.)

with

> 'Sire, fait il, tost vos armés, . . .
> De bien faire apensés soiés, . . .
> Ci voi venir III chevaliers,
> Trestos armés sor lor destriers;
> Je pense et voir vos en cuic dire.
> Prendre vos vienent, u ocire.' (Bl, 973-80.)

(*b*) Both Enide and Hélie are alarmed at the prospect of a fight one to three, and fear that their companion will be "killed or taken." Cf.

> Or iert ja morz ou pris mes sire;
> Que cil sont troi, et il est seus. (E., 2834-5.)

with

> Pris u ocis fust maintenant. (Bl, 999.)
> Il n'a pas force vers'vos trois. (Bl, 1013.)

(*c*) Renaud, unlike the author of LD, makes the three come separately at the knight, and goes out of his way to make an explanation of it. In this he follows Chrétien. Cf.

> Adonc estoit costume et us
> Que dui chevalier a un poindre
> Ne devoient a un seul joindre. (E., 2826 ff.)

with

> Et à cel tens costume estoit
> Que quant I hom se conbatoit,
> N'avait garde que de celui
> Qui faisoit la bataille à lui. (Bl, 1055 ff.)

(*d*) It is important to observe that in *Erec* the three are said to be robbers, pure and simple ("qui de roberie vivoit," 2797), although they have these knightly customs, and that they set upon Erec and Enide merely for the sake of plunder.

> Mout covoitent le palefroi
> Que Enide va chevauchant. (2800-1.)

The one who first sees them claims the right to begin the fight. All he wants for his share of the spoil is the palfrey; his companions are welcome to the rest.

In BI, on the other hand, as in LD, the three, far from being robbers bent on plunder, are the companion knights of Bliobliéris (in LD, William's nephews), and attack BI solely to avenge their friend's disgrace. Yet by a slip Renaud calls them "robbers" ("Vinrent poingnant li robéor," 991), showing that he had Chrétien's poem in mind when writing this passage.

(*e*) The descriptions of the fight with the first knight in the two poems show verbal agreement. Cf., e.g., E., 2861-74, with BI 1082-97.

(*f*) In *Erec* the result is told as follows:

> L'un an a mort, l'autre navré,
> Et del tierz s'est si delivré
> Qu'a pié l'a jus del destrier mis. (2905 ff.)

This is exactly the result in BI, where Willaume de Salebrant is killed, Helin de Graies wounded, and Le Sire des Aies unhorsed and obliged to submit. (See 1097, 1119, 1152 ff.) In LD none are killed. On the contrary, all are forced to go to Arthur.

(*g*) Cf.
> Quant cil le vit vers lui venir,
> Si s'an comança a fuïr. (E., 2889-90.)

with
> Robers les vit vers lui venir;
> Si s'en commença à fuïr. (BI, 965-6.)

(*h*) In *Erec* the horse of the first of the robbers is described as "blans": — "Li premiers fu blans come lez" (2911).

In BI we seem to have a curious reminiscence of this, for there the first of the three companions is *Elins li blans*. Indeed, it is possible that it was the use of this adjective in *Erec* which suggested to Renaud the introduction of this particular name, which could not have been in the original, but which occurs elsewhere in the romances of chivalry.[1]

(*i*) The part Enide and Hélie play in the two adventures is very

---

[1] Cf., e.g., the Prose Romance of *Tristan*, ed. Löseth, p. 283 (395²), and p. 351.

similar, and differs much from that played by Elene in LD. Enide is in great distress lest Erec should suffer mishap.

> Enide vit les robeors
> Mout l'an est prise granz peors. (2831-2.)

So in BI, Hélie is the centre of the excitement. It is she who pleads earnestly that BI be allowed to arm, and declares that it is not fair for three men to attack one.

7. One curious agreement of *Erec* with LD should be noted here. In *Erec* after all are conquered, we read:

> Toz trois an a les chevaus pris
> Ses loie par les frains ansanble. (2908-9.)

In LD after the first is wounded,

> þe dwerȝ Teodolein
> Tok þe stede be þe raine (508-9)

and rode away with it to Elene. In BI this feature is not brought in in this connection. It is after the fight with Blioblićris that we read:

> Robers avait pris le destrier
> Qui ert à l'autre chevalier;
> A son signor tantost le maine. (505 ff.)

This seems to indicate that in this point in which LD and BI differ, LD is nearer the original.[1]

8. The adventure with the sparrow-hawk will be treated in a separate section. It is well to compare here, however, two long passages which are identical in spirit and substance, and show marked verbal agreement as well. There is no similar passage in LD. In BI we read:

> Vers le cort vont, et Margerie
> Tot droit vers l'esprevier le guie.
> Grant gent le vont après sivant,
> Chevalier, borjois et sergant;

---

[1] *Erec* agrees with BI, (1) in their coming separately, (2) in the course of the fight, and (3) in the result; with LD in (1) LD's being ready and riding at once against them, (2) the taking of the horses, and (3) the fear of the third knight when the other two are slain. These features in LD may have been taken from *Erec* by the author of the original of LD and BI, or they may be merely accidental agreements with Chrétien's poem. The former view is the more probable; but in themselves they are of no importance.

Dames et puceles issoient
De lor ouvrois et demandoient
Del chevalier, qui il estoit,
Qui l'esprevier querre venoit.
Pluisor respondent : ' Ne savons.
Mais itant dire nos poons
Que ses elmes est effondrés ;
Bien pert qu'il a esté portés.
Maint chevalier i ont feru !
Tot est effondrés son escu ;
De cols d'espées est orlés,
Et ses haubers est desclošs,'
Ce dist cascuns : ' sans devinaille,
Il est bons chevaliers, sans faille.
Ha Dius ! qui sont ces damoiseles
Qu'il maine o lui, qui tant sont beles?'   (1642 ff.)

and in *Erec :*

Aprés lui ot grant bruit de jant.
Li chevalier et li serjant
Et les dames corent aprés
Et les puceles a eslés.
. . . . . .
Mout chevauche orguelleusemant
Vers l'esprevier isnelemant.   (789–96.)
' Qui est, qui est cil chevaliers ?
Mout doit estre hardiz et fiers
Qui la bele pucele an mainne.'   (753 ff.)
Et mainz an i ot qui disoient :
' Deus ! qui puet cil chevaliers estre,
Qui la bele pucele adestre ? '
' Ne sai.' — ' Ne sai,' ce dist chascuns.   (762 ff.)
Mes mout a cos an son escu,
. . . . . .
Ses haubers est ansanglantez,
Mout est hurtez et debatuz ;
Bien i pert qu'il s'est conbatuz.
Savoir poons sanz nule faille,
Que fiere a esté la bataille.   (1150–60.)

9. In *Erec* the feature of the head-crowned stakes is found in the description of the orchard in which the adventure called *La Joie de la Cort* took place (5774 ff.). This is a magic orchard surrounded

by an invisible air wall, which barred passage. It is possible that this feature was transferred in BI to the Ile d'Or because of the similarity of the place, inhabited as it is by an enchantress, and surrounded, as we find later, by a wonderful orchard. In LD it is part of the description of the castle of Giffroun, the owner of the sparrow-hawk, and it looks as if this were a shift on the part of the English author for reasons of his own. (See p. 168.)

In *Erec* there are many pointed lances, on all but one of which is the armed head of a knight, and on this one hangs a horn. This is to be blown when the knight who dwells in the orchard is overcome, and he who succeeds in this adventure will be honored by all. As soon as the empty lance is covered, a new one regularly appears.

The following passages in *Erec* and BI should be compared:

>Car devant aus sor peus aguz
>Avoit hiaumes luisanz et clers,
>Et s'avoit dessoz les cerclers
>Teste d'ome dessoz chascun. (E., 5780 ff.)

and

>Mult bien faite de pels agus,
>Aguisiés desos et desus.
>En cascun pel ficié avoit
>Une teste, c'armée estoit ;
>Cascune avoit l'elme lacie,
>Qui ens el pel estoit ficie. (BI. 1941 ff.)

10. The reception of BI at the castle of the Ile d'Or, after he has slain the knight, resembles that of Erec and Enide, the newly wedded pair, after they have taken leave of the king and returned to Erec's home.

In *Erec* they come to

>un chastel de grant delit.
>Onques nus miauz seant ne vit. (2317-8.)

In BI

>Il esgarde, voit 1 castel ;
>Onques nus hom ne vit si bel.
>Moult fu li castels bien asis. (1859 ff.)

In *Erec* we read further :

>Tote la janz est aünee
>Por veoir lor novel seignor.
>Einz nus ne vit joie greignor

> Que feisoient jeune et chenu.
> Premiers sont au mostier venu,
> La furent par devocion
> Receü a procession.
> . . . .
> A tant fors del mostier s'an vont,
> El palés real venu sont ;
> La comança la joie granz. (2370-87.)

After BI has slain the knight, the people of the land come to him and declare themselves his subjects. ("Vien ton roiaume recevoir," 2184.) He mounts a horse they bring him.

> Or l'enmainent vers le castel
> U recéus fu bien et bel
> A crois et à procession.
> Grant joie en fisent li baron ;
> El grant palais le ont mené. (2190 ff.)
> Par la vile font joie grant
> Et li viellart et li enfant. (2289-90.)

Renaud probably had in mind also the description of the coronation just at the end of the poem.

> Ancontr'aus s'an ist tote fors
> O reliques et o tresors
> La processions del mostier.
> Croiz . . . . . .
> Lor fu a l'ancontre fors tret. (E., 6899-905.)

11. In both poems all are eager to be of service. Cf.

> Onques nus rois an son reaume
> Ne fu plus liecmant veüz,
> N'a greignor joie receüz.
> Tuit de lui servir se penerent.
>   (E., 2398 ff. ; cf. 2427 ff.)

with

> Moult font le valet grant honor.
> Trestote s'entente et s'amor
> A mis la dame en lui servir ;
> Car faire voloit son plaisir. (BI, 2285 ff.)

12. Enide is spoken of here as follows:

> Aussi iert Enide plus bele
> Que nule dame ne pucele
> Qui fust trovee an tot le monde,
> Qui le cerchast a la reonde.   (E., 2413 ff.)

and the lady of the Ile d'Or in BI:

> Si bele riens ne fu veüe.
> Ceste ne trove sa parelle,
> Tant estoit bele à grant mervelle.
> . . . .
> Que plus bel vis, ne plus bel front,
> N'avoit feme qui fust el mont.   (2197 ff.)

13. Both Erec and BI are inclined to forget their serious missions and to give themselves up to pleasure, the former with Enide, the latter with the *fée*.

Cf.
> Tot mist son cuer et s'antandue
> An li acoler et beisier.   (E., 2440-41.)

and
> Ains le commence à enbracier
> Entre ses bras molt docement.   (BI, 2358-9.)

This is a source of grief to their companions, and in both cases the heroes are prompted to start off again in quest of adventure.

14. A word seems fitting here as to the character of the messenger. In BI it is considerably altered, and certainly not always for the better. Hélie is a very inconsistent creature. At first she scorns the young knight, then she begs him to go back for fear he may lose his life, and says it would be a pity to have such a worthy knight slain. She selfishly tries to prevent his going to the relief of the maiden in distress in the wood, because it would be uncomfortable for her if anything happened to him. Soon, however, she seizes the dog and obstinately refuses to give it up, although her cause is manifestly unjust and she knows that BI will be obliged unwillingly to risk his life to satisfy her caprice. She leads him up to the castle of the Ile d'Or, knowing well the customs of the place, and that no one, knight or king, has passed for five years without being slain, and refrains from telling the young knight the facts until he has got himself inextricably entangled in the snare.

Elene, on the other hand, is a much more pleasing, reasonable personage, and does not treat LD as Hélie treats BI. She acknowledges him to be a brave champion of her own accord, while Hélie has reluctantly to be urged by the dwarf to make this confession. In the forest scene in LD we have Elene praying for the hero's safety, but never objecting in any way to his going to the help of another unfortunate woman, while in BI Hélie abuses him for his desire to go. Elene, moreover, always takes pleasure in telling of the brave deeds of her companion, and she throughout occupies a suitably modest attitude with regard to him.

There is one other important place in which the contrast is significant. When in BI they draw near the castle of the steward of the enchanted princess, which is their destination, Hélie urges BI strongly not to go near the place. When he asks if they had not better lodge there, she replies " nenil mie : De là aler n'aiés envie " (2491-2). Suppose he had taken her advice, what would have happened? In the English poem, however, the situation is different. The messenger, who, up to this time, has in no way led LD into danger, now advises him to go to the castle. She knows it is the place towards which their journey has been directed and which they must enter, and, therefore, although she tells him of the danger he will incur from a fight with Lambard, she encourages him to go on.

'Rid in to þe castell ȝate
And axe þin inn þer ate,
Boþe faire and well.' (1579 ff.)

She stimulates him also by saying that, if he fails, he will ever after be known as a coward.

'And þus may King Arthour
Lesen his honour
For þy dedes slowe.' (1594 ff.)

Indeed, it seems as if she told him that the rescuing of the maiden depended on the fight, for LD replies:

'To do Arthour profit
And make þat lady quit,
To him I will drive.' (1600 ff.)

This account is exactly what we should expect. That in BI appears to be an unfortunate perversion. It looks as if it were a reminiscence of the influence brought to bear on Erec not to undertake *La Joie de la Cort*, which adventure has unquestionably influenced Renaud's poem in many other features.[1] Enide calls Erec's attention to everything, as does Hélie that of BI. Elene, on the other hand, resembles the messenger in Car. and Wig.

15. The whole account in BI, from the coming to the castle of Lampart to the victory over the magicians, is much influenced by similar adventures in *Erec*.

(*a*) Erec, being healed of his wounds, leaves Guivret and starts off with his companion.

Cf.
    Chevauchié ont des le matin
    Jusqu'au vespre le droit chemin. (E., 5367–8.)
and
    Et chevauchierent bos et plains.
    Vers le gaste cité en vont
    Dusques as vespres erré ont. (BI, 2468 ff.)

(*b*) In each case they come to a beautiful castle, surrounded by a moat. In *Erec* it is *Brand-iganz*, in BI, *Gal-igans*. They stop to look at it, and the young knight asks his companion if they had not better spend the night there, but is warned against doing so, for the customs of the castle are such that any knight who enters is almost sure to suffer disgrace, or even lose his life.

Cf.
    'Deus!' dist Erec, . . .
    'Et si ferons nostre ostel prandre
    El chastel, que j'i vuel desçandre.'
    'Sire!' fet cil cui mout grevoit,
    'Se enuiier ne vos devoit,
    Nos n'i desçandriiemes pas.
    El chastel a un mal trespas.' (E., 5415 ff.)
and
    Li chevaliers dist: 'Que ferons?
    Damoisele, herbergerons
    En cest castel ici devant?'
    Cele respondit maintenant:
    'Sire,' fait ele, 'nenil mie.
    De là aler n'aiés envie.
    Car tant en ai oï parler
    Que moult i fait mauvais aler.' (BI, 2487 ff.)

---
[1] See § 16, below.

(c) Erec and Bl are then told of the usage of the castle. In Erec the adventure which any knight who seeks to remain at the castle must undertake, is called *La Joie de la Cort*. The precise nature of this adventure is explained later; meanwhile Erec's companion tells him:

>'Que nus chevaliers de haut pris,
>(Ce ai oï dire et conter)
>Ne puet an cest chastel antrer,
>Por ce que herbergier i vuelle,
>Que li rois Evrains nel recuelle.
>Tant est jantius et frans li rois
>Qu'il a fet ban a ses borjois,
>Si chier con chascuns a son cors
>Que prodon qui vaingne defors,
>An lor meisons ostel ne truisse,
>Por ce que il meïsmes puisse
>Toz les prodomes enorer,
>Qui leanz voudront demorer.' (5480 ff.)

Bl also is told that the citizens of the town never receive any strange knight. The lord of the castle alone extends hospitality.

>'Un usage vos en dirai,
>Dou castel que je moult bien sai.
>Li borjois qu'en la vile sont
>Jà homme ne herbergeront.
>Tot herbergent cis le signor;
>Car il veut faire à tos honor.' (2495 ff.)

(d) In both poems after they enter the castle and ride along the streets, they are the centre of interest of the whole city. The people all leave off their work to follow them and talk about them. In *Erec*, however, they all admire Erec exceedingly and sympathize with him, for they fear he is doomed to suffer; while in Bl they point mockingly at the hero and get ready to shame him. This difference is, of course, due to the different conditions of the encounter.

Cf.
>Tuit an consoillent et parolent. (E., 5503.)

with
>Tot en parolent et consellent. (Bl, 2554.)

(e) In both cases the lord of the castle and the stranger knight salute each other while the latter is still on his horse.

Cf.
>   Li rois Evrains anmi la rue
>   Vint ancontre aus, si les salue.
>   . . . .
>   'Bien veigniez, seignor! Desçandez!' (E., 5547-51.)

with
>   Li Desconnéus le salue,
>   De son ceval ne se remue.
>   Lanpars respont, come afaitiés:
>   'Bials sire, fait-il, bien viegniés.' (BI, 2574 ff.)

(*f*) In the fight which follows, Erec and his opponent have lances of the same description as BI and his.
Cf.
>   N'orent mie lances menues,
>   Einz furent grosses et quarrees. (E., 5940-1.)

with
>   Estes vos que totes les [lances] orent
>   Grandes et roides et quarrées. (BI, 2613-4.)

(*g*) The descriptions of the fight show verbal agreement in the two poems. Cf. E., 5943-60, with BI, 2663-71, and 2628-35.

(*h*) In the descriptions of the attendant crowd we have the following parallel lines:
>   Et [a] grant bruit par totes les rues;
>   Car les granz janz et les menues . . .
>   (E., 5703-4; cf. 750.)
>
>   Et les grans gens et les menues;
>   Plaines en sont totes les rues. (BI, 2650-1.)

(*i*) The following lines also occur in the description of the same conflict:
>   Mout sont doillant et mout sont las;
>   Ne porquant ne recroient pas. (E., 5979-80.)
>
>   Moult se dolousent, moult sont las,
>   Ne por quant ne recroient pas. (BI, 3021-2.)

16. The adventure with the knight in the *Joie de la Cort*[1] in *Erec* corresponds markedly with that of BI with Mabon and Eurain.

---

[1] On this see Paris in *Rom.*, XX, 152 ff. For the magic garden, see Freymond, *Livre d'Artus*, in *Zt. f. franz. Sprache u. Litt.*, XVII, 117, n. 1, where other ref-

Studies on the Libeaus Desconus. 125

(*a*) It follows directly the one just described, in which the lord will lodge every comer himself.

(*b*) The place where the knight(s) is (are), is under the influence of magic.

(*c*) Every one fears the hero's quest will be fatal to himself. No one has availed before. It requires one of unusual powers and exceeding valor to accomplish it.

(*d*) The people of the land look upon the place as the cause of great sorrow to them, and hope to have the trouble ended.

(*e*) They all sympathize with him in his approaching struggle; some accompany him part of the way, but are unable to go farther. (On their way in *Erec* they pass through an orchard. In BI "une forest ont à passer," 2750.) They recommend him to God, and he them (cf. E., 5868–9 and BI, 2816–7).

(*f*) Before he leaves the knight who has lodged him, the latter tells him what he is to expect.

(*g*) He has to go well armed and undergo a terrible fight.

(*h*) A solitary woman is kept in the place who is (or, being transformed, becomes) of exceeding beauty.

(*i*) After the hero conquers his opponent, he receives a lengthy explanation of the reason of the enchantment.

(*j*) The knight who guards the enchanted place is in *Erec* called *Mabonagrain*. Paris has noted the fact that there are many compound Celtic names which have *Mabon* for the first part and a second name joined to the first by *ab* (= the son of),[1] and has suggested that this might be such a form as *Mabon ab Grain* (?). It seems almost certain that the names of the enchanters in LD and BI are due to a misunderstanding. In Car., and in nearly all the traditional forms of this feature of the story (as an examination later will show),

---

erences will be found. On p. 107 of the last named article we read of a garden surrounded with a magic air wall by the King of Denmark. There is but one passage to serve as inlet and outlet. W. Foerster says (*Erec*, *Introd.*, p. xv): "Die '*Joie de la Cort*' ist plump nachgeahmt im Meraugis und besonders ausführlich in Rigomer. Die Luftmauer des Zaubergartens findet sich T. R. IV, 240, vgl. noch ähnliches im 3. Band."

[1] For example, *Mabon ab Deweugen*, *Mabon ab Modron*, and *Mabon ab Mellt*, which are to be found in the index to the *Mabinogion* (see *Rom.*, XX, 153, n. 4). *Mabonagrain* is the name of a dwarf, brother of Helys de Roestoc, in Version P of the *Livre d'Artus*, ed. Freymond, p. 91. There is also a *gue Mabon*, *ib.*, p. 46.

there is but one enchanter. If, then, we suppose him to be originally called Mabonagrain, this name could easily have become divided, and an idea could have arisen that there were really two enchanters, Mabon and Irain.[1] It is probable that the author of the original of LD and BI saw the name in *Erec* in the adventure which resembled the one he was describing, and, whether by mistake or intentionally, introduced it into his poem, splitting it into two words, and thus making two enchanters instead of one. The spelling *Eurain* in BI is easily explained: when Renaud reverted to his *Erec*, he saw in the line following the name Mabonagrain (6348) the name of King Eurain, and, confusing the two, he calls the second magician *Eurain;* whereas the English poem preserves a more natural form, *Irain.*[2]

---

[1] My friend Dr. F. N. Robinson reminds me of a similar explanation by Lipsius of the names *Karinus* and *Leuticus* in the *Gospel of Nicodemus* as a corruption of the single name Λεύκιος χαρῖνος (cf. *Die apocryphen Apostelgeschichten u. Apostellegenden*, I, 85–86). The division into two names would suggest itself more readily, if the author of the original of LD and BI knew of another enchanter called *Mabon*. Such a person, *Mabon le noir*, is mentioned in the prose *Tristan*, ed. Löseth, § 290 a, where he is represented as having no power against Erec (!), "a qui les enchantements ne peuvent nuire, à cause d'une *grace* dont l'a *garni* sa mère *Ocise*, qui s'entendait aux enchantements mieux qu'aucune autre dame de son époque." We have here another point of contact with the Desc. stories. There, also, the wiles of the enchanter Mabon have no effect on the hero because of the latter's parentage. The conqueror of Mabon in LD and BI had to be a son of Gawein.

[2] Paris was near the truth when he concluded that the similarity of the two names in BI with the one in *Erec*, and the likeness of the adventure with the princess in BI to the *Joie de la Cort*, indicated "quelque lointaine communauté de source" between these incidents in the two poems (see *Rom.*, XX, 153, n. 4). In another place (*Rom.*, XX, 156, n. 2) he says of the *Joie de la Cort:* "Peut-être n'avons-nous ici qu'une variante étrangement altérée du conte qui fait l'épisode principal du *Bel Inconnu*, où. . . . les deux magiciens qui retiennent enchantée la future épouse de Guinglain s'appellent Mabon et Evrain." This may be; but it seems clear that, as regards this incident, the agreements between the Desc. poems and *Erec* are due to a borrowing from *Erec* by the author of the original Desc. poem, and not the other way. In all probability this borrowing was more one of incident than language. The close verbal agreement between BI and *Erec* in so many places in this episode is certainly due to Renaud, who has also introduced from Chrétien's poem other features of the adventure as told in BI. [The whole of the present discussion of the name *Mabonagrain* was in type, and Dr. Schofield had left the country, before the number of *Romania* con-

It is not a little significant in this connection to see Renaud write: "Mabons avoit non li plus sire" (3321). This is most natural, for he was, of course, always mentioned first in the combined name. Moreover, we see that the doubling of the enchanters caused the poet difficulty. The reason of the enchantment of the princess originally was that she refused to marry the magician. But when there became two, what was to be done in the matter? The following passage in LD explains itself:

> To dele þey will her diȝte,
> But sche graunte hem till,
> To do Mabounis wille
> And ȝeve him all her riȝt. (1809 ff.)

It is well to note here[1] that the probable reason for the introduction of a second enchanter is found in the fact that in the original, as in Car., the one magician withdrew in the midst of the fight through one door into the palace, hoping to lure the hero in, but, failing in this, reappeared through another. The author of the original of LD-BI may have mistaken these two appearances of the one enchanter for a single coming against our hero of two different ones. We remember also that the English poet, probably following his original, had to summon devils to his aid to get rid of the superfluous Irain, and that in BI the latter escaped from the fight and was not heard of again.

(*k*) When the victory is made known, there is great rejoicing in the city — especially from the hero's three companions. Cf.

> Mout s'an est Enide esjoïe
> Quant ele la voiz antandi,
> Et Guivrez mout s'an esjoï.
> Liez est li rois et sa janz liee:
> N'i a un seul cui mout ne siee
> Et mout ne pleise ceste chose.
> Nus n'i cesse ne ne repose
> De joie feire et de chanter. (E., 6162 ff.)

---

taining F. Lot's interesting conjectures on the same subject (*Rom.*, XXIV, 321-2) reached America. Lot regards *Mabonagrain* as "une fusion des deux noms juxtaposés *Mabon* et *Evrain*." — *Eds.*]

[1] Cf. Mennung, p. 49.

with
>
> Grant joie font et cil et cele.
> Si s'antrebeisent et acolent. (6356-7.)
>
> Tot un venoient en riant.
> Saciés que lor ot joie grant,
> Quant tot ensanble il s'entrevirent;
> De moult bon cuer se conjoïrent.
> L'uns acole l'autre et enbrace;
> N'i a celui joie ne face. (Bl, 3396 ff.)

(*l*) The young knight is then speedily disarmed by the people, who run up to him.
Cf.
> Trestoz li pueples i acort
> . . . .
> D'Erec desarmer s'aprestoient. (E., 6180-4.)

with
> Por Giglain desarmer corurent.
> Si le desarment en la place. (Bl. 3407-8.)

(*m*) In both poems the barons and people gather in a great assembly when they learn the joyful tidings.
Cf.
> Furent assanblé li baron
> De tot le païs anviron,
> Et tuit cil qui la joie sorent
> I vindrent, qui venir i porent;
> Granz fu l'assanblee et la presse.
> Chascuns d'Erec veoir s'angresse.
> Et haut et bas, et povre et riche. (E., 6365 ff.)

with
> Comment de Galles li baron
> Et li evesque et li abé
> Et tot li prince, et li casé,
> Vinrent, quant sorent la novele
> . . . .
> Puis n'i ot nule retenue,
> Que tot ne venissent à cort,
> Por la grant joie qui lor sort.
> Tot li palais vint cele part,
> Petis et grans, moult lor est tart,
> Qu'il aient lor dame véue
> Moult i est grans lies méue. (Bl, 3431-43.)

(*n*) There is music and singing in token of their joy. Cf. E., 6380 ff., and BI, 3447.

(*o*) But each author declares he wishes to tell the events briefly. Cf.

    Mes je le vos vuel assomer
    Briémant, sans trop longue demore. (E., 6386-7.)

with

    Dorenavant vos vuel conter
    Briement, sans trop longue raison. (BI, 3429-30.)

(*p*) Erec and Enide go to Arthur directly after this adventure, and are heartily welcomed at court. So do LD and Elene; so does Blonde Esmerée, although she is not accompanied by BI, as she should have been.

17. When Giglain, after all his painful waiting and longing, receives a message from the *fée* of the Ile d'Or to come to her, his spirits revive, and he starts off at once. On the way, the messenger leads him through a magnificent orchard. Such an one could not be seen elsewhere. All sorts of trees and herbs are to be found there in abundance. The birds keep up a constant song, and spices and flowers fill the air with sweet odors. Renaud doubtless had this addition suggested to him by the account of the similar orchard in *Erec*, which the knight has to traverse before he reaches the dwelling of Mabonagrain.

Cf.

    Li rois fors del chastel le mainne
    An un vergier qui estoit pres. (E., 5730-1.)

with

    Si se sont d'autre part issu,
    Parmi un huis en un vergier. (BI, 4204-5.)

Cf. also *Erec*, 5755 ff.:

    Ne soz ciel n'a oisel volant,
    Qui pleise a home, qui n'i chant,
    Por lui deduire et resjoïr,
    Plusors de chascune nature.

with BI, 4238 ff.:

    Tos jors i avoit cris d'osials,
    De calendres et d'orials.
    De merles et de lorsingnals;
    Et d'autres dont i ot asés,
    Ne jà lor cans ne fust lassés.

and *Erec*, 5760 ff. :

> Et terre, tant com ele dure,
> Ne porte espice ne racine
> Qui vaille a nule medecine,
> Que l'an n'an i eüst planté,
> S'an i avoit a grant planté.

with BI, 4229 ff. :

> Dius ne fist herbe de bonté
> Que el vergier n'éust planté
> . . . . .
> De ce ot asés el gardins.

Both orchards are surrounded by a wall. In *Erec* it is invisible, but none the less impassable.

18. In describing the castle of the Ile d'Or, on BI's return to it, Renaud reverts to the description of Brandigan in *Erec*. Cf.

> Chevauchié ont des le matin
> Jusqu'au vespre le droit chemin
> Plus de trante liues galesches.
> Et vienent devant les bretesches
> D'un chastel fort et riche et bel,
> Clos tot antor de mur novel ;
> Et par dessoz a la reonde
> Coroit une eve mout parfonde.   (E., 5367 ff.)

> Brandiganz a non li chastiaus.
> Qui tant par est et forz et biaus
> Que roi n'anpereor ne dote.
> Se France et Angleterre tote,
> Et tuit cil qui sont jusqu'au Liege,
> Estoient anviron a siege,
> Nel prandroient il an lor vies.   (E., 5389 ff.)

with

> Cevaucié ont des la jornée,
> De si que vint à la vesprée,
> Plus de XXX liues galesces ;
> Tant qu'il vont devant les bretesces
> De l'Ile d'Or, le bon castel,
> Dont li mur sont et fort et bel.
> Moult fu li castials bons et fors.
> Se cil qui sont dèsqu'à Limors[1]

---

[1] This name does not occur in LD. It also is taken from *Erec*, 4717.

I fuissent à siege XXX ans
N'enterroient-il pas dedens.
Moult estoit bials à demesure. (Bl, 3882 ff.)
Tot entor coroit la marine. (3900.)

19. Renaud seems also to have got the hint of the description of the beautiful room in the Ile d'Or from the account of the castle of Brandigan in *Erec*.

Cf.
Une chanbre fist ançanser
D'ançans, de myrre et d'aloé.
. . . . . .
An la chanbre antrent main a main,
. . . . .
Mes por quoi vos deviseroie
Les peintures, les dras de soie,
Don la chanbre estoit anbelie?
Le tans gasteroie an folie,
Ne je ne le vuel pas gaster,
Einçois me vuel un po haster. (E., 5564 ff.)

with
Et adonc par le main le prist.
Atant par le canbre s'en vont;
Très parmi l'uis trové il l'ont.
Quant en la canbre entré sont,
Tot maintenant trové i ont,
Une si très douce flairor,
Dont asés mius valoit l'odor
K'encens, ne pètre, ne canele;
. . . . . .
La canbre sanbloit paradis.
Asés i ot argent et or,
De tos biens i ot grant tresor.
Parée fu de dras de soie
De mult cier pris. Que vos diroie?
Mais moult en i ot de divers,
. . . . . .
Mais por sa grant joie conter,
Que moult en avoit grant mestier,
Ne le vuel entendre et descrire;
Que trop me costeroit à dire. (Bl, 4642–86.)

Renaud here adopted the incident of their entering the chamber hand in hand, the incense with which the room is filled, its beautiful embellishments "les peintures, les dras de soie," all of which are found in the *Erec* passage. We also find Chrétien's plea that he cannot linger longer over the description; he must hurry on. The only difference is that, despite his protestations, Renaud does describe at length, elaborating the ideas he got from Chrétien. The latter gives the headings which Renaud fills out. We may note also that not even the additions are his own, but are borrowed from other parts of *Erec*. Cf. E., 6876 ff. and BI, 4675 ff.

20. It is also from this passage that Renaud takes the lines descriptive of the torrent over which BI finds himself in the night.

Cf.
>Coroit une eve mout parfonde.
>Lee et bruianz come tanpeste. (E., 5374-5.)

with
>Une grant iaugue sos avoit,
>Rude et bruiant plus que tempeste. (BI, 4468-9.)

It is then perfectly clear that Renaud has made wholesale use of *Erec*, and that its influence is constant from the beginning to the end of his poem. From it he has taken hundreds of lines, from it he has borrowed many new features. He was, however, very skilful in his borrowings, and the most striking parallels are not in passages which deal with the same incidents in the two poems. It is, moreover, not unusual to have two passages following each other directly in BI clearly taken from passages in *Erec* some two or three thousand lines apart. Renaud must have known the *Erec* almost by heart, and he introduced Chrétien's characteristic turns of expression and his method of treating his subjects, whenever an opportunity offered. Not unconsciously, however, for he seems to have done his borrowing deliberately, and frequently passages are found in which Renaud has changed only the rhyming word — apparently with the idea of concealing his obligations. He tried to be original, and to cover up his footsteps; and, indeed, we cannot withhold from him a due share of praise for the skilful way in which he has worked over his narrative. He entered into the spirit of his master with wonderful ease, and wove Chrétien's ideas so naturally into his own composition that, although it has long been known that he was indebted to Chrétien for some features of the poem, the extent of his borrowings has escaped the notice of scholars.[1]

Mennung has already pointed out[2] several of the episodes in the LD-BI group which are taken from the *Erec*. These are, in his opinion: (1) the fight with the three robbers; (2) the sparrow-hawk adventure; (3) the recognition scene between Hélie and Margerie; (4) the heads on stakes; (5) the knight who will joust with all who come to his castle. He thinks, moreover, that the fight with the giants was taken from *Erec*, — an idea which Paris has shown to be improbable (p. 152). As to No. 3, I am of the opinion that this was introduced first by Renaud, although one cannot be certain in the matter, inasmuch as LD omits the character of Margerie altogether. The other features (Nos. 1, 2, 4, 5 above) were certainly in the original of LD and BI, and were doubtless borrowed from *Erec*. In this same version there were probably, however, more features taken from *Erec* than Mennung supposes, e.g. the *Mabonagrain* episode (see pp. 126 f.).

Of course the objection may be raised that if there was borrowing from *Erec* by the author of the original of LD and BI, then the passages which I have maintained were taken by Renaud from *Erec* might be regarded as borrowings on the part of the author of Renaud's original. This possibility, however, becomes smaller and smaller the more it is considered. Doubtless there were some verbal agreements between *Erec* and the original of LD-BI in those features which they had in common; but anything like the extended agreement which exists now between *Erec* and BI is not to be thought of. This will be clear if we remember that the borrowings in BI are not limited to the adventures which Renaud's poem has in common with *Erec*, but are found from the very beginning to the very end of the book, some of the most striking parallels being in parts which in general are entirely unlike in BI and *Erec*, and many being in the second half of BI, which is certainly Renaud's own addition. Moreover, the English poem shows practically no trace of these borrowings. Most of the verbal agreements between LD and BI have been

---

[1] Renaud does not hesitate to repeat himself. Cf., for example, the fight between BI and Bliobliéris, and that between BI and the enchanter (451 ff., 3006 ff.).

[2] *Der Bel Inconnu*, p. 49.

pointed out by Kölbing,[1] and they are altogether too slight to interfere in any way with my argument.

Before leaving this part of our subject I would call attention to the fact that the following 42 names seem to be common to BI and *Erec*,[2] but are not found in LD (except perhaps in the case of *fius Do*).

Aguizans, li rois d'Escoce. BI, 5372; E., 1970.
Amangons. 5452; E., 1726.
Arés. 42; E., 1528.
Bans de Gomeret. 5737; E., 1975.
Beduiers. 61; E., 1735.
Bliobliéris. 333; E., 1714.
Breton. 5695; E., 652.
Bruians des Illes. 5454; E., 6730.
Caraés. 41; E., 1727.
Carados. 44; E., 1719.
Cadoalens. 5657; E., 315.
Cadoc. 5694; E., 4515.
Cornouaille. 1844; E., 6647.
Do (Gilles li fius). 1789; E., 1729.
Erec. 39; E., 19.
Escoce (see Aguizans).
Fineposterne. 5424; E., 1952.
Gales li cals. 6020, 41; E., 1726.
Gaudelus. 5432; E., 1701.
Gaudins. 5444; E., 2227.
Gorhout. 5434; E., 1695.
Gormans. 5434; E., 1695 (Gornemanz).

Grahelens de Fineposterne.[3] 5424; E., 1952 (Graislemiers de F.).
Guingamer (ses frère). 5426; E., 1954.
Guivres. 5388; E., 4951.
Gringars (Grigoras ?).[4] 173; E., 2005.
Cil de la *Haute Montaigne*. 5418; E., 1939.
Keu, le seneschal. 5574; E., 1739.
Li *Lais Hardis* (de *Cornuaille*). 5394; E., 1697.
Los. 33; E., 1737.
Limors. 3889; E., 6495.
Melians de Lis. 5435; E., 1698.
Orguillous de la Lande. 1472; E., 2175.
Parcevals le Galois. 5406; E., 1526.
Li rois de la *Roge Cité*. 5386; E., 2192.
Sagremors. 5905; E., 1733.
Tors, li fius le rois Arés (*Atels*). 42 (5487); E., 1728.
Tristans. 5488; E., 1713.
Truerem. 5420; E., 1941 (Treverain).
Tintaguel. 51; E., 1959.
Uriens. 33; E., 1706.
Ydés. 5460; E., 1724 (Yders).

It is well also to examine to some extent the names of those persons called differently in the two poems, LD and BI.

---

[1] In *Engl. Studien*, I, 121–169.

[2] Cf. Paris, *Hist. Litt.*, XXX, 118: "La plupart des noms qui y figurent ne sont pour nous que des noms: au poète et à ses auditeurs ils rappelaient les aventures des héros qui les portaient." The names in the accompanying list are spelt as in BI. Only one of the places where each name occurs is usually given.

[3] Cf. Zimmer, *Zt. f. franz. Sprache u. Litt.*, XIII, 1 ff. BI should have no influence in settling the form.

[4] Cf. the name of King *Grigorz* (with long *i*) in Wolfram, *Parzival*, iv, 926. Cf. *Perc.*, 8480.

Studies on the Libeaus Desconus. 135

1. *William Salebraunche* is the name in LD of the first knight whom the hero encounters. Of the three avengers only one has a name: the eldest is called *Sir Gower*. In BI the knight is called *Blioblièris*, the three avengers:

> Elins li blans, sires de Graies
> Et li bons chevaliers des Aies [1]
> Et Willaume de Salebrant. (521 ff.)

The only name common to both is *William Salebrant* (Salebraunche). *Sir Gower* is probably an addition of the English poet. In the original, as in *Erec*, probably none of the avengers were named, and William Salebrant was doubtless the name of the first knight, as in LD. The name *Blioblièris* [2] is in *Erec*, and Renaud perhaps had one other name suggested by the *Erec* passage [3] (see above, p. 115).

2. The maid rescued from the giants in LD gives her name as *Violette*, and that of her father as *Sir Antore*.[4] In BI she says it is *Clarie*, and that of her brother *Saigremor*. Here we have nothing to guide us to the original names. It is possible that the original story did not give any special names to either the maiden or her father

---

[1] I adopt this reading in accordance with the suggestion made by Seiffert in his *Namenbuch zu den altfranz. Artusepen*, Part I, Greifswald, 1882, p. 42.

[2] It is of frequent occurrence. See Heinzel, *Ueber die franz. Gralromane*, in the *Denkschriften der Wiener Akad.*, XL, 1892, Part III, p. 80, note. Cf. Freymond, l.c., pp. 81, 116.

[3] It is curious to note the following passage in the spurious introduction to *Perceval li Galois*, ed. Potvin, I, 7, which, if we put the name of the son for the father, would describe the adventure in BI.

> Li premiers chevaliers conquis
> Ot à nom Blihos Bliheris;
> Sel conquist mesire Gauwains,
> Par grant proece dont ert plains;
> Au roi Artu l'envoia rendre;
> Cil monta, ains n'i vot atendre,
> Tresqu'à la cort si fu rendus.

[4] In Version P of the *Livre d'Artus*, ed. Freymond, p. 63, alongside the story of the love of Gawain and Florie, we read: " *Claudas* wird von *Antor* [brother of Ban and Bohor] besiegt und sein Land wird verwüstet. Claudas zieht mit einem neuen Heer vor die Stadt Trebes, wo sich die Königin *Helaine* befand."

(brother); but we may note that, (1) the names in LD have a French form, and are not the sort the English poet would be likely to make up; (2) it is more probable that the maiden would give the name of her father than brother, and (3) *Saigremors* is found in *Erec*, 1733.

3. In LD the owner of the dog is called *Sir Otes de Lile;* in BI, *Orguillous de la Lande*. Here again we note that the former is obviously a French name,[1] and the latter is in *Erec*, 2175.

4. The lady of the Ile d'Or is in LD called *La dame d'Amour*, which would not be a word invented by the English author,[2] and was almost surely in his original. It suggests clearly the seductive character she must have had at first (see pp. 197 ff.). In BI we find her called *la pucele* (*dame*) *as blances mains*, and we remember that the most beautiful woman in *Erec* was also called *la pucele au chainse blanc*. Of course the latter appellation would not be suitable in BI; but the idea of calling the *fée* always by a name made up from a peculiar feature of her dress or appearance still lingers. The expression used in BI was very common,[3] and would naturally suggest itself.

5. The knight who defends the sparrow-hawk is called in LD *Giffroun* or *Giffroun le fludus*, in BI, *Giflès li fius Do*. Some have regarded these names as identical, and *le fludus* is generally considered a corruption of *li fius Do*. We have, however, another character in LD called *Gifflet*. *Gi(r)fles li fius Do* was a well-known personage, and the name is in *Erec* (1729). It is just possible that Renaud, dropping out the character of Gifflet *the squire* in LD, made

---

[1] Bartsch, *Die Eigennamen in Wolfram's Parzival*, Germanistische Studien, II, 142, says that *Schionatulander* may be *Li joenet à l'alant*, "The Youth with the Dog," in allusion to the cause of the knight's death. Such a name would be very appropriate here. It could easily become confused with the more familiar name which Renaud writes, probably following Chrétien. It is well to note that the owner of the dog in the *Lay of the Great Fool* (see below, p. 171), is called "the Gruagach (enchanter?) of the white hound." The hero swears he shall have to give up the name thereafter.

[2] Cf. Paris, *Rom.*, XX, 299.

[3] It was, as is well known, regularly applied to *Ysolde*. In *Meraugis*, p. 5, last line, we read of her who claimed the sparrow-hawk: "ot la pucele et blanches mains." Cf. *Yvain as blances mains, Perceval*, 29140; Prose *Tristan*, p. 123. In *Peredur*, Ygharat has the appellation "à la main d'or." See note by Loth, in *Les Mab.*, II, 75.

use of the name in another connection, having before him the exact form he has used.

A few other names deserve notice :

1. In BI the knight who takes Margerie home is not named. In LD the corresponding knight, who takes the hawk to Arthur, is called *Claudas*. This is not an English name, but occurs frequently in French.[1]

2. The name of the castle *Bel Leu* in BI was probably an invention of Renaud's, and may have been suggested by *Erec*. Cf.

> Un fort chastel,
> Qui mout seoit et bien et bel,
> . . . . . .
> Car mout estoit pleisanz li leus. (E., 5185-90.)

and

> Un castel de pris ont veü,
> Qui moult estoit et bons et bels.
> Bel leus avoit non li castels. (BI, 1486 ff.)

3. The name of the steward in LD and BI, viz. *Lampart* (*Lambard*), is also found elsewhere. It is, e.g., the name of Perceval's great uncle, and occurs in the Prose *Tristan*, ed. Löseth, p. 357. See further, Zimmer, *Zt. f. franz. Spr. u. Litt.*, XIII, 47, 52 ff.

4. As to *Guinglain*, Zimmer points out[2] that there is no form *Winwaloen* (given by Paris), although the Breton *Winwaloe* exists. *Winwaloeus*[3] is a Breton saint of the sixth century, whose life was written before 884, — nowadays called *Saint Guénolé*. Of this saint it is told how, a serpent having bitten the foot of one of the saint's disciples, he not only cured the wound, but, calling the serpent, forced it to leave its cave, and made it perish by the application of the sign of the cross. Since the names of the heroes are so similar, we are reminded of the serpent transformation in our poems ; and we remember that in *Peredur* and Wig. the sign of the cross availed the knight. But the coincidence is doubtless only accidental. As

---

[1] Cf., e. g., Prose *Tristan*, ed. Löseth, p. 36, etc. In the *Livre d'Artus*, ed. Freymond, p. 63, he is the vassal of the King of Gaul.
[2] In *Zt. f. franz. Spr. u. Litt.*, XIII, 17 ff.
[3] See Mennung, pp. 65-6. Cf. *Revue Celtique*, XV, 245.

Paris says,[1] "C'est un miracle familier aux saints, et notamment aux saints celtiques, que de guérir de la morsure des serpents et de faire périr ceux-ci." We have here, then, in his opinion, probably a purely ecclesiastical legend, of a kind similar to those associated with the names of St. Paul and St. Patrick.

Zimmer also points out that the form *Guiglain* (without the first *n*)[2] occurs in *Perc.*, 33402, 33435, 33592, in the Prose *Tristan*, etc., and makes it probable that this was the original form. He suggests a form *Guiganlois* (cf. *Guigan-bresil; Loies* appears in numerous Breton names),[3] giving *Guigal(l)ois*, which he compares with *Wigalois* and the form *Gingeleus* (or *Guigeleus*) of a MS. of the *Parzival* of Philipp Colin of Strassburg (*Hie vindet gawin sinen sun gingeleus*, Keller, *Romvart*, p. 672). The change of *Guigalois* to *Guiglain* (*Guinglain*) might have taken place, he thinks, under the influence of *Gauvain* (cf. *Gau-vains, Y-vains*, and *Agra-vains*, who are brothers, as also are *Aglo-val* and *Perce-val*), with which the name is often united, in rhyme even, since Gauvain is the father of Guinglain.

The latest suggestion (March 27, 1895) on this point is that of E. Freymond,[4] based on likenesses to our poems, especially to Wig., in the prose *Livre d'Artus;* viz. that the name is due to *Gui(n)galois* + *Alain*, the latter being in that text the grandfather of *Guigalois. This does not seem so probable as Zimmer's supposition, on the whole.

5. The situation of Arthur's court is different in the four poems of our cycle: in LD, Glastinbery; in BI, Charlion; in Wig., Karidôl (= Carduel, Cardevile, = Carlisle) ; in Car., Camelot (see p. 186).

6. The city of the enchanted princess is called *Sinadoun*, which is, of course, *Snowdon*. As Paris notes, it occurs also in the Latin

---

[1] *Romania*, XX, 302. He adds, "Le rapprochement même des noms s'efface si on réfléchit que le nom de Guinglain n'a été mis que tardivement, dans les contes celtiques, en rapport avec l'aventure du fier baiser."

[2] In the French prose romance it is written *Giglan*. *Giglain* is the form in the Hippeau text of BI; but Foerster says (*Zt. f. rom. Phil.*, II, 79) that *Guinglain* is the constant form in the MS. of the Duc d'Aumale.

[3] See *Zt. f. franz. Sp. u. Litt.*, XII, 237.

[4] *Zt. f. franz. Sp. u. Litt.*, XVII, 50, note 2.

romance of *Meriadocus* in the British Museum.[1] Ward speaks of the name as "essentially English." In the *Lai du Cor*[2] of Robert Biket, it is the king of Sinadoun who tries the horn next after Arthur.

RENAUD'S USE OF THE PERCEVAL.

BI shows traces of Renaud's acquaintance with Chrétien's *Perceval*. It also contains passages which, but for possible chronological difficulties,[3] one would unhesitatingly pronounce borrowings from the continuation by Gautier (Gaucher). Thus in two places BI seems to show the influence of Gautier's account of Perceval's visit to the Castle of Maidens: the description of events at the Ile d'Or, and at the castle of Senaudon. First as to the latter.

Perc. and BI come to a castle, which in both cases is "mout rices" and surrounded by a stream, over which the hero passes. In *Perc.* the castle is described as follows:

        Si vit .1. moult rice castiel,
        Dont tout li mur et li quariel
        Èrent de marbre coulouré,
        De vermel et de gausne ovré ;
        Tour i avoit haute et bien faite,
        Ausi com s'ele fust portraite. (26487 ff.)

In BI we read :
        Li murs estoient bon et bel,
        De mabre sont tot li quartel ;
        .   .   .   .   .
        Et furent de maintes colors ;
        Taillié a bietes et à flors.
        Et sont li quartel bien asis,
        Indes et vers, gaunes et bis ;
        Et a v toises tot entor
        Ot adiès une haute tor. (2835-44.)

---

[1] *Hist. Litt.*, XXX, 174, n.; see Ward, *Catal. of Romances*, I, 375.
[2] F. Wulff, *Le Lai du Cor* [1888], v. 415.
[3] Birch-Hirschfeld, *Gral*, p. 110, and Nutt, *Studies*, p. 95, think that Gautier followed Chrétien after no long interval. Heinzel, *Gralromane*, p. 3, expresses no opinion. Mennung, p. 17, believes that Gautier borrowed some incidents from BI (but see p. 192, below).

The city is apparently uninhabited. In both cases it (or the hall) is said to be *gaste*.

>Pierchevaus moult s'esmervella
>l'or çou que il ne vit nului. (26504-5; cf. 26916.)

In BI:

>Et la cité home n'avoit
>Tote gaste la vile estoit. (2847-8.)

This does not deter him.

>Ens est entrés parmi la porte. (*Perc.*, 26499.)
>Par la porte dedans entra. (BI, 2850.)

Nothing delays him:

>Perchevaus ne s'est atargiés. (*Perc.*, 26496.)
>Que de rien ne s'en va targant. (BI, 2888.)

When he enters the hall the door is closed behind him. In *Perc.*:

>la porte estoit fremée
>Tantost com l'oi je hui passée.
>(26879-80; cf. 26505-6.)

and in BI:

>Derier l'uis ot 1 jougléor
>Qui en sa main tint 1 tabor,
>Et li a l'uis après fermé. (2889 ff.)

The hall is splendidly lit by torches. In *Perc.*:

>I ot moult cierges alumés
>Que moult fu grande la clartés. (26837-8.)

and in BI:

>En la sale avoit grant clarté
>Des cierges qui laiens ardoient. (2892-3.)

In the centre of the hall was a table. Cf.

>Une table ot mise desus
>. . . . . .
>Bien .v. piés, au mien ensient. (*Perc.*, 26517-21.)

with

>Une grant table en mi avoit,
>Qui séoit desus VII dormans. (BI, 2896-7.)

He remains beside the table, waiting to see what will happen. Cf. *Perc.*, 26703-4 with BI, 2899 ff.

Getting separated from his horse, he finds it again. In *Perc.*:

> Revenus est à son cheval
> Là ù prèmiers ot pris estal. (26621-2.)

and in BI :

> Iluec estoit tot à estal ;
> Liés fu quant il ot son ceval. (2961-2.)

After the meeting he is in great terror, and returns to the centre of the hall. Cf. *Perc.*, 26618 ff. with BI, 3065 ff.

But the hero is exhausted and goes to sleep, and when he wakes up it is day. In *Perc.*:

> Si lassés ert et si aquis,
> Delés la dame est endormis. (26945-6.)
> Travelliés estes et penés. (26958.)

So in BI :

> Moult estoit Giglains travilliés ;
> . . . .
> De dormir li est talens pris,
> Car lassés est et travilliés.
> Dormi a, puis est esvilliés.
> Grant jors estoit, quant s'esvilla ;
> En la sale grant clarté a. (3227-34.)

Cf. *Perc.* :

> Perchevaus toute nuit dormi
> Tant que li biaus jors esclarci,
> Et que li solaus fu levés. (26971 ff.)

Perc. is told that the castle "si biel" was built without the aid of masons or laborers (26899 ff.). With this and the description of the castle already given, compare that of the Ile d'Or in BI :

> Moult i avoit rice castel,
> Li murs en furent rice et bel,
> Dont li castels tos clos estoit. (1867 ff.)
> En la vile ot II tors vermelles ;
> Qui beles èrent à mervelles,
> Et furent de marbre vermeil,
> Qui moult reluist contre soleil.
> . . . . . .
> Un palais i ot bon et bel.
> Cil qui le fist sot d'encanter,
> Que nus hom ne l'puet deviser

De coi il fu ; mais bel estoit.
Cristal la piere resanbloit,
Dont li palais estoit tot fait
Et à conpas trestos portrait. (1881-94.)

When Perc. is well received by the maidens, it seems to him "qu'il soit entrés en paradis" (26770) ; so to BI, when he entered the room of his loved one, it "sanbloit paradis" (4655).[1] Moreover (and the agreement here is specially striking), we find both Perc. and BI going to sleep in the evening in the castle, and, when they awake in the morning, they are out in a forest with their arms and equipment, and marvel at the change.[2]

Cf. *Perc.*:

with BI :
    Delés la dame est endormis. (26946.)
    S'est endormis dalès s'amie. (5299.)

Then also cf. *Perc.*, 26974 ff. :

    Esvelliés s'est, si s'est trouvés
    Desous .I. grant caisne fuellu ;
    Lés lui sa lance et son escu
    Et ses armes et son diestrier,
    Tout atourné por chevaucier.

and BI, 5303 ff. :

    Quant Giglains au matin s'esvelle,
    De ce qu'il vit ot grant mervelle ;

---

[1] Cf. also Perc.'s asking explanation from the beautiful lady of the strange experiences he had in the castle (26879 ff.) with that asked by BI of his enchantment at the Ile d'Or (4776 ff.).

[2] In the Prose *Tristan*, ed. Löseth, § 290ᵃ, we learn of Erec's going to sleep in a castle and the next morning finding himself when he wakes up in a boat in the middle of a lake. When he reaches the bank, he finds his horse and arms. In *Li Romans de Claris et Laris*, ed. Alton, Marine and her company meet with a similar adventure on their way to Denmark (see p. 820). Heinzel says (*Ueb. die franz. Gralromane*, p. 31) : " Ein märchenhaftes Motiv ist benutzt, wenn Gawan, nachdem er in der Gralburg eingeschlafen ist, den andern Morgen auf freiem Feld erwacht, 20304 ; s. erste Interpolation zu Pseudo-Gautier, Potvin, III, S. 372, V. 170. Heinrich vom Thürlein Krone 14884. . . . Das Erwachen Percevals bei seinem ersten Besuch auf der Gralburg, Crestien 4537, hat nichts Zauberhaftes. Er wird nur in unhöflicher Weise allein gelassen. Gleichwohl wird diese Einsamkeit des Gastes am Morgen nach der glänzenden Geselligkeit den Abend vorher den Anlass zu Einführung des Märchenmotivs geboten haben."

>   Car il se trova en un bois.
>   Dalès lui trova son harnois,
>   Son cief tenoit sor son escu
>   Et devant lui si r'a véu
>   Son ceval qui fu atachiés.

In both cases the hero is astonished. In BI, Robert, of course, takes part.

In *Perc.*:

>   Perchevaus moult s'en esmervelle. (26981.)

In BI.:

>   Quant li uns a l'autre véu ;
>   Moult en sont andui esperdu. (5315-6.)

The hero gives expression to his surprise.
Cf.

>   Dont à primes garde entor lui ;
>   'Diex aïe !' fait-il, 'jou fui
>   Anuit el castiel as Pucèles
>   .   .   .   .   .   .
>   Or ne voi borde ne maison,
>   Ne mur ne porte ne riens née ;
>   .   .   .   .   .   .
>   Mais de chou ne me douc je mie
>   Que ne fusce mout aaisiés
>   Et en trop rice lit chouciés ;
>   Et or sui ci desous ce kaisne.' (*Perc.*, 26987-27003.)

with

>   Li uns a l'autre regardé :
>   'Robert, dist Giglains, que dis tu?
>   Avons nos ci à nuit jéu ?
>   Er soir me couçai je aillors,
>   Dalès m'amie à grant honor ;
>   Or me sui en un bois trovés,
>   Tos esbahis et esgarés.
>   Et tu, venis tu ci er soir ?'
>   Ce dist Robers : 'Naie por voir.
>   Er soir en mon lit me dormi ;
>   Or me resui trovés ici.' (BI, 5318 ff.)

But both decide to arm and ride on.
Cf.

>   Sans atargier le hauberc vest,
>   Le hiaume lace sans arriest,

with

L'escu au col, l'espée au lés,
Est desus son cheval montés.   (*Perc.*, 26983 ff.)

Atant cauce ses esperons.
Li escuiers l'aubert torsa
Et cil sor son cheval monta.   (BI, 5342 ff.)

They commence their journey.
Cf.

with

Tant a erré par la gaudine
Qu'il vint en une grant valée.   (*Perc.*, 27006–7.)

Tant [ont] erré par lor jornées,
Et tant lor droite voie tinrent,
Qu'al castel des Puceles vinrent.   (BI, 5358 ff.)

This last line in BI would almost be sufficient to suggest borrowing, for we have the Castle of Maidens[1] introduced here without any reason. It was surely not in Renaud's original. BI is made to come to the castle at which the adventure in *Perc.* took place. The agreements in the above passages are too close to permit of any other theory than borrowing, whether by Renaud or by Gautier (see p. 192, below).

It looks also as if from this passage an explanation might be found for the origin of two of the proper names in BI which are in no other version. In *Perc.* (26582) the lady who first appears at the castle is said to be *esmarie*, and also "moult avenans et bele." In BI, also, she is very beautiful, and is given the name of *Esmerée*. Further, the chief of the maidens is compared in *Perc.* to a "*Rose* de noviel *espanie*" (26797), and we remember that the *amie* of Gifflet in BI was called *Rose espanie*. We have already noted, also, that in both cases the epithet *gaste* is applied to the places in the two poems which are described in similar words;[2] and elsewhere (p. 137) a suggestion is made as to the origin of the name *Bel Leu*. If these be accepted, most of the names which Renaud made up have been explained.[3]

---

[1] On this name see Ernst Martin, *Fergus*, *Einl.*, p. xix.
[2] Cf. above, p. 140.
[3] There is a *gaste cité* in the prose romance of *Perceval li Galois*, which later becomes peopled (as Mennung points out, p. 18).

Studies on the Libeaus Desconus. 145

RENAUD'S KNOWLEDGE OF TRISTAN.

Renaud must also have known some form of the *Tristan* story[1] (probably that by Chrétien), for the name of that hero occurs in BI no less than ten times. He is among the knights at Arthur's feast at Charlion (35), and he is one of the barons whom the king calls to counsel him how to induce Giglain to return (5160). He takes also a prominent part in the tournament (see 5210, 5488, 5518-5541, 6018). The fight of BI with the enchanter was not equalled by that "del grant Morholt, ne de Tristant" (3011); and of BI and the fairy it is said :

Car plus l'uns por l'autre se deut.
Qui ne fist Tristans por Yseut. (4335-6.)

We hear also of *Isex la blonde* in 4260, of *Yseuls la bele* in 5492 ; and *Mars de Cornouaille* is mentioned in 5448.

THE ORIGIN AND DEVELOPMENT OF THE STORY.

No satisfactory theory has as yet been offered to explain the origin of our cycle of poems. Mennung[2] thinks that the most primitive elements are the episodes with the *fée* and the enchanted princess. These, he holds, first existed amongst the Bretons as independent tales, but were later told by some Breton singer as the adventures of a single hero. This fusion he calls Version Y (the Breton elements being X[1] and X[2]). To the combination Y was added a new adventure ; viz., the fight with the giants, which was, he thinks, taken from *Erec*. These three incidents are found united in Version Z, and from this form are drawn independently the Italian Car. and another version, which he calls U. In U the earlier story is lengthened by a second borrowing of several incidents from *Erec*. In this version the hero is for the first time called *Guinglain*, "The Fair Unknown," and is also made a son of Gawein. From U, LD and BI are drawn independently ; and from BI comes Wig.

---

[1] Cf. Léopold Sudre, *Les Allusions à la Légende de Tristan dans la Littérature du Moyen Age*, in *Rom.*, XV, 534 ff.; see also pp. 598, 602.

[2] *Der Bel Inconnu*, pp. 44 ff.

L

Paris[1] regards all this as "judicieux et vraisemblable," except as to the first borrowing from *Erec*, which he is right in thinking unnecessary. He thinks,[2] moreover, that the author of Version Z added the account of " l'enfance solitaire et sauvage du héros."

We thus see that, in the opinion of Paris and Mennung, the kernel of the story is the *märchen* of the *fier baiser*, which became combined with another *märchen* (the *fée* episode), and one hero was made to perform both adventures. From this was elaborated, by the addition of different episodes taken at different times from other poems, a biographical romance telling the deeds of a young knight, who finally received the name of Guinglain and was called by Arthur and his knights Libeaus Desconeus. In the course of the development of this romance it occurred to some one to make the hero a young boy brought up alone in the woods, ignorant of his noble parentage and of the outer world, who came to Arthur's court anxious to be knighted. He is made to undertake the series of adventures which had already become collected around the original *märchen*. This prefatory account, which now is tacked on to a story with which it had originally nothing to do, is most familiar to us as the account which is regularly given of the youth of *Perceval*, although a similar story is told of the boyhood of other heroes, e.g., Cuchulinn, Tyolet, Fergus, The Great Fool, etc. This is, then, the only connection which the Desc. poems, in the opinion of Paris and Mennung, have with the Perceval cycle.

I should like now to propose an entirely different theory, which will, I think, be found to explain the situation much more clearly and simply.

I hope to be able to show that the *fier baiser*, instead of being the beginning of the whole cycle, was not attached to it until a series of other adventures had grown up around a young hero who had been brought up in the woods; and that the account of the latter's boyhood was part of the story from the beginning, and not a late addition. In a word, that *Libeaus Desconus* is only *Perceval* with a new name, and that originally the adventures ascribed to the former in

---

[1] *Rom.*, XX, 299–300.
[2] Mennung (p. 43) thought wrongly that this might have been first added by Pucci.

the early versions of our cycle of poems were those that had previously been ascribed to the latter only, with the single exception of the elaborated account of the *fier baiser*.

These conclusions are based on the similarity which will be seen to exist between that form of the Fair Unknown story which is the most primitive attainable by analysis and one version of the Perceval story, namely the *Peredur*, not merely in the account of the hero's youth, but in the general framework of his subsequent adventures.

The Welsh story, *Peredur*,[1] contains, amongst others, the following features :

1. A mother, having lost her husband and several sons in battle or tournament, determines to prevent her only remaining son, who is very young, from suffering a like fate, and flees with him to a forest, where she brings him up in entire ignorance of the outside world. Discovering by accident the existence of other human beings, he is seized with a desire to go to Arthur's court. His mother, unable to dissuade him from going, gives him instructions as to his future conduct. He starts off, leaving her behind in sorrow (pp. 45–49).

2. He goes to the court, anxious to be made a knight. Just then a man is needed for an adventure demanding great valor and strength. No one of the courtiers wishing to undertake it, the young man offers himself, and at once sets out. Much to the surprise of all, he is successful. Owein helps him to put on his new armor, taken from the knight whom the boy has just slain, and he departs in quest of adventure, bent also on revenge for a wrong done him by one of Arthur's knights (51–55).

3. He first has an encounter with a single knight who has robbed and killed many knights before, and who refuses to let him pass. P. overthrows him ; but the knight begs for mercy, and his life is spared on condition that he go and give himself up to Arthur, telling him by whom he has been conquered. The knight swears to do so, and at once fulfils his promise (55–56).

4. P. rides on and next meets several knights, all of whom he overthrows and disgraces, and sends to Arthur as before (56).

5. As he is riding through a wood, he hears the piercing cries of a woman in distress. He fights with the one who has caused her

---

[1] The translation of Loth has been used.

trouble and conquers him. The vanquished man is forced to go and deliver himself up to Arthur, promising further to look after the woman he has caused to mourn (cf. Wig.). There is joy at court (60-62).

6. Soon P. comes to a great castle surmounted by numerous strong towers. He is welcomed there, and his armor is removed. A woman enters the room who is more beautiful than any he has ever seen. She also welcomes him, throws her arms about his neck, and sits down beside him. A meal is prepared, and they place themselves at the table. When the suitable time comes, a room is prepared for P. and he retires to his bed. Later the young woman comes to him and offers to be his wife or mistress. She is the sole heir to the lands about, but is in distress because of a knight who wishes to marry her. She is anxious to get rid of him, as are also her people. The time has almost arrived when she must submit to him. Nothing further, however, passes between P. and the lady that night. P. frees her from her oppressors, but is unwilling to marry her, and departs (62-68).

He then comes to another castle ruled over by a lady, where he is again well received. They sit down to a repast, after which he is advised to leave the place, for the land is in the power of sorcerers. Nevertheless, he stays one night, during which he hears frightful cries, goes to the rescue of the one in trouble, and overcomes a sorceress, who declares he alone could have done this: fate had so decreed (69-70).

7. The next day he departs. Later he comes to a hall where some valets are playing chess. One of three ladies near by weeps because she knows the fate that is to attend him if he is like all previous comers; for all who come there without permission must risk their lives in combat with the lord of the castle. P., however, is permitted to defer the fight until the next day, and in the evening there is eating, drinking, and conversation. According to the rules of the place, he fights with the knight, and finally forces him to beg for mercy (82-84).

8. This knight then gives information of a great serpent not far away who has injured him. He instructs P. how to find the monster. On his way P. meets a wonderfully beautiful woman. She knows the object of his coming, and tells him that the *addanc*, whom he must

first overcome, kills his victims "non par vaillance, mais par ruse." The monster, invisible himself, lies in wait at the threshold and slays every comer with a poisoned dart. On condition that P. will love her (which he already does), this lady gives him a stone which makes him invisible and the *addanc* visible. With this aid P. slays the *addanc*. On coming out, he finds three companions, who greatly rejoice and offer him a share of the kingdom (84-89).

9. A knight now begs to be taken as P.'s attendant. The latter is willing, and they ride on together (89).

10. The serpent is then found and killed. P. shows his prowess in a tournament, marries the princess who has aided him, and governs the land with her for many years, "à ce que dit l'histoire" (91-96).

11. In the course of the story we also learn that Arthur's court is at *Kaerllion;* that P. becomes famous there, and that at each bit of news from him the knights long for his safe return; that some of them start out to bring him back; that Gawain and he are special companions and friends; and that P. has his revenge before he goes back to court.

It is impossible not to see in these incidents a striking resemblance with what must have been an early form of the story of the Fair Unknown. Practically the culmination of that part of the Welsh narrative which here concerns us is the killing of a serpent. The young knight does this with the aid of the most beautiful woman he has ever seen, — one for whom he has already avowed his affection. As a result she marries him, and together they govern her land for many years. All that was really needed was for some one familiar with the widespread *märchen* of the *fier baiser* to combine, under the influence of this *märchen*, the serpent killed by P. and the beautiful woman who aids him into the single character of the princess in serpent form, and to adopt the special incident of the disenchanting kiss. This easy combination once made, the next step, also a very natural one, would be to make this disenchantment the special mission on which the young knight leaves Arthur's court. Naturally, upon the happy conclusion of his mission, he would return to Arthur, and the story would end with the marriage of the lovers and their joint rule over the wife's lands. These changes would necessitate the coming of the messengers to court to obtain aid, and their accompanying the champion who is given them. Other than this little that is new is needed.

I do not maintain, of course, that *Peredur* is the source from which our Desc. poems had their origin, for it itself must in all probability be regarded as a working over of an earlier narrative; but I think its likeness to the poems of our cycle shows clearly that the latter are originally nothing but stories of the exploits of the youthful Perceval. It is important here to observe:

1. That we need, under any circumstances, to assume the influence of the Perceval saga to explain the introduction, telling of the boyhood of the hero, his life in the woods, his going to court, etc.

2. That practically every incident in Car. is accounted for by the Welsh story modified as above.

3. That LD contains only two new features; viz. the dispute about the dog, and the sparrow-hawk incident.

4. That BI has only such further additions as can readily be explained (see above, pp. 106 ff).

5. That the incidents in the Welsh come in precisely the same order as in LD.

Moreover, *Peredur* explains unique features in the different poems.

I. It agrees, e.g., with LD in the following points: (1) the boy is furnished with armor at Arthur's court, and he is clad in this armor by one or more of Arthur's knights;[1] (2) the adventure with the company of hostile knights follows directly that with the single knight, and *all* are sent to Arthur (unlike BI, where another adventure intervenes, and only one of the company is made to go to the court); (3) the hero takes a knight as his attendant when he is near the end of his journey, although the latter has really little to do;[2] (4) the *addanc* uses poisoned weapons.

II. *Peredur* agrees with BI in the description of the events at the Ile d'Or: (1) the reception by the beautiful lady; (2) the hero's retiring after their meal to the bedchamber prepared for him;

---

[1] In *Peredur* it is Owein; in *Perc.* and *Wig.* it is Gawein; in LD, which here appeals for authority to a French source, we have both Owein and Gawein, as well as Perceval and Agrafain, bidden to do this service. I may add that, except Gawein, who is now made the boy's father, Perceval is the one of Arthur's knights oftenest mentioned in LD.

[2] See p. 111, above.

(3) the visit of the lady after he is there; (4) the fact that the hero and she do not pass the night together; (5) disturbance of the hero's rest by sorcery (for the features of the two castles ruled over by women would easily become united); (6) the piercing cries in the night;[1] (7) the knight who wishes to marry the lady, but whom she and her people dislike; (8) the fact that the duration of her resistance has almost reached its limit. *Peredur* also strengthens the contention that the Ile d'Or episode was only an incident in the journey, and that there was no love lost in the whole affair, for in the Welsh the lady is forced to act as she does by her brothers.

We may also note that (1) the great danger in the struggle with the *addanc* is on crossing the threshold; (2) the hero is warned of his foe's deceits before he goes to the conflict; (3) when he returns victorious he finds his three companions awaiting him; (4) it is specially stated that he alone can overcome the sorcerers: it had been so decreed by fate.

But it is with Car., even more than with LD and BI, that we should expect *Peredur* to correspond in points in which the four poems of our cycle disagree. For Car. is admitted to be based on a version earlier than the source of LD-BI,—on a version, in fact, in which Gawain had not become the father of the hero, and in which the boy was not yet called Libeaus Desconeus or Guinglain. Our expectations in this regard are not disappointed; for if we compare Car. and *Peredur*, we find that in both: (1) the father of the boy has been killed, and it is to keep her son from any knowledge of warfare that the mother flees to the woods; (2) when she finds him determined to leave her, she gives him instructions as to his future conduct; (3) the boy leaves the court intent on revenge for a wrong done him by one of Arthur's knights; (4) he has absolutely no real affection for the lady at whose castle he lodges; (5) it is not necessary to fight before he is offered the privilege of spending a night with her; and (6) he does not lie with her.

The correspondences pointed out in the last four paragraphs certainly support our hypothesis (p. 146) as to the development of the Desc. story.

---

[1] I.e., in BI, the cries of the hero when in terror from the enchantment practised by the *fée;* in *Peredur*, the cries of the victim tormented by a sorceress.

Mennung's view,[1] that there were *two* distinct borrowings made from the *Erec* before the composition of BI, is thus made improbable. The adventure with the giants in *Erec* is no more like that in the Desc. poems than is that in the *Peredur*, and certainly gives no ground for belief in a "direkte Entlehnung."[2] There is no necessity, then, for version Z in Mennung's *Filiations-Tafel*, and, consequently, for putting the composition of the version from which *Carduino* is drawn after the year 1160. Doubtless the *Erec* was used by the author from whose poem LD and BI are drawn; but I can see no ground to suppose that it had any influence on the form of the story on which the Italian poem was based.

We must believe that there was some version of the story such as that of which I have already spoken, containing, perhaps, all the adventures which are common to *Peredur* and the Fair Unknown story, with the changes necessary to unify them into a continuous account of the young hero, his boyhood, his arrival at Arthur's court, his undertaking the adventure proposed by messengers, which had as its aim the freeing of an enchanted princess, the difficulties and battles on the way, the final success, the journey of the princess with her deliverer to the court, their marriage and return to the wife's country, over which they rule happily for many years.

It seems probable that the Italian poet had before him more than he used, e.g., the fight with several knights and the adventure with the knight who was later called Lampart. Still one cannot be certain, and there is no need to dogmatize.

Though *Peredur* has been used in the foregoing comparison, it should be observed that the soundness of the results arrived at does not depend on a particular theory as to the position of the Welsh story in the Perceval cycle. *Peredur* is, as Nutt says,[3] "an obvious piecing together of all sorts of incidents relating to its hero, the only connecting link being that of his personality," and "its author may be supposed, when compiling his work, to have stretched out his

---

[1] *Der Bel Inconnu*, p. 45.

[2] Paris (*Rom.*, XX, 300) has already, for other strong reasons, rejected Mennung's view on this point. He holds "que l'épisode des géants dans la source de *Carduino* et du *BI* ne provient pas d'*Erec*, qu'il représente un lieu commun des contes celtiques."

[3] *Studies*, p. 144.

hand in all directions for material;" but, of course, no one would hold that the agreements between Per. and the Desc. poems could be due to a borrowing by the former from the latter. Only a few of the elements which we have regarded as significant in our comparison are peculiar to Per. and are not found in other forms of the Perceval story.[1] These few features are matters of detail which are much more likely to be remnants of a primitive form than to be modifications produced by outside influence. It is hardly conceivable that the author of Per. or of its source should have been so impressed by these details as intentionally to have altered his original in accordance with them or to have had his memory confused by them. Nor would any one contend that the Desc. poems are taken from *Peredur*. That, of course, is out of the question. What we may well hold, however, is that they both are, to some extent, based on one original, from which they have developed independently of each other, worked over for different purposes by different hands. This investigation may then, I think, be said to show that *Peredur* is not a mere working over of the *Conte du Graal*, but is based to a large extent upon some earlier version of the Perceval story, which, we may add, went back, in all probability (though not necessarily directly) to a Celtic story. But it is not with the origin of the *Peredur* that we have now to do. When we return to the Desc. poems we see, as I have said, that not only the introduction, but the groundwork of the form we have thought most primitive, is but a development of the Perceval saga. Here, however, the story branched out along different lines. The author of the earliest poem of our cycle had doubtless no desire to keep close to his original. Indeed, he could better show his originality by choosing, as he has done, a few only of the incidents to elaborate in a way peculiar to himself. He added the *märchen* of the *fier baiser*, and changed his story to suit the new situation. The hero is given a new name, and the separation of the poem from its original cycle is now complete.

We are now in a position to decide with comparative certainty what were the leading features of the oldest ascertainable form of

[1] Cf. Nutt, *Studies*, pp. 132 ff. That the *serpent* episode is not found in the other versions does not interfere with our argument. The adventure of the *fier baiser* might easily have become attached to our hero, even if there was no such hint in the original.

our story. In this reconstruction we are justified in including (with some reservations) those significant features which *Peredur* has in common with Car. or BI or LD, and those which Car. has in common with LD or BI or Wig.

VERSION A.

In all probability, then, there was a form of the story which ran somewhat as follows :

1. *Introduction.* A possible invocation for help in telling the story (as in Car., LD) ; then, in brief, an account of the death of the hero's father (P. and Car.) ; of the flight of his mother to the woods to keep her son ignorant of warfare ; his being brought up in isolation there ; his roaming about the woods hunting wild beasts until he learns by accident of the existence of other human beings than those he had before known, and his determination, despite his mother's wishes, to go to King Arthur's court (P., Car., LD) ; his mother's instructions as to his future conduct ; a possible stop at some place on the way (P., Car.) ; and his arrival at court, unknown and unexpected (P., Car., LD, BI).

2. *At the Court* he is welcomed by the king, who at once inquires who he is, and is told by the boy that he does not know anything of his father, but that he himself wishes to be made a knight. His request is granted and a feast is prepared for him. While all are at table, a beautiful young lady rides up, accompanied by a dwarf, and begs that some very brave knight be given her to free a lady who is in distress. The young knight at once offers himself, and the king approves; but his youth being apparent, he is declared by one of the messengers to be unequal to the task, and a request is made for a more experienced warrior. The king, however, holds to his decision, and the messengers must accept him or none. The boy is properly equipped, takes leave of the king, joins the messengers, and as they ride to the land of the princess in distress they meet with several adventures.

3. The first of these is with a knight whose habit it is to fight with and plunder all knights who come that way. He challenges our hero, who, not being able to pass otherwise, accepts the struggle, in which he overthrows his opponent. The latter calls for mercy, and

this is granted on condition that he go and deliver himself up to Arthur, telling him who has sent him.[1]

4. The agreement of P. with LD and BI makes it probable that there came next a fight with several knights, all of whom are overthrown and sent to Arthur.

5. Then follows a fight with two giants for the rescue of a maiden of noble family whom they have carried off by force from her father's castle near by, and whom one of them is then holding in his embrace, whilst the other is roasting some flesh on a spit over a great fire. The travellers, after they have settled down to spend the night in a wood, hear the cries of the unhappy maiden. The hero cannot refrain from rushing off to her rescue alone. In his fight with the giant by the fire, the latter probably defends himself by using as a weapon the spit he is roasting with; but the young knight pierces him to the heart with a spear. The second giant probably defends himself with a stick of some kind which is near by, but he also is killed. The maiden, now freed from her persecutors, tells who she is and how she happens to be in that plight. They all sit down full of joy and regale themselves with some food taken from the giants (probably the flesh they were roasting). When morning comes, the hero, the messenger, and the dwarf continue their journey (and possibly nothing more is said of the rescued maiden).[2]

6. Then follows a stay of one night at the home of an enchantress.

---

[1] One cannot be certain whether the first adventure took precisely this form so early. In P. and Car. the boy is incited by motives of revenge, and it is possible that the knight may have been killed outright, as in Car. and Wig.

[2] As this account is almost the same in Car., LD, and BI, we are justified in supposing it to be the form of the version which we are reconstructing; but some of the details are not in Peredur. These may have been introduced from some source other than the Perceval saga, or their absence in Peredur may be due to omission. We have the cries of the woman in distress heard by the young knight in the wood, and his hastening to the rescue, in both P. and Erec; but in both cases her cries are caused by her lover's being ill-treated or killed. There is no fire or roasting, and the adventure is not one of the night when the company have settled down for rest. On the whole, we may conjecture that the incident as told in P. gave the suggestion, which was filled out with considerable changes by the author of the version now under consideration. Wig. agrees with P. in having one giant's life spared on condition that he look after the maiden and go to Arthur. He does so at once, and there is great rejoicing at court. In LD the heads of the giants are sent to Arthur.

This was not a specially important feature of the story. It was merely an incident in the journey, and was never again referred to. There is no love lost between the young hero and the enchantress, and he has no desire to return. He probably seeks lodging at the castle and is received in a friendly way by the people, as well as by the lady of the place, who is sole ruler and is much skilled in sorcery. They have a repast, and then the knight retires. During the night he is subjected to some sort of unpleasant deception, probably because he disobeys orders which the enchantress has previously given him. He may have received a warning from his companion, after the meal, not to linger in the place. In the morning he is quite willing to set out on his journey. Whether there was as yet a fight to free the lady from the power of some one who wished to marry her is hard to tell. The Welsh makes it probable, whilst its absence in Car. and the lady's general character as a sorceress make against it.

7. He probably comes next to another castle and obtains admittance, but is obliged by the customs of the place to fight with the lord.[1] He is expected to suffer the fate so many others have met before him; but he surprises all by overthrowing his opponent. The evening is spent in eating, drinking, and conversation. The next day the young knight is given information by this same lord about the serpent near by and the way to reach it.

8. At any rate, before he enters the place where the serpent is, he is told something of what he is to expect and what he is to do and what to leave undone there.

9. This serpent is a transformed princess who is kept in this shape by magic. There is probably but one magician, and he possibly makes an attempt to lure the hero over a threshold, to cross which would have caused his death; but the knight, being informed of his cunning, does not fall into the snare. The hero kills the magician, and then voluntarily, although with much trepidation, kisses the serpent on the mouth. Immediately she is transformed into a most beautiful woman, who at once offers her love to her rescuer. He accepts it gladly, and, after a time of great rejoicing at the disen-

---

[1] For this not uncommon feature cf. Foerster, *Erec*, *Einl.*, p. xv (*Yvain;* P. Paris, *Rom. de la Table Ronde*, III, 359); prose *Lancelot* (P. Paris, *op. cit.*, V, 266); *Claris et Laris*, 4171 ff., 26855 ff.; *Livre d'Artus*, Version P (Freymond, *Zt. f. franz. Sp. u. Litt.*, XVII, 46, 65); *Blancandin*, ed. Michelant, 894 ff.

chanted city, the two set out together for Arthur's court, where they are heartily welcomed. The parentage of the young man is made known; possibly his mother appears; and he, receiving the king's approval, marries the princess. A great throng accompanies the wedded pair on their way back to the wife's country. The hero is made ruler there, and lives happily for many years with his beautiful wife (who perhaps bears him a son who later rivals the glorious achievements of his father).

This version I shall call *A*. We do not know in what language it was written, but it was probably French.

VERSION B.

Version A is next worked over by a French poet, in whose hands it becomes longer and more detailed. The hero is made to undertake at least two new adventures on his way to the enchanted city, while new features are added and changes are made in the adventures of version A.

1. The introduction is left much as it was; but the following changes are made :

(*a*) There is now no question of a slain father, for we are told at once that the boy's father is no other than *Gawein*, and that his own name is *Guinglain*, although he has always been called *Belfil* by his mother; that he comes to court in ignorance of his own name, and that the king, because of his beauty and the mystery of his birth, calls him *Li Beaus Desconeus*. After having been favorably received, he begs Arthur for permission to undertake, as a test of his valor, the first adventure that presents itself. His request is granted, and he is given over to Gawein for instruction in knightly ways. He receives suitable attire. All the court wash and go to meat.

(*b*) The name of the messenger is (*H*)*élie* (*Elene*). She rides a white horse, and some little account is given of her appearance.

(*c*) The dwarf is called *Tidogolain*. He is skilled in music, and is also described. Probably he, as well as Elie, makes objection to the sending of Libeaus.

(*d*) Lib. at once claiming the adventure, the king readily accedes, and is not moved by the entreaties and sneers of the messengers. They must be satisfied with Lib. or none.

(e) Probably the messenger rides away in anger without the proffered knight, who overtakes her later.[1]

(f) Possibly at Arthur's command four of the best knights, Gawein, Perceval, Iwein, and Agravain, arm Lib. with splendid armor.[2]

(g) Lib. receives Arthur's blessing. He sets out for the city Senaudon.

2. The first adventure with the single knight occurs at a place called *Perilous*. The knight's appearance is described. He is always there on the lookout for passing knights, and is ever ready to fight with them. If defeated, they suffer shame and are deprived of their belongings. Contrary to expectation, Lib. is the victor. Up to this time at least, the messenger has had no confidence in him, and has not ceased to chide him. The knight is forced to promise to go to Arthur. He is to say that he has been sent by *Li Beaus Desconeus*.

3. The result of this conflict paves the way for a new adventure which is now introduced. The conquered knight meets on his way to Arthur's court three other knights (possibly his nephews). He tells them how he has been shamed, and gives them the young knight's name. They start off at once to take revenge. The next morning they overtake Lib. and his companions going along gleefully, challenge Lib. to fight, and find him ready for them. He conquers all, and one or more of them are sent to Arthur. Lib. and his companions continue their journey until nightfall, when they prepare a place in which to spend the night.

4. In the adventure with the giants little change is made. The giant holding the maiden is the one who is killed first. The rescued maiden expresses her gratitude to Lib., and tells how she was carried away from her father's garden by the two giants, who were in a place of concealment there. We cannot be sure how the young woman was disposed of.

5. A new adventure was probably inserted here. As they are riding along, they see a most beautiful little dog of all colors, which Élie at

---

[1] In this point BI and Wig. agree. In Car. the hero and the dwarf go together, the messenger apart. In LD all three go together.

[2] This is only inserted because the English author declares it was in his French source. His statement may or may not be true.

once admires and covets. Lib. catches it and gives it to her, and they go on, talking joyfully by the way. Soon, however, the owner rides up. He is finely dressed and carries a bugle. He asks for the dog, but Lib. refuses to return it, and meets his threats with defiance. The knight goes back in anger to his castle to get his arms, and returns later. There is a fierce conflict, but at last the knight is overcome and forced to go to Arthur. Élie keeps the dog.

6. Another new adventure now follows, viz. the competition for the sparrow-hawk. This needs to be discussed by itself, and is therefore left for a separate section (see below, p. 164).

7. Some important changes have been made in the visit to the castle of the enchantress, although probably the general features remain the same. As we have only BI and LD to help us here, and as they are almost entirely unlike in this part of the story, we cannot with any certainty tell just what was the exact form of their original. There are, however, some new features which must have distinguished it from the older version.

(*a*) The name of the city is the *Ile d' Or*.

(*b*) The privilege of lying with the enchantress can only be had by overcoming a knight (or giant) who is ever in readiness to fight with all who come to the castle.

(*c*) His name is *Malgiers*, and he has been at his post for some time.

(*d*) He is heartily disliked by the lady of the castle, as well as her followers, and all long to get rid of him.

(*e*) Lib. kills him, after a terrible struggle, and the people show their joy. They conduct him to the palace. Here his armor is removed, and he is lovingly welcomed by the lady, who is very beautiful and skilled in magic.

(*f*) She at once offers to marry him, and he makes no objection.

(*g*) Élie, seeing his infatuation, brings him to reason by calling to his memory his real mission, and the dishonor any delay in performing it would bring on him and Arthur.

(*h*) He is thus for a time enthralled by the charms of the lady; but before he departs he repents of his passing weakness.

These features (*a–h*) must have been in Version B. When we try, however, to decide whether Lib.'s opponent was a courageous but tyrannical knight in splendid attire, or a hideous heathen giant;

and whether there was a custom that the lady of the castle could only be won by a knight who should defeat all comers for seven years, the present knight having but two years more to serve, or whether a giant had *beleid* the castle round about and was filling the people with terror, we are certainly at a loss. If we were to decide the case on grounds of probability, we should have to conclude that the first alternative in each case, i.e., the account as given in BI, is the more likely, and the narration in *Peredur* would strengthen this opinion. Still we may feel confident that, in its present shape, BI, with its details and elaborations, does not represent this part of Version B in more than general features. As we have seen (p. 108), above, Renaud identified the lady of the castle with his loved one, and many changes were doubtless made on this account. It is probable that in Version B she was called *la dame d'Amour* (see above, p. 136). Renaud, doubtless, did not hesitate to change the original name for one he thought more suitable, especially when the latter was very common and was the name given to Ysolde, the best exemplar of true love. It is of course possible that, in Version B, the enchantress was also called *la fée as blances mains* and yet that every trace of this should disappear in LD.

It is not improbable that, during the night at the castle, Lib., because he was not *chast*, and could not wait until they should be married before attempting to gratify his desires, had to suffer "traie and tene" by being mortified in the extreme by just such events as happen to the hero in BI when, on his return visit, he spends his first night in the castle. These events almost certainly belonged here, as the similar ones have this place in Car.; and although the English poet omits them, he leaves a clear trace of them. There is not the slightest necessity to believe, with Kaluza, that the words "aftirward at þe last," in LD, 1505, refer to a second visit to the place, and that therefore the English poet must have seen BI. It is very clear that he does not tell the whole story of the specific enchantments, though he probably had it before him; he sums up the account with a few vague generalities. Kaluza's interpretation of these words (*Lib. Desc.*, p. cxxxviii.) is rejected by Paris, *Rom.* XX, 298, who shows that, on Kaluza's theory, the English poet would, in using them, have been guilty of a gross inconsistency. The convincing arguments of Paris need not be here repeated. The words "aftirward at þe last" merely refer to the delay in the execution of the hero's mission which was caused by his giving in to the enchantress's wiles.

In this connection we should observe that the English poet is reckless about the amount of time he assigns to different adventures. If Kaluza's reading be right,[1] LD stays no less than a year at the Ile d'Or; he remains with Sir Otes a fortnight; he gives a feast at Cardevile which lasts forty days; he stays feasting with Arthur another forty days; and takes as well a side-trip into Ireland and Wales, where he sees terrible adventures which, fortunately, the poet does not specify. And yet this is the poet whom Kaluza pictures as having such a keen appreciation of what was fitting in a romance, who cut out a vast deal of his original because he thought it was unnecessary or marred the beauty of the whole, who shifted the adventures about when he saw they were out of place, who changed the characters of his hero and the messenger that they might suit his taste better, who omitted one of the leading personages altogether, and who dropped whatever was improbable or inconsistent, — and thus, strangely enough, felt his way back each time to what we know to be a more primitive form of the story. Certainly to a poet who would go about his work in this way, "zusammengehöriges auch zusammen zu behandeln, vorhandene unebenheiten auszugleichen," etc. (*Introd.*, p. cxxxiii.), the following remark would be applicable : "Alles in allem genommen zeigt der verfasser des Lib. Desc. eine weit grössere selbständigkeit im verhältniss zu seiner vorlage, als mancher andere me. romanzendichter" (*Introd.*, p. cxlv.).

As to the length of time which these different stays occupied in LD, as opposed to the other poems, we may say that the statements are entirely harmless, and to a great extent meaningless. The main thing is that the English author never thinks of telling us what went on in these periods. Never is the progress of the story impeded in any way, and we skip comfortably over the break which our author *tells us about*, almost heedless of his remark.

Kaluza informs us (p. cxxxiv.) : "Gar zu unwahrscheinliche dinge werden von den englischen bearbeitern gern weggelassen oder auf

---

[1] The Ashmole and Naples MSS. give the time as *three weeks*. Strangely enough this is the length of time Peredur lingers at this point in the story.

M

natürlichere weise erklärt. So vermissen wir z. b. in LD die stimme der fee, welche in BI, v. 3186 ff., nach erfolgter entzauberung der dame dem helden über seine abstammung aufschluss giebt, ihm seinen wirklichen namen 'Guinglain' nennt," etc. This is certainly doing honor to the English poet, but we must remember that he did not in all probability find this particular feature in his original, and could not therefore leave it out, and further that his practice in other cases does not justify Kaluza's high opinion of his artistic insight. For example, we learn (what is not in BI) that when LD returns to find Irain, whom he left lying on the ground when he went to fight with Mabon, he is terrified to see that invisible powers have carried him away. What is a magic voice compared with this? We are asked to believe that the English poet leaves out the magic voice because it is improbable, when in the next breath he introduces a greater wonder. We might ask also how much more probable the English author made the struggle with those who were angered at LD's refusal to give up the dog. In BI the knight rides to the castle, arms, and returns *alone* to fight with the hero. The author of LD, however, is supposed to have changed the account thus: The knight goes to his castle, summons all his friends, and tells them of his trouble. They all arm and mount their horses "for har lordes sake" and come against LD together.

>Wiþ bowers and wiþ arblaste
>To him þey schote faste
>And made him woundes wide. (1174 ff.)

But this does not trouble the hero. He soon dispatches them all. He is now afflicted "wiþ grimly woundes sare;" but what matter? Twelve fresh knights put in an appearance, the lord himself among them, with no mild intent.

>þey smitte to him at ones
>And þouȝte to breke his bones
>And fille him doun in fiȝt. (1198 ff.)

LD slays three, and four flee. The lord and his four sons remain "to sell har lives dere," and LD fights all five at once. He is knocked off his horse; but three strokes of his axe suffice to remove the heads of three of his opponents' horses, and the lord deems it policy to flee. LD, however, has energy enough left to ride after him, and he succeeds in overtaking him and making him promise to go to Arthur. Not satisfied with this, the English poet summons "gentill men fiftene" to accompany Elene to the castle. Far from being offended at the death of such a goodly company of his friends,

> þe lord was glad and bliþe
> And þonked fele siþe
> God and seint Michell,
> þat swich a noble kniȝt
> Schulde winne in fiȝt
> His lady fair and hende. (1270 ff.)

To complete the confusion, the author thus makes this very knight a some-time follower of the princess of Senaudon, who has fled for fear into Wirral(!) on the enchantment of his mistress. It is surely impossible, in the light of these facts, to maintain such a contention as that made by Kaluza.

But to return from this long digression, we may say tnat it seems probable that the head-covered lances were a feature of the castle of the Ile d'Or, as in BI, and not of the castle belonging to the owner of the sparrow-hawk, as in LD.

8. It is quite probable that in Version B it was told that, on leaving the castle, Lib. took with him the steward and made him his squire.

9. A good many new features have been introduced into the adventure with the last knight, which now runs as follows. Just before the party reach Senaudon, they arrive at a beautiful castle, where every knight who comes obtains lodging only by jousting with the lord, who is called *Lampart*. If the stranger wins, he is treated with distinction; if he loses, he is turned away in shame and pelted with mud and fen by the people of the town. This information is given Lib. by Élie, who fears for his safety if he goes to the place, but nevertheless urges him to go. A fight is soon arranged with the lord, who is delighted at the prospect of an encounter. The conflict is fierce. Lances are broken; but finally Lampart is knocked off his steed, and he yields to Lib. He is the steward of the transformed princess, and receives the young hero gladly. They sit down to supper, and in the morning Lib. sets out for the enchanted city.

10. The account of the adventures at Senaudon probably remained in B much as it was in A. B contained, however, the following

variations: (*a*) Whatever description of the city is given, is given by Lampart. (*b*) The hall is full of minstrels playing on all sorts of instruments with torches before them. They can disappear suddenly. (*c*) There are *two* magicians whose names are *Mabon* and *Irain*. (*d*) Lib. kills one ; but the other, although badly wounded, escapes. He was probably carried off mysteriously. (*e*) The serpent kisses Lib. (not the reverse). (*f*) After the kiss has been given, it is revealed to him (in all probability by the rescued princess herself) that he is the son of Gawein.

The Sparrow-Hawk Adventure.

It is not easy to determine what were the exact features of this adventure in Version B, in which it seems to have been for the first time introduced into the Desc. story. It was probably a borrowing from *Erec*,[1] and, if so, we might expect its form to be somewhat like that in Chrétien's poem ; but the different setting of the incident in the two poems must have affected its features. In *Erec*, for example, we have the hero riding along *alone*, and he is forced to get some fair companion if he wishes to enter into the competition for the sparrow-hawk, while in *Desc.* the hero has already a companion. Then too the defender of the hawk Erec finds to be his enemy upon whom he had vowed revenge for a wrong which does not enter into the *Desc.* poems, and thus this feature would have to be omitted. Further Erec falls in love with the young woman whom he champions, and later marries her. In neither LD nor BI could this be, for in these poems the only suitable ending for the story is to have Lib. marry the princess whom he frees from her serpent form. These important features being inadmissible from the nature of the case, we may conjecture better what Version B contained.

BI and Wig. agree in introducing here a new female character whom the hero meets by the way, and who tells him of the adventure. She is very beautiful and has merited the prize, of which, however, she has been forcibly deprived by a knight who wished it for his *amie*. The young woman is now in great distress, and the hero volunteers to aid her to obtain her rights. The party ride on to the castle together.

---

[1] See Mennung, p. 49; Paris, *Rom.*, XX, 300; W. Foerster, *Erec*, *Introd.*, p. xv.

This agreement between BI and Wig. seems to indicate that this new character was also in Version B.[1] If so, it was probably introduced in order that the French poet might get on common ground with Chrétien in the account the latter gives in *Erec*. The story in LD, however, is so reasonable and has itself so many points of agreement with *Erec*, that we cannot admit the introduction of this new character into Version B without some misgivings. At any rate we can understand what led the author of LD to make the young knight's companion the one who is put into competition for the prize. Be it noted first that in *Erec*, as in LD, the young lady strives only once for the hawk, and in no version except BI is there any mention of a previous lover killed in the undertaking. Enide, moreover, becomes the constant companion of Erec, and shares his adventures. In the same way it is for his constant companion, Elene, that the hero in the English poem fights. Further, in LD, as in *Erec*, the young lady is unexpectedly asked to compete, and must make special preparation. A glance, however, at the respective positions which Enide and Élie occupy, with regard to the hero, may account for the change made in LD. In the French poem it is Enide with whom the young knight is in love; she is the heroine of the story, whom the hero is to marry. It would not have been artistic, it would not be acceptable to us even, to have her less beautiful than an unnamed minor character in the story, — the *amie* of a knight, mentioned only in this connection. In LD, however, Elene is only the messenger who brought news of the princess's trouble and who is now merely acting as a guide. LD has no love whatever for her. She merely gives him an opportunity to show his valor; and we are not surprised or disturbed at her not winning the prize.

This brings us to the other questions as to the form of this adventure in Version B: Was the competition a special event occurring just then, or could any passer-by proffer claims for the prize at any time? Was there any real trial of beauty, and, if so, who were the judges?

It would seem most probable that there was a special gathering, a great tournament, to which people were summoned from all parts,

---

[1] For Wig., as I shall try to show later (see pp. 215 ff., below) is not derived from BI but independent of it.

and that the young knight and his companion happened to come while it was in progress, or soon after the decision was made. There is such a gathering in *Erec*, B, *Durmart*,[1] *Meraugis*,[2] *Wigalois*, and *Geraint*; LD alone does not tell of an assembly of this sort, although a crowd of spectators seems to have been easily secured. If then we conclude that there was in B a great gathering, the important feature of which was to be the presentation of a splendid sparrow-hawk to her who came attended by a champion and was the most beautiful, it seems almost certain that there must have been some sort of decision as to the claims of the several competitors. This we have in LD, Wig., and *Meraugis*; but not in *Erec*, B, and *Durmart* (the last two, however, probably borrowing directly or indirectly from *Erec*[3]). The decision was probably given by the spectators, and in every case it seems to have been unanimous, one lady being by general consent far more beautiful than the others. In LD (949 ff.) the decision is told thus:

> Boþe men gonne hem bring
> Two chaiers into þe cheping,
>   Har beaute to descrie.
> Þan seiden eld and ȝinge,
> For soþ, wiþ oute lesing,
>   Betwene hem was partie.
> 'Giffrouns lemman is clere,
> As rose in erbere.
>   For soþ and nouȝt to lie.
> Elene. Þe messengere,
> Semeþ but a lavendere
>   Of her norserie.'

In no other poem is the decision given against the hero's companion; but the reason why it is so in LD is not far to seek. Here alone is that companion a mere messenger and not a loved one. This relation is emphasized in the passage just quoted.

The decision, however, seems in no case to have been final. If

---

[1] Vv. 2005 ff.
[2] Raoul de Houdenc, *Meraugis de Portlesguez*, ed. Michelant, Paris, 1869, pp. 8 ff.
[3] See Kirchrath, *Li Romans de Durmart le Gallois* (in Stengel, *Ausgaben u. Abhandlungen*, XXI), 1884, p. 62. Cf. Mennung, p. 17.

any knight was dissatisfied, he could still win the prize by overcoming the champion of the successful young woman. LD, BI, Wig., and the rest all have to fight with another claimant; but, of course, in each case the hero of the story is victorious. In *Meraugis*, probably by confusion, these two features have no connection. There are *two* prizes, one for the most beautiful woman, and the other for the most valiant knight; and the fight which takes place is only to decide the claims of the knights for the latter.

The change which the author of LD seems to have made, in that the adventure is not the great event of a tournament but merely due to a passing challenge, explains some other variations in his account. In *Erec*, BI, etc., the hawk is placed on its perch, in sight of all, before the claimants arrive, while LD and Elene are obliged to wait until one of Giffroun's squires brings it with him to the place. Moreover, the knight is not prepared to fight at once when LD comes. Both have to wait until preparations are made. It is not an event anticipated by either party.

LD agrees with *Erec*, as opposed to BI, in the following points:

1. There is no special provoking cause for the hero's undertaking the fight.

2. The hero remains where he is when he first hears of the affair all that night, and sets about the undertaking early in the morning. BI does not wait at all.

3. In both cases he makes two trips in the morning, first with only one companion (although with a different object in the two poems), returning later to fetch the maiden who is to compete for the prize. The object in *Erec* is to attend mass. In LD it is for this object that the lord of the castle is up.

4. The young knight wears armor in which he has never before fought, — armor given him by a friendly old knight with whom he has lodged, in *Erec* by his host, in LD by Sir Antore; while in BI special attention is called to the way his helmet, shield and hauberk are battered; no new armor is given him.

The fact that BI agrees with LD, unlike *Erec*, in making the lord of the castle the rival claimant, seems to settle that this was in their original B; and, if so, it becomes less probable that there was a great concourse of knights to contend with the knight who was their host. Perhaps, after all, LD represents best Version B in this point also.

This does not mean, of course, that LD represents the original and best form of the general sparrow-hawk story as it is found in so many places; but merely that it is perhaps most like the adapted form which the author of Version B made to suit the changed conditions.

Having made the changes he did, it was quite suitable for the English poet to bring in here the feature of the armed heads on the lance points, for this gives a reason for the willingness of the lord of the castle to receive any one who may care at any time to claim the prize. His offer is a perpetual wager[1] — a means by which he lures people to the place that he may fight with them. The knowledge of this wager is sufficient to incite a young knight, himself eager to display his prowess, to undertake so perilous an exploit despite the persuasions of his companions.

In the description of the fight there is, for obvious reasons, much more resemblance between BI and *Erec* than between LD and *Erec*. The incident in Version B must have been very much shortened, for even Renaud has only sixty lines corresponding to two hundred in *Erec*.

What conclusion the adventure had in Version B it is hard to decide. Erec discovers that his opponent is the knight on whom he was anxious to revenge an insult to himself and Queen Guinovere and sends him to Arthur. BI, bearing him no ill-will, spends the night with him in enjoyment, having, however, made him promise to go to the court. Wigalois also sends Hojir, whom he conquers, to Arthur; but LD's opponent has to be borne from the place on his shield and we hear no more of him. The gerfalcon is, however, sent to Arthur by a knight, Claudas, together with a letter telling how the prize was won. There is thus practical unanimity in all versions except LD in the sending of the conquered knight himself to the court, and we must conclude that this was probably the result in Version B. It is well to note, nevertheless, that the English author is consistent in the account he gives. Elene has expressed no desire for the prize, and does not really deserve it for her beauty, and it

---

[1] For a curious account of a sparrow-hawk used as a perpetual challenge to a trial of strength, see Mandevile's *Travels*, ed. Warner, Roxb. Club, p. 73, where is told of " Le Chastel Despuere," or " þe Castell of þe Sperhawke," and of the hawk sitting on a perch, kept by "a fair lady of Fairye" who rewards all those who fulfil certain conditions. Cf. also Lady Charlotte Guest's *Mabinogion*, II, 153.

can therefore appropriately be sent to Arthur; whereas Margerie has travelled far to win it and does deserve it. The whole question hinges on the introduction of this last-mentioned character.

In *Erec* there is great rejoicing at court on the arrival of the vanquished knight. In LD, when the news is received, Arthur is so delighted that at once

> An hundred pound honest
> Of florins wiþ þe best
> He sente to Cardevile toun. (1045 ff.)

With this money LD gives a great feast. But in BI a long time after, when the disenchanted princess, having seen her deliverer's wounds healed, her affairs put in order, and extensive preparations made for her journey, overtakes on her way to the court a company of knights, she finds it to be composed of all those whom at different times BI has forced to promise to go to Arthur, and who in some inconceivable way have come together and are still (!) on their way. They must surely have been in a pitiful condition and badly used up by BI to have made such poor time.

The young woman for whom our hero fights in BI and Wig. has to be got rid of again. BI finds she is a daughter of King Agolans of Scotland, and obtains from Gifflet a knight to take her home (cf. Claudas in LD). In Wig. it is said in the beginning that any one can tell from her appearance that she is of king's kin. Renaud now works in another feature from a different place in *Erec*.[1] After Erec has succeeded in the *joie de la cort*, Enide discovers, when the young woman in the garden gives an account of her parentage, that they are relatives. In the same way Élie learns from Margerie's words that the latter is an old friend.

We have yet to speak of the prize in the different versions. In *Erec*, BI and *Durmart*, it is a sparrow-hawk (*esprevier*); in LD it is also a *gerfalcon* or hawk; while in Wig. there are two prizes,—a marvellous horse, and a wonderful parrot kept in a cage of gold. In *Meraugis* there are also two prizes,—a swan for the bravest knight, and a sparrow-hawk for the most beautiful woman. Kirchrath[2]

---

[1] Cf. W. Foerster, *Erec*, p. xvi. It is just possible that, as Mennung thinks, this feature may have been in the common original of LD and BI. (See p. 133.)
[2] See *Li Romans de Durmart le Gallois*, pp. 55 ff.

thinks we have in the last poem a misunderstanding. A swan is certainly a remarkable present for a brave knight, and the two presents seem to be due to a confusion. In LD the gerfalcon is described (773) as "whit as swan," and in Wig. (2543) we read: "das pfert was *blanc alsam ein swan*." It looks as if Version B described the sparrow-hawk as being white as a swan and it was this version that Raoul de Houdenc knew. This might help also to account for the peculiar relations which exist between *Meraugis*, *Erec*, BI, and *Durmart*, as to which see Kirchrath, pp. 50 ff.

Kirchrath thinks that BI is the medium between *Erec* and *Durmart*, and that Raoul borrowed about the same time as Renaud, but independently, from *Erec*. Inasmuch, however, as *Meraugis* also shows agreements with *Durmart*, he is of the opinion that "Durmars bildet eine Erweiterung und theilweise Verschmelzung des Desconeu [i.e., BI] mit Meraugis."

I may call attention to the following points in which *Durmart* agrees in this adventure with BI.

(1) In both the meeting with the lady for whom the hero fights is accidental. (2) It is from her that he learns first about the whole affair. (3) In both he is incited to fight for her by her weeping for the loss of her previous companion. The lady had been attracted to the tourney by her desire to win the prize of the most beautiful, having confidence in the powers of a defender who has failed her in her need, and the hero comes to her rescue to save her from sorrow. (4) She is of royal birth — in BI the daughter of a king, in Dur. a queen herself (cf. Wig.). In these four points the two poems differ from *Erec*, where (1) the lady plays a very subordinate part and is not by any means the leading figure. (2) It is from her father that Erec learns the custom of the place. (3) He is prompted to fight by mingled feelings of love, desire for adventure, and revenge. (4) The maid whom he defends has never before entered the contest, and has had no other lover or defender. She has not thought of competing for the prize. (5) She is the daughter of an extremely poor knight. (6) The hero marries her later.

The name of the lord of the castle is in BI *Giflet li fius Do*; in LD *Giffroun le fludous* (as to which see p. 136 above). In Wig. he is identified with the Red Knight.

The Adventure with the Dog.

We have seen that in Version B two new adventures were introduced, — the sparrow-hawk contest and the capture of the dog. The former, it seems, was borrowed from *Erec*. I should like now to call attention to the fact that we have a very close parallel to the latter in Celtic tradition. It is to be found in the *Lay of the Great Fool*, which presents other features in common with the Perceval stories.[1] I shall quote from O'Daly's translation of the *Lay* in his *Fenian Poems*, Second Series.[2]

Amadan Mor (= The Great Fool) and his beautiful companion are making their way through a pleasant valley when

> To the place in which they stood
> A deer approaches with antlers fierce;
> And a red-eared white hound
> Barking loudly in his track.

The Great Fool kills the deer.

> He then lays hold of the white hound
> And ties him gently with a thong;
> 'I shall keep thee to amuse me
> Until pursuers or some one follows me.'

"'Twas not long till they saw approach them in the valley" the owner of the dog. He comes up and salutes them. The Great Fool demands his name and station, and the other gives his name as "The Knight of the Mantle," and says he is the owner of the white hound. The Great Fool retorts that the knight shall not any longer be called by the latter name. The knight begs that the dog be given back to him, but the rough hero refuses bluntly.

> ''Twas I that slew the deer,'
> Saith the Amadan in firm tone,
> 'And whoever of us has the stoutest arm,
> Let him have the deer and white hound.'

The knight is forced to give in.

---

[1] See Nutt, *Studies in the Legend of the Holy Grail*, pp. 152 ff.
[2] *Transactions of the Ossianic Soc. for 1858*, Vol. VI, Dublin, 1861, pp. 169 ff.

> Then the gentle young woman said,
> 'Give to me the white hound;'

and it is given over to her charge. Campbell's version in his *Popular Tales of the West Highlands*[1] corresponds to this closely. The following additional feature is of interest. The scene opens thus:

> They heard the hunt in the glen,
> The voice of the hound and music sweet.

With this should be compared the opening in the English poem LD:

> As þey ride on a lowe,
> Hornes herde þey blowe
> And houndes grete of gale. (1057 ff.)

There can be no question that we have here the same story which is told in LD and BI.[2] As has been noted, the Celtic poem agrees with LD, as opposed to BI, in the opening. It also agrees with the former in the whole course of the poem. It is the hero himself (a strong, burly fellow — no polished chevalier, be it noted) who catches the dog and refuses scornfully to surrender it at the demand of the knightly owner. He gives it to his companion, and tells the knight that if he wants it he must fight for it. Moreover, the latter is provoked by the hero so that he tells his name and station before the fight. It will be remembered that in this adventure *Wigalois* is very similar to the account in LD, and very unlike that in BI. It is curi-

---

[1] Edin., 1860–62, III, 160; orally collected. The story is also told in prose by Patrick Kennedy in *The Bardic Stories of Ireland*, Dublin, 1871, pp. 152–3. Nutt gives a summary of the *Lay* in his *Studies on the Legend of the Holy Grail*, pp. 160 ff.

[2] There are some slight analogies to this adventure in *Durmart*, 1675 ff.; but they are of no moment. On the recurrence of this episode in Gautier's *Perceval*, see Mennung, p. 17, and below, p. 192. Nutt (*Studies*, pp. 161–2) compared the *Lay of the Great Fool* in this adventure with the *Conte du Graal*, and concluded thus: "While the general idea is the same, the way in which it is worked out is so different that it is impossible to conceive of the one story having been borrowed from the other. What can safely be claimed is that the Great Fool counterpart of Peredur-Perceval in the adventures of his youth and up-bringing, is also, to a certain extent, his counterpart in the most prominent of his later adventures, that of the stag-hunt." Cf. *Rev. Celt.*, XII, 202, 203.

ous that Wig. preserves a feature in common with the Celtic not found elsewhere. BI and Wig. agree in describing the dog as being white, having ears of a different color, while LD is content to say that the dog was "of all colours." Cf.

> das was *blanc* über al. (Wig., 60, 26.)

with

> Plus estoit *blans* que nulle nois. (BI, 1275.)

Only, however, in Wig. is it said as in the Celtic that one of the dog's ears was *red*.

> Niwan *ein ôre* was im val,
> das ander *rôt alsam ein bluot*. (60, 27-8.)

In BI, on the contrary, we read:

> *Orelles noires* comme pois. (1276.)

LD and Wig. also describe the owner of the dog as being finely dressed. In LD he is "y-clothed in inde," and the notes of his bugle reveal "in what stede he wer" (1101). In Wig. every lock of his hair is "bewunden wol: mit sîden und mit golde: gezieret als er wolde" (61, 4 ff.), and he is dressed "mit grüenem tymît." In the Celtic tale he comes "in full splendour of gold" and is "of the handsomest mien." In BI, however, we learn that he wears a "corte cote . . . d'un burel":

> D'une houses estoit hosés;
> Estrangement estoit hastés. (1299-1300.)

Further, BI varies from the *Lay* as well as from LD and Wig. in having the owner see the maiden catch the dog. The last three represent a little time as elapsing between the taking of the dog and the arrival of the knight. There is one point, however, in which BI is closer to the *Lay*: viz., in representing the hound as following a deer "with antlers fierce."

> Un cerf vit, qui lès lui passa,
> Langue traite, vait effréés;
> De xvi rains estoit armés. (1266 ff.)

But the resemblance of the *Lay* to our poems does not end here. As in LD, the hero and his companions go with the knight to his castle and are well received; tales are told of the hero's valor.

>'Twas not long till they saw in the valley
> A city that shone like unto gold;
> There was no colour which eye had seen
> That was not in the mansion, and many more.
>'Twas then the young maiden asked,
> ' What golden city is that
> Of the finest appearance and hue,
> Or could it be betrayed or traversed?'

She is told that it is called *Dun an Oir* (Fort of the Gold), and, moreover, that the glen through which they have passed is full of magic.

> They found a woman in the Dun.
> A sight like it was never seen;
> Her person was fairer than the snow,
> Blue her eyes and bright her teeth.

She is also gifted with a knowledge of magic, and it is at this castle that the Great Fool gets back his legs, of which he had been deprived by drinking an evil potion.

This continued agreement is remarkable. It is especially to be noted that in LD the adventure at the city of the Ile d'Or follows directly that with the hound, while in BI the sparrow-hawk episode intervenes. Moreover, in LD the owner of the dog rides back to his castle cordially with the hero and his companions, while in BI they part as soon as the knight is conquered, the latter starting off at once for Arthur's court.

The descriptions in LD of the Golden City and of its lady are very general. In BI they are more definite, and are closer to the Celtic. In the French we read:

> En la vile ot 11 tors vermelles;
> Qui beles èrent à mervelles,
> Et furent de marbre vermeil,
> Qui moult reluist contre soleil, etc.   (1881 ff.)

This is, indeed, the City of the Golden Isle,[1] or, in the words of Campbell's version, the city "filled with the glitter of gold."

---

[1] As we have seen (p. 158, above) this name is supposed to have entered our cycle (in Version B) at the same time with the adventure with the dog.

Of the mistress of the place, BI says:

> El palais ot une pucele,
> Onques nus hom ne vit si bele. (1915-6.)

Further, "les oels ot vairs" (2214), and a line wanting in the MS. of BI at this point very probably told of the beauty of her teeth. In LD, also, she is called "a lady, whit as flour" (1489), which is like the French "Plus estoit blance d'une flor" (2210). Compare now with these passages the last stanza of the Great Fool here quoted (p. 174, above), which reads as follows in Campbell's version (stanza 32):

> A young wife that I found in the tower
> The sight of an eye no better was,
> Whiter than very snow is her form,
> Gentle her eye, and her teeth like a flower.

We have already seen reason to believe that the Desc. poems had their origin in some form of the Perceval cycle. The fact that we have some of the episodes in them closely paralleled in a Celtic poem which itself shows other points of agreement with the same cycle, is certainly of interest and importance. It will doubtless give some comfort to those who advocate the Celtic origin of the Perceval stories.[1]

HEADS ON POLES.

"This grim stroke of fancy" (as Professor Child calls it) is of very common occurrence. As we have seen, it is a feature of one of the castles in *Erec*, LD and BI.[2]

1. In Old French it is found, for example: (*a*) in *La Mule sanz Frain*,[3] where there are four hundred stakes, all but one of which are surmounted with a bloody head. (*b*) In Version P of the prose

---

[1] It may be noted that we have also in Campbell's collection (III, 403) the story of the transformation of a hideous being into a beautiful woman. For an early case in Celtic of transformation from a spell see MacInnes and Nutt, *Argyllshire Tales*, pp. 467-8; cf. Nutt, *Academy*, April 30, 1892, and note in Miss Weston's translation of Wolfram's *Parzival*, 1894, I, 319.

[2] A large number of the instances which follow will be found collected in Professor Child's *English and Scottish Ballads*, Parts II, 417; IV, 507; VI, 507; VIII, 459; IX, 216.

[3] Méon, *Nouveau Recueil*, I, 15 (vv. 429-37).

Livre d'Artus,[1] where, as in *Erec*, when one spear is covered a new one appears. (*c*) In *Mériaduec* Gawein kills his opponent and sticks his head up on a pole along with forty-four others whom the latter has conquered (see below, p. 238). (*d*) In *Ider* we read also of " le manoir, qu' entourent des pieux chargés de nombreuses têtes coupées " (see *Hist. Litt.*, XXX, 205). (*e*) In the prose *Lancelot* (P. Paris, *Romans*, V, 266) Hector is led into a garden " fermé de grands pieux aigus." He is shown an ivory horn and told to blow it. He does so, and the owner of the place appears. Hector conquers him in fight.

2. In Middle High German it occurs also in *Wolfdietrich B*. The heathen whom Wolfdietrich afterwards overcomes at knife-throwing, threatens him thus :

> ' Sihstu dort an den zinnen fünf hundert houbet stân,
> Diu ich mit mînen henden alle verderbet hân?
> Noch stât ein zinne lære an mînem türnlîn :
> Dâ muoz dîn werdez houbet ze einem phande sîn.'[2]

3. We have the same feature of one stake with no head on it in the Finnish *Kalevala*.[3] Lemminkäinen, going to the Northland, is warned by his mother that he will find a courtyard planted with stakes, with a head on every stake but one, on which his head will be stuck.

4. In Persian we have the incident of the heads in the story of *The Fair One of the Castle*, the fourth in the poem of *The Seven Figures* (or *Beauties*), by Nisami of Gendsch († 1180). Many suitors, having essayed unsuccessfully to obtain a Russian princess shut up in a castle made inaccessible by a talisman, had their heads arrayed on the pinnacles of the castle.

Most of the instances are, however, to be found on Celtic soil.[4]

---

[1] Ed. Freymond, *Zt. f. fr. Sp. u. Litt.*, XVII, 46 (§ 68), 65 (§ 111).
[2] St. 595, Jänicke, *Deutsches Heldenbuch*, III, 256.
[3] Schiefner, Rune 26, vv. 315-22, p. 163.
[4] Indeed, as Mr. Alfred Nutt says, " heads play as large a part in the olden Irish sagas as they presumably do in the tales of the head-hunting Dyaks, or as scalps in Red Indian stories." He is, however, hardly justified in adding, " When, therefore, in the *Conte du Graal*, Perceval, after having slain the Grail king's enemy, cuts off his head and brings it to the Grail king, who, forthwith, has it fixed on a stake on the top of the highest tower in his castle (Potvin's ed., VI,

5. One of the adventures of Cuchulinn was the cutting off of the heads of four charioteers, and placing them on the four points of a pronged pole.[1]

6. In Campbell's *Tales of the West Highlands*[2] we read: "'Many a leech has come,' said the porter. 'There is not a spike on the town without a leech's head but one, and may be it is for thy head that one is.'"

7. In the tale of Conall Gulban,[3] Conall "saw the very finest castle that ever was seen from the beginning of the universe till the end of eternity; and a great wall at the back of the fortress, and iron spikes within a foot of each other, about and around it, and a man's head upon every spike but the one spike. Fear struck him and he fell a-shaking. He thought that it was his own head that would go on the headless spike."

8. The giant of Loch Léin had a great castle, around which were seven hundred iron spikes; and on every one but one of these spikes was the head of a king, a queen, or a king's son.[4]

9. The king of Erin[5] promises his daughter to the Shee an Gannon

---

131), I look upon this as evidence of the original Celtic character of the *Conte du Graal*." (*Folk and Hero Tales*, II, 453.) This habit of putting heads on stakes was doubtless common in actual practice. In the *Image of Irelande*, by John Derricke (1581; edited with an Introd. by John Small, Edin., 1883; see plate VI), there is a plate representing Sir Henry Sidney, the Lord-Deputy, setting out on his state progress through Ireland. The heads of several of the rebels are displayed on poles over the gate of Dublin Castle. Above, the following lines are printed:

    These trunckles heddes do playnly showe each rebelles fatall end,
    And what a haynous crime it is, the Queene for to offend.

[1] *Táin bó Cuailgne, Lebor na h'Uidri*, p. 58, col. 1 (in Sullivan's *Introd.* to O'Curry, *Lectures*, p. cccxlv, note). Dr. F. N. Robinson has given me the following note: "For a Celtic poem illustrating the custom, see the *Dean of Lismore's Book* (ed. by M'Lauchlan and Skene, Edinburgh, 1862), p. 58, and Additional Notes, p. 151. Connal Cearnach M'Edirskeol avenged the death of Cuchullin by killing all his enemies, and in this poem he carries their heads on a withe and tells their names. The poem is usually known as the *Lay of the Heads* (*Laoidh nan ceann*), and is said by the editor to be well known in the Highlands. Cf. Aubrey de Vere, *Children of Fochlut Wood.*"
[2] I, 312 (*The Ceabharnach*).   [3] Campbell, III, 202.
[4] Jeremiah Curtin, *Myths and Folk-lore of Ireland*, Boston, 1890, p. 37.
[5] Curtin, p. 114 f.

if he can tell what will put a stop to the laughing of the Gruagach Gaire. "There are twelve iron spikes out here in the garden behind my castle. . . . I'm greatly in dread that your head'll be on the twelfth spike," said the king. The other eleven were covered by the heads of kings' sons who had been unsuccessful.

10. In the story of *Shaking-Head*,[1] two hundred and ninety-nine kings' sons have failed in their attempt to win a king's daughter, and their heads are on iron spikes in the garden of the castle. The king fears the present suitor will be the three-hundredth. Be it noted that the princess has here a knowledge of magic, and plays tricks on the hero (cf. BI).

11. The king of Albainn and the "big lad" come to the castle of the king of Eirin, the walls of which are surmounted by a row of iron spikes. All but two of these are covered by those who have previously gone to inquire after the king's condition.[2]

Other similar instances may be seen in (12) *The Bare-Stripping Hangman*;[3] (13) Carleton's *Three Tasks;* (14) Hyde's *King of Ireland's Son*, p. 39 ; (15) *The Lad with the Skin Coverings;*[4] (16) *Geraint and Enid, Mabinogion*, trans. Loth, II, 170 (in the passage corresponding to that in *Erec*).

The Celtic examples would seem to favor the view that this feature was originally connected with the castle of the Ile d'Or, as in BI. Indeed, there is a striking resemblance between the whole situation in the Desc. poems and in some of the traditional stories, especially in No. 15. In both cases we have a poor lad (originally clad in skin coverings) coming to the castle of a princess skilled in the black art. This is defended by a monster (surely Maugis in LD can be called such ; see 1333, 1339-41), who apparently aspires to the hand of the princess. She, however, is ill-disposed toward him and sympathizes with the young knight. This giant ever guards the entrance to the castle and lets no armed man pass without fighting. If the

---

[1] Curtin, p. 193.
[2] *Righ a bh' air Albainn*, in *Folk and Hero Tales*, Argyllshire Series, II, ed. MacInnes and Nutt, London, 1890, p. 79; cf. p. 453.
[3] Argyllshire Series, III, ed. MacDougall, London, 1891, p. 81.
[4] Argyllshire Series, IV, *The Fians*, collected by J. G. Campbell, 1891, pp. 261 ff. Nos. 13 and 14 are cited by Nutt, *Folk and Hero Tales*, Arg. Series, II, 453, who also refers to *The Dialogue of the Elders*, p. 76.

latter is defeated his head is cut off and put on a stake. When the monster sees the young hero come, he tells him to look out or he is sure to be worsted (cf. LD, 1372-4). The princess watches the fight from the windows of the castle along with her maidens (cf. BI, 2095 ff.). The young knight overcomes the giant and cuts off his head (cf. LD, 1484). He is offered the hand of the lady, who would only marry the one who had killed the giant; she also displays her knowledge of sorcery.

We have already seen that the Welsh *Peredur* presents in continued narrative a series of adventures bearing close resemblance to those of the poems of our cycle, relating them in exactly the same order in which they occur in the English poem, which is the least artistic and seems to represent best Version A of the Desc. group. It is a matter of no small importance that we have also in Celtic literature and tradition separate parallels to most of these adventures and to others in our stories not found in *Peredur*. It is well known that the stories of the youth of Cuchulinn resemble those of the *enfances* of Perceval.[1] Of the former hero it is also related how he overcame three brothers, powerful knights, and slew others whose heads he cut off and put on pointed stakes. In the *Lay of the Great Fool* we find a very close parallel to the adventure with the dog in our Desc. cycle and a suggestion of the Golden City and the enchantments there. Now we have a story which is strikingly like that told of the giant Maugis guarding a princess who is anxious to get rid of him and is willing to marry the knight who shall slay him. Had the knight failed, however, his head would have been placed on a stake alongside those of many others who had been unsuccessful in the adventure. We read also of hideous beings transformed into beautiful women when they are embraced by heroes who are not frightened by their repulsiveness. And so on. Have not these considerations some bearing on the vexed question of the Celtic origin of the Perceval stories?

---

[1] See Zimmer, *Gött. Gel. Anz.*, 1890, XII, 519.

GLIGLOIS.

The poem called *Gliglois* is preserved in a unique MS. (fr. 23, pp. 63–81) of the Royal Library of Turin. The rubric runs: "C'est de Gliglois comment il eut grant painne pour s'amie," and Paris, in his review of Stengel's *Mittheilungen*,[1] noted the resemblance of the name to that of the hero of BI, adding, "la forme *Gliglois* (l. *Guiglois?*) se rapproche du *Wigalois* allemand." Kölbing did not heed this suggestion in his study of LD,[2] and Stengel in his review of Kölbing[3] called attention to the fact, being evidently of the opinion that there was a close connection between the two poems. Foerster, however, after a careful examination of the *Gliglois*, felt forced to say that it "mit dem Gedichte Renauts leider in keiner Beziehung steht."[4] Paris then made another examination of the poem and came to the same conclusion.[5] My knowledge of this poem is limited to the summary and extracts given by Paris; but I hope to show that the poem has something in common with that of Guinglain, and that the author, "en plaçant son action dans le cadre des romans de la Table Ronde," has left the incident in the same setting in which he found it, merely telling at greater length and with increased charm an old story of the hero whose name forms the title of his poem, and who is none other than *Wigalois*, Perceval *li Galois*, who elsewhere became known best as *Li Beaus Desconeus*.

Gliglois is a youth of noble birth who betakes himself to Arthur's court that he may learn the profession of arms. He is given over to Gawain for instruction. Soon a beautiful maiden named Beauty comes to the court. Her father and mother are dead, and she and her elder sister are the heirs of the country of Landemore. Gawain falls in love with her; but his suit is unsuccessful, and Gliglois is given to her as a servant in order that he may advance his master's cause. The young knight, however, falls desperately in love with her himself, and finally avows his love. She rejects it scornfully, but lets his offence pass. Meanwhile all have been invited to a great tourney, to which each knight is to bring his *amie*. Gliglois, however, is bid-

[1] In *Rom.*, III, 110. [2] In *Engl. Stud.*, I, 121–169.
[3] In *Zt. f. rom. Phil.*, I, 486. [4] See *Zt. f. rom. Phil.*, II, 77.
[5] See *Hist. Litt.*, XXX, 161.

den to remain at home. Beauty also decides not to go; but she changes her mind soon after the rest have departed, and Gliglois gets her a passing knight as a companion. The youth persists in following them, until Beauty, realizing his great love for her, sends him with a letter to her sister revealing her own love for him, and asking that he be furnished with the best of armor and sent to the tourney. The sister receives him kindly, has him splendidly equipped, reveals to him Beauty's love, and sends him to the tournament. It is well to note that she marvels at the boy's beauty and concludes that it is no wonder her sister loves him. Needless to say Gliglois distinguishes himself by his prowess, and, although unknown to all, is acknowledged the victor of the joust. He returns quietly to Arthur's court. Beauty " révèle son nom à la reine ; après quoi Beauté raconte comment elle l'a aimé, comment elle l'a fait faire chevalier, et déclare qu'elle ne veut pas d'autre époux que lui ; la reine l'approuve. On appelle le roi et les autres chevaliers ; Arthur demande à Gliglois de faire partie de sa *mesnie;* Gauvain, enchanté du succès de son écuyer, l'embrasse et dit qu'il veut être désormais son compagnon. Mais la reine fait part à son mari de l'amour de Gliglois et de Beauté et annonce leur prochain mariage." The poet ends with some reflections on the perseverance in love which succeeded so well in the case of his hero.

If now we look again at *Peredur*, which we have seen to be so intimately connected with the Desc. stories, we find an adventure which might easily have suggested the romance of *Gliglois*. We are there[1] told how Peredur, while in confinement at a king's palace, learns of a great fight that is to take place ; how the princess, who is deeply in love with him, obtains for him splendid equipment, and how he goes off alone to engage in the struggle. He conquers all, but returns to his prison without having been recognized. The princess, however, reveals the name of the victor, and tells how she has aided him, and the king offers him his daughter's hand. Of course Peredur cannot accept it, but the young lady tells him in parting, " C'est toi, seigneur, l'homme que j'aime le plus."

If we fit to this single incident the general features of the beginning and ending of the story of which it is a part, the resemblance

---

[1] *Les Mabinogion*, trans. Loth, II, 102 ff.

becomes still more striking. There also the hero is a youth of noble birth who betakes himself to Arthur's court to serve him and is given over to Gawain for instruction in knightly ways. There too, shortly after the youth's coming, a beautiful maiden also arrives. Her father and mother are dead, and she and her elder sister are sole heirs of their land. This is exactly the introduction in *Carduino*, in which, it will be remembered, the messenger is a sister of the enchanted princess. But Beauty gives no reason for her coming. She comes to stay; that is all. May we not, in this fact, see evidence that the introduction in *Gliglois* has no immediate connection with the form of the story as there told, but is a reminiscence of the introduction to the whole history of which the adventure described in *Gliglois* was but an incident? We remember that the young hero in all the Desc. stories is remarkable for his beauty, that he is received with great joy at court on his return, that Arthur makes him one of his *mesnie*, that Gawain, above all, is delighted at his success and proud of his exploits, and that he is married to the woman whom he loves and who loves him.

It may be noted also that there are no names in *Gliglois* which are not in BI, except *Lindemore*, which is of common occurrence elsewhere,[1] and *Beauty*, the addition of which is readily understood; while the connection of the poem with the rest of the Perceval *li Galois* cycle explains the remarkable agreement, heretofore obscure, in the names of the heroes.

If my conclusions in this matter are justified, it is evident that for the first time the poem *Gliglois* has been shown to be connected with the cycle of poems with which every one felt it ought to be connected, and also that another strong argument has been adduced in support of my contention that the Desc. poems all go back originally to some form of the *Perceval* story and are not confined, in their resemblance to that story, to the introductory portion.

---

[1] For example, *Fergus*, ed. Martin, p. 6, 4 (cf. p. xxi), and " pucele de Landemore " in *Meraugis*, p. 8.

CARDUINO.

The relation of *Carduino* to the other stories in the Desc. cycle has always been somewhat perplexing. It is quite evident that it is not based on either LD or BI or their direct original. While LD and BI make the hero the bastard son of Gawain, who is delighted when he discovers that the young knight is his son, *Carduino* represents that flower of chivalry as no other than the murderer of the boy's father, and as forced to kneel before Car. and crave mercy lest his life should be taken away. None of the characteristic names in LD and BI are known to the Italian poet. Some of the most important adventures in these poems have no counterpart in the Italian, and, where the three stories have incidents in common, Car. in general presents a much more primitive form of saga-material. It is clear that we have now to deal with a poem which owes its immediate origin to some other source than that which we are able to postulate directly for LD and BI, and yet was certainly a branch of the same tree.

How then are the points in which Car. varies from the other poems to be accounted for? Heretofore no satisfactory explanation of the problem has been given. All investigators have agreed that Car. represents in some of its features an older form of the story, or an earlier tradition than that we have in LD and BI; but, nevertheless, I hope to be able to show that a large part of it is based on a later work than either of the other two, and that in its present form it is but a late *rifacimento*, in which are introduced important variations from its original. This becomes evident when one notes the striking resemblance which a large part of the poem bears to incidents in the French prose romance of *Tristan*.

If we think again of the first part of the story as it is found in the Italian poem, we remember that there the hero is represented as the son of a knight who was a great favorite of King Arthur's and therefore aroused the jealousy of the other courtiers. He was murdered by the three brothers, Calvano, Agueriesse, and Mordarette, who, however, did not thereby incur the displeasure of the king (because, of course, the murderers were not known to him) but continued to live at his court. The widowed mother, knowing that her only son, then very young, would be likely to suffer a like fate, to avoid this, fled to a wild forest, where she continued to live alone for many years before her whereabouts became known. She aimed to bring up her son so much apart from the world that he would never become a knight. The boy was accustomed to roam about in the forest, killing the wild beasts with his javelins, entirely ignorant of the outer world. One day, however, he saw by chance some knights in shining armor, and the sight of them aroused in him a desire to give up his solitary life. His mother with sorrow saw him depart. The boy went to Arthur's court, was there made a knight, and soon set out on a mission to prove his valor. The reports of his exploits delighted Arthur, but, we may suppose, afflicted Calvano and Mordarette, who were still at court and feared his revenge on them for the murder of his father.

This introduction differs markedly from any other we have preserved, and has always appeared an inexplicable perversion of what was thought to be the original form of the story. If, however, we examine the account of Perceval which is included in the prose romance of *Tristan*,[1] we find the matter explained, for the summary I have just given of the opening of Car. might equally well be a summary of the story of Perceval's youth as found there. The chief difference is that in *Tristan*, although Gauvain is indeed represented as the murderer of Perceval's father, the animosity of Gauvain and his brothers is also directed against Perceval's brothers, especially Lamorat, whose death they finally bring about. In Löseth's summary we read (§ 302): "Le roi Pelinor a eu cinq fils, qui se distinguent à la cour d'Arthur au point d'éveiller les plus vives jalousies; Arthur lui-même les estime beaucoup. . . . Les fils de Pelinor sont haïs de Gauvain et de ses frères à cause de leur gloire." And again (§ 246): "Mais Gauvain et ses frères en sont *tristre et dolent;* ils haïssent Lamorat, car ils savent que Gauvain a tué le roi Pellinor, le père de Lamorat, et ils craignent toujours la vengeance. . . . Gauvain et ses frères, Agravain, Mordret et Guerret ne pensent qu'à le mettre à mort. Lamorat lui-même ne se doute de rien; il se croit aimé de tout le monde." One day while Arthur is at Camelot news comes that Lamorat has won in the tourney to

---

[1] Löseth, *Le Roman en Prose de Tristan*, Paris, 1891, §§ 302, 306–310. See also §§ 246, 254, 255.

which most of the knights have gone. "'Si Lamorat savait qui a tué son père, il le vengerait bien,' dit-on à la cour, où le meurtrier n'est pas connu. Gauvain est très mécontent de ce nouveau triomphe de Lamorat, et Gaheriet aussi (§ 255)." Soon Gauvain and his brothers succeed in killing Lamorat and Driant. News of the murder is brought to Arthur, but the names of the murderers are concealed. It is then told (§ 308) how Agloval "arrive dans un pays *sauvage* et *divers*, près de la tour où sa mère s'est retirée avec le jeune Perceval et où elle pleure la mort de Pelinor, de Lamorat et de Driant; elle espère au moins empêcher son fils cadet de devenir chevalier. Agloval rencontre Perceval, qui *aloit tot contre val la plaigne gitant et lancent javeloz que il tenoit, et corroit une heure avant et l'autre arrieres, une haut et l'autre bas.* Les armes d'Agloval . . . brillent au soleil." This is something new and attractive to Perceval and "il désire aller à la cour d'Arthur pour être armé chevalier de la main du roi" (§ 309). The mother, who "se désole d'abord de l'arrivée d'un chevalier," is overcome with grief at her son's departure. The two brothers, however, go to Arthur's court, where the king knights Perceval. Gauvain and his brothers fear that the boy will take vengeance on them for the murder of his father and brothers.

It is now easy to explain most of the names which are found in the Italian poem. The three brothers, *Calvano, Agueriesse*, and *Mordarette*, are none other than *Gauvain, Guerrehes*,[1] and *Mordret*. *Dondinello* is the French *Dodinel*. True, Dodinel is not the young knight's father: he is nevertheless mentioned in the same connection, as having been conquered by one of Perceval's brothers.[2] When the Italian poet decided to call his hero *Carduino* instead of *Perceval* it is not remarkable that he discarded the name of the father also (if indeed, *Pelinor* was the form in the *immediate* source he had before him).[3] The name *Carduino*[4] may have been suggested by that of

---

[1] *Guerrehes* and *Gaheres* are constantly confused in the MSS., according to Löseth, *Tristan*, p. 22, n. 4. [2] § 307.

[3] Possibly the surname of Dodinel, *le Sauvage*, may have had something to do with his being made the father of Carduino.

[4] Rajna thought the name *Carduino* suggested by *Carduel*, and pointed out that *Carados* is usually found in Italian in the form *Caradosso* (*Introd.*, pp. xiii-xiv, and note 1). Paris is of the opinion that it may be an alteration of the Celtic name *Cardroain*, found, for example, in *Durmart* (*Hist. Litt.*, XXX, 187, note 2).

Carados, who plays an important part in the prose romance. In the *Conte du Graal*, 12595 ff., we have an account of the dubbing of a youth Carados by Arthur at a Pentecostal feast at Carduel; and the name is in this passage spelt *Caradun*. A diminutive of this would easily give the name of our hero: *Caradun*, *Caradunino or **Cardunino, Carduino*.[1]

It is also a confirmation of the opinion that the prose *Tristan* influenced the Italian poem that the author of Car. represents Arthur's court as being at Camelot, which is never mentioned in BI or LD, but which is the regular situation in the prose *Tristan* (although Perceval does, indeed, go to Carducil). Further, the name of *Merlin* enters into both Car. and the prose romance in this connection, as constantly, while Merlin is nowhere mentioned in BI or LD. The only other personal name in Car. (except those of the three wise men of the East, in the invocation) is *Beatricie* " dal viso rosato,"[2] by which name the princess in serpent form is called. This is evidently an invention of the Italian author.[3]

But not only does the prose *Tristan* explain the introduction and general setting of the Italian poem : it also accounts for the variations in the other adventure in which Car. has been supposed to differ most from its original, viz., the fight with the single knight. It will be remembered that in LD and BI we have a knight who refuses to let the young hero pass until he fights with him, for he is accustomed to challenge every warrior who appears at that place. In Car., however, we read that the boy and his companions are riding

---

Curiously enough, in *Meleranz* von dem Pleier, 3575, etc., we have a knight whose father is *Kardeuz*, and who, when asked, gives his name as *Lybials*.

[1] In the *Conte du Graal*, 12714, 12719, we have the name spelt *Caradieu*. This form, with a diminutive ending added, might also give the Italian name — *Caradieuino, *Caraduino, *Carduino*. Child, *Ballads*, I, 264, notes also the occurrence in the *Möttuls Saga* of a form *Karadin* which he suggests may be for *Karadiu*.

[2] In the *Tristan* poem in the same MS., published by Rajna along with the *Carduino*, we read also of " Isotta bella *col viso rosato* " (5, 2).

[3] Mennung, by a curious mistake (p. 34), gives the name *Giovane* to the widowed mother merely because the adjective happens to be spelt with a capital letter as the first word of the line: " Giovane e fresca e bella di natura " (i, 6, 2). He might have noticed the very same line in the *Secondo Cantare* (9, 2), where it is used to describe the enchantress.

along the way when a knight appears, who, happening to notice the beauty of Car.'s companion, at once demands that she be given over to him; otherwise Car. shall lose his head. But Car. will fight first, and manages to kill his opponent. He learns that the latter is Agueriesse,[1] one of his father's murderers, and thus his revenge is partly performed.

In the prose *Tristan*, in direct connection with the story of Perceval and his brothers (§ 304) which we have just considered, we are told how "Gauvain rencontre un chevalier, accompagné d'une belle dame, qu'il veut lui enlever." The knight is "sans armure" (Car. has no arms except his two rude spears) and is overcome; but assistance arrives and Gauvain is finally worsted. In Car. this fight is said to take place not with Gauvain, but with Agueriesse. This change seems to be due to the fact that the first fight which Perc. has in the *Tristan* is with Gaheriet. He fights to avenge his father's death, and is victorious. "Perc. quitte la cour pour se mettre en quête de Lancelot . . . Perc., conduit par une demoiselle, arrive dans la *Forest perilleuse*, près d'une île où sa sœur, désirant venger la mort de Pelinor et de ses frères sur Gauvain, a fait construire deux tours; . . . Perc. y vient et lutte victorieusement avec Gaheriet; sur le conseil de Perc., qui ne se doute pas que sa sœur est dans l'île, tous deux s'enfuient ensemble du château" (§ 288ᵃ).[2] These two incidents combine to form the account in Car., where also, we may note, Car. hurries on for fear his killing Agueriesse may be revenged.

There is one more point in which Car. varies from LD and BI, namely, in the fact that Car., before he returned to court, is said to have begun a war against those who had murdered his father (ii, 67, 7-8). This also may have been suggested by the *Tristan*, where we read (§ 313): "Gauvain et ses frères se décident à chercher Perceval, dont ils craignent la vengeance, pour le mettre à mort." It was then natural for the Italian poet to make Carduino (i.e. Perceval) enter into a struggle with his enemies before he

---

[1] "Ce récit [i.e. the incident in Car.] est en contradiction avec les traditions reçues: dans l'*Artus*, dans le *Lancelot* et dans le *Tristan*, Gaheriet est le plus loyal, le plus preux et le plus sage des quatre fils du roi Loth." P. Paris, *Rom.*, IV, 141.

[2] This last incident is from MS. 12599; see Löseth, pp. 191, 213.

returned home. In *Tristan* they were away from Arthur's court in search of him.

My belief that Car. is based partly on the account of Perceval given in the prose *Tristan* is strengthened by the fact that there occurs in the same codex (Riccardiana, 2873) with it a little poem entitled, *Cantare quando Tristano e Lancielotto combatetero al petrone di Merlino*, first edited by Rajna, along with the *Carduino*, in 1873, and, of course, founded on the Tristan story. The greater part of it might, indeed, almost be taken from the very form before us. This will be seen if we glance only at the short *résumé* of MS. 758, printed in the Preface (pp. vi ff.) of Löseth's edition of the prose romance. On pp. x—xi we read: "*Messire Tristans, qui s'estoit partis blechiés de cest tournoiement, jeut grant piesche mallades a ung chastel nommé Daras [le chastel Daras], qui estoit assés près du chastel aux Pucellez. Et quant il fu garis il prist congié au seigneur de laiens et cevaulcha p'usieurs journees sans plenté d'aventures trouver qui a conter faiche. Et tant esra qu'il vint a ung perron nommé le Perron Merlin, assés près de Kamaelot, et pour che que luy et Pallamedes avoient prins jour de combatre en ce lieu.* Lancelot arrive; Tristan le prend pour Palamède et le défie. Ils s'abattent l'un l'autre, les chevaux sur les corps. Puis ils chamaillent, et le combat devient terrible; leurs armes sont mises en pièces, et ils sont couverts de blessures; à la fin leurs épées leur tournent dans leurs mains. Ils se reposent, forcément, et Tristan demande à Lancelot son nom. Apprenant qui il est, Tristan est ravi, s'excuse de l'avoir combattu et lui exprime son affection et son admiration; ils *s'entrefirent la plus grant joie du monde.*"[1] Whether this poem was in reality drawn from the French *Tristan* or the Italian translations does not concern us now. It is sufficient that in direct connection with the *Carduino* we have another little poem in the same style dealing with Tristan. But this is not all. Rajna brings forward three other Italian poems, the *Bataglia de Tristano e Lancelotto e della Reina Isotta*, the *Morte*, and the *Vendetta di Tristano*, and concludes (p. lix) that these three formed part of a series of

---

[1] With this cf. further §§ 202—203. Be it noted that this account makes Tristan arrive at the stone first, that we have the court at Camelot, and mention of the castle of Daras. For a summary of the Italian poem see Rajna, *Introd.*, pp. xliv ff., and for a discussion of the source see pp. xlvi ff., and P. Paris, *Rom.*, IV, 143.

little poems which had Tristan for their principal subject. He is disposed to put the date of our poem, along with the *Morte* and the *Vendetta*, in the second half of the fourteenth century. Gaspary[1] fixes the position of these three poems and Car. more definitely, at about the year 1379. Thus we have before us a series of short poems of chivalry dealing with separate adventures of knights of the Round Table, in all of which Tristan is the prominent figure. They are all in the same *ottava rima* and in the same style. Is it remarkable that the author of *Carduino* (who may have been the author of the rest of the series) should have reverted to the story of Tristan for his version of the boyhood of his hero?

But who was this poet? And would the style of poem we have before us in Car. and the method of treatment of the subject be in accord with what we know of him? D'Ancona and Rajna feel confident that the author of our poem was Antonio Pucci, the Florentine poet, who was born in the beginning of the fourteenth century and died about 1390. He was not of noble birth, but, as D'Ancona says,[2] he represented the most perfect type of the popular poet of his age; indeed, he was a sort of higher ballad-singer, even if he did not use his calling to earn money. Almost all of his poems were intended for the people. They were written with an eye single to popular presentation, and not for lengthy recitation in the halls of the nobility. We should not then be surprised to find that he treats his sources with freedom; and his poems would have been unsuited to their purpose had they been long and detailed. This explains why the little Italian poems deal briefly with a few episodes only, extracted from the general fund of the stories of chivalry. It helps us to understand the mode of treatment of the story in Car., where we have the whole account given in 115 stanzas of *ottava rima*, while the *Tristan* poem following is completed in 42 similar stanzas. Be it noted, moreover, that the former poem, being longer than the others, is divided into two *cantari*, as if arranged for recitation on two occasions.

In it we have also (what was undoubtedly an addition of Pucci's) the three opening stanzas telling of the significance of the wise men

---

[1] See *Gesch. der ital. Lit.*, II, 256-7.

[2] *La Poesia Popolare Italiana*, Leghorn, 1878, p. 43; cf. D'Ancona and Bacci, *Man. della Lett. Ital.*, Florence, I, 530, and Gaspary, II, 81 ff.

of the East. The second *cantare* opens in a like manner, and both openings[1] bear witness to the popular character of Pucci's works. They remind us of the opening of the English poem, which was also a popular production; but they contrast markedly with that of BI, written, as it was, for a very different purpose.

But, as Gaspary points out in his discussion of *die Ritterdichtung*,[2] the knightly poetry flourished in its Franco-Italian form in upper Italy at the end of the thirteenth and the first half of the 'fourteenth centuries, and from there went to Tuscany, where it generally clothed itself in the *ottava rima*, and became somewhat ennobled in style. For a long time, however, it remained the property of the people. "Die höheren Kreise der Gesellschaft interessirten sich nicht weniger für die aus Frankreich gekommenen Erzählungen; aber sie bedurften nicht so sehr der Uebertragungen und Umformungen und konnten die Originale selbst lesen." Of the romances of the Breton cycle, adds Gaspary, "finden sich nur wenige ältere Versionen in italienischer Sprache." These are especially the two prose redactions of the *Tavola Rotonda*, one in a MS. (Riccardiana) perhaps of the beginning of the fourteenth century, the other (Laurenziana) much later and showing reminiscences of Dante's *Comedy*, together with those poems we have already spoken of as belonging approximately to the year 1379. The people had before preferred the French national cycle of Charlemagne and his paladins, the stories of Arthur, Tristan, and Lancelot being more suited to please the cultivated classes.

Heretofore Car. has been regarded as occupying a somewhat unique position among Italian Arthur romances. The position to which we have been able to assign it by the help of the light thrown on the subject by the prose *Tristan*, accords better with what we know of the history of the Arthur cycle in Italy. Mennung's view (p. 43), "dass wir es hier [i.e. in the *enfances* of Car.] *unbedingt* mit einer primitiven Gestalt der Parzival-Sage zu thun haben," can no longer be maintained. If Car. preserves some primitive elements, they are remnants of the form of the story on which it is based. It is clear that most of the account in Car. is drawn from a late, distorted prose version. Mennung's second idea that *all* the *Dümmlingsmärchen* (as

---

[1] Cf. also the opening stanza of *Tristano e Lancielotto*.
[2] See *Gesch. der Ital. Lit.*, II, 256 (chap. xx).

he calls it) is an addition of Pucci's, and had no place in his original, the present investigation has shown to be erroneous. We have not to do with a fusion of two elements which were previously distinct and separate, — a fusion which therefore "notwendig irgend einem Reimer zugeschrieben werden muss," for an account of the hero's youth was almost certainly an essential part of the Desc. cycle from the beginning (see pages 146 ff., above). The fact that it is found in the English poem LD shows that it was, at any rate, in the original on which Car. was based.[1]

In regard to this introductory part of the Desc. stories, it is important to remember that in the first continuation of the *Perceval* (that by the so-called Pseudo-Gautier) it is twice related how Gauvain had a son by a maiden whom he found in a tent[2] in a forest, and that an imperfect summary of this boy's youthful exploits is given,[3] — a summary which shows some resemblances to the *enfances* of Perceval and those of the hero of the Desc. poems, but which has nothing to say of the *fier baiser* and which does not give the boy any name. Paris (*Hist. Litt.*, XXX, 185, n. 2) calls attention to a possible relation between the Pseudo-Gautier story and the account of LD's origin given at the outset in the English poem (see LD, 8-9). The second continuator of the *Perceval*, Gautier (or Gaucher), introduces Li Beaus Desconeus by name as the son of Gawain,[4] and in a fashion which suggests that he knew the story in Pseudo-Gautier and intended to identify Li Beaus with the unnamed boy told of by the latter.[5] The name itself Gautier may have got from Version B of the Desc. story.[6] It is hazardous, however, in the present state of *Perceval* investigation, to attempt to fix precisely the relation between Gautier and the Desc. poems. Mennung thinks that Gautier

---

[1] Paris, *Rom.*, XX, 299.
[2] Pseudo-Gautier, 11987-12450, 16856-17525. Cf. Paris, *Hist. Litt.*, XXX, 192, n. 2; Waitz, *Die Fortsetzungen von Chrétiens Perceval le Gallois*, Strassburg, 1890, pp. 6, 22, 27, 28.
[3] Pseudo-Gautier, 20380-831. See Paris, *Hist. Litt.*, XXX, 192-194.
[4] Gautier, 24584; see also 33402-4. Cf. Paris, *Hist Litt.*, XXX, 194.
[5] This may perhaps serve as a reason (in addition to those given by Heinzel, *Gralromane*, pp. 52, 53) for believing that the work of Pseudo-Gautier was not (as Paris thought, *Hist. Litt.*, l.c.; *Litt. fr. au Moyen-Âge*, 2d ed., p. 99) unknown to Gautier. [6] See p. 157, above.

borrowed two features from BI and perhaps a third:[1] (1) the stealing of the dog (cf. BI, 1260 ff., with *Perc.*, 22603 ff.) ; (2) the knight in love with an ugly lady (cf. BI, 1708 ff., with *Perc.* 25380 ff.); (3) the *gue amorous* (cf. BI, 318 ff., with *Perc.*, 24207 ff.). In the first and third of these places there is no necessity of postulating an obligation on the side of either author. In the second instance, if there was any borrowing (which is by no means certain) a strong case could be made out for Renaud as the borrower. In a previous section (see pp. 139 ff., above) it has been pointed out that indications of Renaud's having borrowed from Gautier are not lacking. If, now, Gautier may be supposed to have been acquainted with Version B and Renaud to have been acquainted with Gautier's work, all the apparent relations between BI and Gautier would be explained, and we should have made some advance towards a chronology at once of the lost Desc. poems and of the continuators of Chrétien's *Perceval*. But I refrain from entering upon these dubious matters at present, reserving a discussion of them for a future opportunity.

In his effort to make the introduction in Car. represent a very early form of the Perceval story, Mennung has laid much stress on the agreements between Car. and the late English metrical romance of *Sir Percyvelle*,[2] where also there is no reference to the Grail Quest, and has even gone so far as to believe (see pp. 43-4) that Pucci got his account of the boy's youth from an Englishman who made known the *Percyvelle* form of the story when on a visit to Italy. The relations I have pointed out between Car. and the prose *Tristan* of course make this conjecture impossible ; but, inasmuch as Pucci has preserved in Car. some of the features of the original Desc. story, combined with his borrowings from the *Tristan*, it is well to examine the points wherein his poem agrees with the English *Perc.* and the French *Perceval li Galois*.

Mennung points out (pp. 40 ff.) the following agreements of Car. with the English *Percyvelle*:

1. In P. the boy's father is a brother-in-law of the king and beloved by him. In Car. he also is a favorite of the king.

---

[1] *Der Bel Inconnu*, pp. 17, 18. With regard to the third feature Mennung expresses himself with some reserve.

[2] *Thornton Romances*, ed. Halliwell, 1844.

2. The death of the father is explained, and the boy later takes revenge on the slayer. [But Car. is told of the whole situation before he leaves his mother, and she prompts him to revenge. As to P., " he wiste never that he hade a fader to be slayne " (571–2).]

3. The murder was due to jealousy. [But in the one case the victim is killed openly in a tournament, without any secrecy, by one knight only. In the other several knights conspire and slay him secretly. They do not incur the displeasure of the king, for they are not known. In P. the Red Knight becomes the plague of the king. In Car. the murderers stay peaceably at his court.]

4. Spears play an important part in both poems, and in each case it is said that they were found. [But in Car. the boy accidentally finds two in the woods which have been left there by hunters. His mother is disturbed by the accident, for all her efforts have been directed against his seeing anything which may arouse his curiosity to know of the outer world. In P. the mother gives him one little Scots spear which she had carefully brought with her from home. She merely *tells* him she found it.]

5. There are, however, certain agreements in the way in which he questions his mother as to his new treasure.

> 'O madre mia, de! dimmi inmantanente:
> che è questo che lucie e taglia tanto?'   (i, 13, 1–2.)

> 'Swete modir,' sayde he
> 'What manere of thyng may this bee,
> That ȝe nowe hafe takene mee?'   (197 ff.)

He asks also how they are called. Cf. 'Come son chiamat[e]?' (i, 12, 8) with 'What calle ȝee this wande?' (200).

6. In each case he is clothed in skins. [This is common to all versions.]

It will be noticed that whatever agreement there is between Car. and the English *Perc.* is, then, in the part of the latter which precedes that in which the English author follows Chrétien's narrative closely.

We find, also, that Car. presents the following points of resemblance to the interpolated introduction to the French *Perceval* in places in

o

which the latter differs from the English *Percyvelle*.[1] (1) The mother takes her treasures with her to the woods. Cf. *Perc.* 1117-8 with Car. i, 6, 8. (2) It is told how, when she had reached the depths of the forest, she had a dwelling built. Cf. *Perc.* 1197-9 with Car. i, 7. 1-3. (3) Mention is made of the trouble at court because of their friends' ignorance of their whereabouts. Cf. *Perc.* 1208 ff. with Car. i, 7, 5-8. (4) The boy believes what his mother tells him of their condition. Cf. *Perc.* 1224 ff. with Car. i, 10, 4-8. (5) There is an account of the boy's going out into the woods twice. It is on the second occasion that he sees human beings like himself. On his return home each time he is welcomed by his mother. (6) Javelins are his sole weapons in both. He always carries them (*Perc.* 1263).

All these agreements are, as I have said, with a part of *Perc.* not written by Chrétien. With the main body of the poem Car. shows no significant agreement, and we are safe in concluding that Pucci did not know it. The English *Perc.*, on the other hand, cannot be said to show any agreement of importance with the part by the interpolator, but is strikingly like Chrétien's narrative.[2] Why may we not conclude that the author of the spurious *Perceval* introduction, the author of the original of Car., the author of the English *Perceval*, and the rest, drew from similar stories which are not now preserved? That stories of youthful heroes of this kind were very common outside of our cycle and without any connection with the Quest of the Grail, is well known.[3]

---

[1] Rajna (*Introd.*, pp. xvi ff.) has cited some of these agreements; cf. Mennung, pp. 41-3.

[2] See Steinbach, *Ueber den Einfluss des C. v. T. auf die altengl. Lit.*, Leipzig, 1885; cf. Golther, *Chrestiens Conte del Graal*, in *Sitzungsberichte der k. b. Akad. der Wiss. zu München*, June 7, 1890, pp. 203 ff.; and Kölbing, *Germ.*, XIV, 180. On *Das Percevalmotiv ohne den Gral*, see Heinzel, *Ueber die franz. Gralromane*, in Vienna *Denkschriften*, 1892, XL, iii, 22. On the similarity of the Pseudo-Chrétien introduction with that of Wolfram, see Martin, *Zur Gralsage*, p. 16 (cf. Heinzel, p. 81).

[3] Some of the most important of these are: (1) Cuchulinn in the *Táin bó Cúalgne*: analysis in O'Curry, *Manners and Customs*, II, 358 ff.; cf. Zimmer, *Zt. f. vergl. Sprachforschung*, XXVIII, 446 ff., 661 ff.; *Gött. Gel. Anz.*, 1890, p. 519, n. 1. (2) *Fergus*, ed. Martin, 1872; see *Einl.*, pp. xvii ff. (3) The *lai* of *Tyolet*, edited by Paris, *Rom.*, VIII, 29 ff., cf. 40 ff. (cf. Golther, Munich Acad.,

It is now necessary to discuss the relations between Car. and LD and BI.

I have already accounted for about half of the Italian poem in showing the origin of the introduction and of the fight with one of the murderers of the boy's father. The striking agreements between the remainder and the LD-BI group admit of two theories only: either Pucci borrowed from LD or BI (or their direct original), or from a form of the story such as might come from Version A. That the former of these is almost impossible all will admit. Pucci shows no trace of ever having known LD or BI or Version B. We cannot imagine his turning the father of the young hero (Gawain, above all others) into the murderer of the boy's father, the latter becoming an unimportant knight.[1] It is surely incredible that he could have omitted such striking incidents as the adventures about the dog, the sparrow-hawk, and the like, and have reverted in the adventures he did relate to a more primitive form of the story, at the same time leaving no trace of any of the striking names which are peculiar to the Desc. cycle.. We can only believe that Pucci had before him some form of the story drawn from Version A.

Some will doubtless be disposed to ask why, if Car. is in parts so much like the story of Perceval as told in the prose *Tristan*, and if this latter work is supposed to be largely based on Chrétien's lost poem,[2] we may not suppose that Pucci, or the author of his original, drew directly from Chrétien's *Tristan*. This, indeed, is a tempting theory, for, if Chrétien had embodied in his earlier poem some account of the youth of Perceval, this would explain, perhaps, why, when it later occurred to him to connect Perceval with the story of the Grail, he began in the middle of the account of the boy's youth, taking it for granted that his readers were familiar with the previous account of the father's death, etc., and thus leaving a lacuna, which, being soon observed, caused an interpolator to prefix the omitted beginning. I refrain from following this theory farther at this time. We may confidently put aside the suggestion that the

---

Sitzungsberichte, 1890, p. 214). (4) The prose introduction to the *Lay of the Great Fool*, Campbell, *Pop. Tales of the West Highlands*, 1862, III, 146 ff.; cf. Nutt, *Studies*, pp. 154 ff., and *Folk-Lore Record*, IV (*Aryan Expulsion-and-Return Formula*). See also Paris, *Hist. Litt.*, XXX, 194.

[1] Cf. Mennung, pp. 46-7. [2] See Löseth, *Préface*, p. xxv.

introduction to Car. may have been drawn from Chrétien's poem, because it is not credible that in the early accounts Gawain could have been represented in such an unfavorable light as that in which he appears in Car. and the prose romance. This is not only at variance with Chrétien and all the early poets, but also with the rest of the poems of our cycle. Even Wirnt von Gravenberg was unwilling to believe that Gawain had to give in to another knight, albeit the latter wore a magic girdle, and declares that he would never have put such a thing into his narrative had it not been positively asserted by his squire in spite of the poet's "striving" with him in the matter (Wig., p. 20, vv. 15 ff.).

Whether Pucci followed his original closely or not is, of course, uncertain, and is a point we can never hope to settle definitely. It seems probable that, except in the points which I have already pointed out, he did not vary much from the story he was following; but he probably introduced new details of his own invention, or from other stories with which he was familiar, and relied for some of his material on the popular tradition of his own land. This accords, it will be noticed, with what we know of the Italian poet.[1] There can be little doubt that Car. was specially prepared for recitation in the open air to an audience of common people, who delighted in the marvellous but cared little for the refinements of chivalry. Indeed, there was no possibility of detailed elaboration, for the poem had to be of such a length as would not weary its hearers. Pucci, therefore, doubtless felt no qualms of conscience about departing from his original. He was not writing for critics; he was merely striving to please an ignorant populace. It was for this latter reason, as we have seen, that he gave the distinctively Christian tone to the whole poem, which is not found in BI. There the characters go to mass occasionally, and sometimes call on God for aid, in a formal way; but it is quite evident that the author is worldly-minded. The people for whom his BI was intended were not anxious for moral lessons, nor did the writer feel any desire to give them. His aim was to interest, not to edify, his hearers or readers. We find also in Car. rude touches which would appeal to an uncultivated audience: for example, the

---

[1] Cf. D'Ancona, *Una Poesia ed una Prosa di Antonio Pucci* in *Il Propugnatore*, II, 2, p. 407; also separately, Bologna, 1870.

great eating powers of the hero, the roasting of the hind with its skin and hoofs on, Car.'s slinging it over his shoulders to carry it off, and the like. It may be that Car.'s always keeping by him the primitive weapons he used in the forest may be due to a similar reason.[1]

THE STAY WITH THE ENCHANTRESS.

That which is of most interest to us in connection with this part of our story is the character of the enchantress, in which regard LD, BI, and Car. differ. In BI she is very human, and her powers as a sorceress do not make her unlike other women. She only differs from them in being more beautiful. She confesses to having placed all her love on one man. When he thoughtlessly leaves her, she determines to have revenge; but, when she sees him again, she finds it impossible to conceal her love. She makes him uncomfortable for a time by playing tricks on him; but later they laugh heartily over them together, and she explains to him how she came to have her skill in magic. It was taught her by her father as a special sign of his love to her, his only heir. She was a diligent student and profited by his teaching. There is nothing remarkable, then, according to her own report, in her knowledge. She is simply the daughter of a king "qui moult fu sages et cortois," and her knowledge of sorcery was an accomplishment laboriously acquired. All traces of the supernatural element in her nature have nearly faded away, and the reason is not hard to see : Renaud identified her with his own loved one.[2]

In LD this change had not yet been made, and the lady of the Ile d'Or is there a regular sorceress, who has no real affection for LD, but keeps him with her by continued exercise of her magic. Her

---

[1] Before going on to consider some of the important incidents in Car., I should like to suggest that the lines in which the messenger tells Arthur that he ought to know about the enchanted city, for it was under his sway (i, 35, 1-4), may be due to the fact that Pucci was confused at having *Gales* made the land of the princess whilst *Carduel* was also put in that country.

[2] Bethge, *Wirnt von Gravenberg*, Berlin, 1881, p. 36, gives an odd reason for the omission, by Wirnt, of the *fée* episode : " Es bewog ihn dazu auch wol die absicht seinen helden nirgend in schlechtem licht erscheinen zu lassen : dass Guinglain bei dem zweimaligen verlassen der dame die er doch liebt und die ihm ihre volle liebe geschenkt hat nicht gerade als ein edler karakter erscheint ist klar." Golther, *Gesch. der deutschen Litt.*, 1893, I, 170, repeats this idea.

retention of him must surely have been for purposes of sensual enjoyment. Therefore the author laments that LD was not "chast," and curses the enchantress for her deception of the hero. LD stayed merely because he was victimized by her wiles. "Sche blered his iȝe," we are told, with "fantasme and fairie" (see 1516 ff.).[1] There was doubtless in the original some account of different deceptions to which she subjected LD; but these the English author passed by, making general statements, which, however, point back to specific enchantments. When LD finally breaks away, it is as if he had got happily out of a bad scrape. The woman is not mentioned again. The hero was fascinated by her wiles, not overcome by love.[2] Be it noted that she is suitably called *la dame d'amour*.

When we come to Car., we find ourselves really in the domain of folk-lore, for we are now introduced to a being resembling in some measure a Lamia. She is a charming and attractive "gientil donna," who fascinates our hero. She has, however, no love for him, and her desires are purely sensual. She even excites his passions by telling him of the "gran gioia e gran diletto" he shall have with her, and he waits impatiently for the desired time to come. Any knight would have served her purpose as well. Indeed, it was the rule of the castle that every man who came there armed should lie with her, if he satisfied one condition, which was that he should come to her only when she told him not to come and refuse to obey when she called him. That this was too hard a request to make of most mortals is evident from the fact that knight after knight, according to the dwarf's statement, had been victimized by her (ii, 19, 7-8). As in LD, so in Car., she has no distinct personality. She is the representative of a type. In Car. also the hero is glad to get away, and no mention is made of her again.

It is important to note that in this adventure in Car. the hero does not in any way act as a deliverer. He has no fight to free the young lady from the persecutions of a hostile knight or giant. There is, indeed, nothing honorable for him in the whole encounter. He is only a befooled searcher after sensual pleasure. This could then

---

[1] Cf. Paris, *Hist. Litt.*, XXX, 186.
[2] Cf. the visit of Filisel de Montespin and the lady messenger to the castle of the *magicienne*. *Amadis de Gaule*, Antwerp ed., 1572, bk. xiii, chap. xvi.

hardly have been the form in the original. Every other adventure which the young hero undertakes is calculated to show his heroism and redound to his honor. This is the case, moreover, with this very adventure in LD, BI, and *Peredur*, and must surely have been so in Version A. It thus seems probable that the author of Car. reverted to some popular tale, such as were common in Italy, and changed his original to suit.

The specific enchantments which he underwent during the night need not be dwelt upon. In Car., as he is crossing the threshold, the lady roars loudly like the sea in a tempest. House and walls disappear, and soon he finds himself suspended by four giants on the end of a huge fork over a great river, where he remains until morning with his feet dangling just above the water.[1] In BI he is twice deceived. His first attempt to cross the threshold results in his imagining himself on a narrow plank over a tempestuous stream, whereas he is really hanging to the perch of the sparrow-hawk. Again he tries; and this time he fancies the ceiling to be falling upon him, but the servants, attracted by his cries, find him with his pillow over his head.

Similar enchantments seem to have been common enough in Italian stories. Examples may be found in the tricks which Filenia plays upon her suitors in *Il Mambriano* of Il Cieco da Ferrara, and many analogues have been collected by Rua and Prato.[2]

DISENCHANTMENT BY MEANS OF A KISS.

The idea of the *fier baiser* is one of the most widely spread in the domain of folk-lore, and in some places is in full force to the present day. It occupies such an important position in our stories that we must enter to some extent into an examination of the subject. For instances of disenchantment by this means see the following places:[3]

---

[1] Cf. Paris, *Rom.*, XV, 16.

[2] To these Professor Kittredge has kindly called my attention. See Rua, *Novelle del Mambriano esposte ed illustrate*, Turin, 1888, pp. 85 f.; and Prato, *Zt. für Volkskunde*, I, 112-3.

[3] The majority of these are collected by Professor Child (*Ballads*, Pt. II, 306-8; IV, 502 ff.; VI, 504). Others were communicated to Mennung (p. 20) by Reinhold Köhler.

(1) Ulrich von Zatzikhoven's *Lanzelet*, 7836 ff., translated from the French before 1194 and "sans doute sensiblement plus ancien."[1] (2) Legend of the daughter of Hippocrates in Maundeville.[2] (3) An account of the liberation of the daughter of Hippocrates by Espertius in *Tiran le Blanc*, written about 1400.[3] (4) *Historia del principe Sferamundi* in the 13th book of *Amadis of Gaul*.[4] (5) The English ballad of *Kemp Owyne*, preserved in a number of versions.[5] (6) *The Laidly Worm of Spindleston Heughs*.[6] (7) *Hjálmtèrs ok Ölvers Saga*, caps. 10, 22.[7] (8) The Danish ballad *Jomfruen i Ormeham*.[8] (9) Angelo de Tummulillis, *Notabilia Temporum*.[9] (10) Bojardo, *Orl. Innamorato*, ii, 26, 7 ff. (11) Mone, *Anzeiger f. Kunde des deutschen Mittelalters*, III, 89.[10] (12) Müllenhoff, *Sagen, Märchen u. Lieder der Herzogthümer Schleswig-Holstein u. Lauen-

---

[1] Paris, *Rom.*, XX, 301; cf. Golther, *Gesch. der deutschen Litt.*, II, 168-9, 225.

[2] Ed. Warner, Roxburghe Club, 1889, p. 12; pp. 23 ff. of Halliwell's ed., 1839. Clouston, *Orig. and Analogues of some of the Cant. Tales*, pp. 518 ff., tries to connect this with the *Wife of Bath's Tale*, and in this he is followed by Professor Skeat, *Works of Chaucer*, III, 449, but the *Wife's Tale* belongs to a different cycle. André Dacier gives a delicious bit of interpretation by way of explaining the legend of the daughter of Hippocrates as a medical allegory (*Vie d'Hippocrate*), prefixed to his translation of the *Œuvres d'Hipp.*, Paris, 1697, I, cvj ff. The legend is repeated in Faber's *Evagatorium*, ed. Hassler, III, 267. See also Sathas, *La Trad. hellénique et la Lég. de Phidias*, etc. [1882], pp. 13 ff.; Paris, *Hist. Litt.*, XXX, 191.

[3] Ed. Caylus, II, 334-9. Dunlop (ed. Wilson, I, 406) notes "a like story in the 6th tale of the *Contes Amoureux de Jean Flore*," written towards the end of the 15th century.

[4] Pt. II, c. 97, pp. 458-62, Venice, 1610. See Child, *Ballads*, Pt. II, 308-9.

[5] Child, Pt. II, 306 ff.; IV, 502 ff.; VI, 504; IX, 213.

[6] Child, Pt. II, 311-13. This, though the composition of a Mr. Lamb, is, in Professor Child's words, "not only based on popular tradition, but preserves some small fragments of a popular ballad." It is closely related to *Kemp Owyne*. Another version of *The Laidly Worm* is *The Hagg Worm* (Child, Pt. IV, 503 ff.).

[7] Rafn, *Fornaldar Sögur*, III, 473 ff., 514 ff. See Child, Pt. II, 307.

[8] Grundtvig, *D. G. F.*, No. 59, II, 177. For further references as to similar Danish stories, see Child, Pt. II, 307; VI, 504; VIII, 454.

[9] Ed. Corvisieri, Rome, 1890, pp. 124-6; see the review in *Giornale Storico*, XVII, 161 f. Angelo tells of the adventure as an historical fact occurring in Cesena in 1464. Professor Kittredge kindly called my attention to this version.

[10] Also in Desaivre, *Le Mythe de la Mère Lusine*, 1883, p. 202 (see review in *Mélusine*, II, 22). Cf. Schönhuth, *Die Burgen u. s. w. Badens u. der Pfalz*, I, 105.

burg, Kiel, 1845, No. 597, p. 580. (13) Panzer, *Bayerische Sagen u. Bräuche*, Munich, 1848, No. 214, I, 196. (14) Vernaleken, *Alpensagen*, Vienna, 1858, No. 100, p. 123. (15) Menghin, *Aus dem deutschen Südtirol*, Meran, 1884, p. 8. (16) Stöber, *Die Sagen des Elsasses*, St. Gallen, 1852, No. 190, p. 248. (17) Sommer, *Sagen, Märchen u. Gebräuche aus Sachsen u. Thüringen*, Halle, 1846, No. 16, p. 21, etc. (18) Curtze, *Volksüberlieferungen aus dem Fürstenthum Waldeck*, Arolsen, 1860, p. 198. (19) *Id.*, p. 201. (20) *Walliser Sagen* gesammelt u. erzählt v. Sagenfreunden, Sitten, 1872, p. 150. (21) Grimms, *Deutsche Sagen*, Berlin, 1816, No. 222, I, 304;[1] cf. p. 17. (22) Lenggenhager, *Volkssagen aus dem Kanton Baselland*, Basel, 1874, p. 91.[2] (23) Kreutzwald, *Ehstnische Märchen*, tr. by F. Löwe, Halle, 1869, No. 19, pp. 268 ff. (24) Wucke, *Sagen der mittleren Werra*, Salzungen, 1864, I, 1.[3] (25) J. W. Wolf, *Hessische Sagen*, Leipzig, 1853, No. 46, p. 33. (26) H. von Pfister, *Sagen u. Aberglaube aus Hessen u. Nassau*, Marburg, 1885, p. 75. (27) *Sagen vom Thurmberg bei Durlach*, Mone's *Anzeiger*, VII (1838), 476. (28) Schönhuth, *Die Burgen u. s. w. Badens u. der Pfalz*, I, 107. (29) *Traditions et Légendes de la Suisse Romande*, Lausanne, 1872, pp. 103–5. (30) Decurtins, *Märchen aus dem Bündner Oberlande*, in Jecklin, *Volksthümliches aus Graubünden*, Zürich, 1874, p. 126. (31) A Breton tale in *Rev. des Trad. Populaires*, III, 475. (32) Another, contributed by Luzel to the *Annuaire des Trad. Pop.*, II, 53 ff. (33) Kuhn, *Westfälische Sagen*, Leipzig, 1859, No. 276, p. 242.[4] (34) Schambach u. Müller, *Niedersächsische Sagen*, Göttingen, 1855, No. 132 (cf. Nos. 124–31).

A comparison of all these tales with one another and with Car., LD, and BI, yields the following results :

1. *The Person transformed*, when her station is mentioned, is always of noble birth and beautiful. It is often said that she is the

---

[1] Also in Stöber, *Sagen des Elsasses*, p. 346.

[2] Also in Dobeneck, *Des deutschen Mittelalters Volksglauben*, Berlin, 1815, I, 18; and in Grimms, *D. S.*, No. 13, who get it from Praetorius, *Weltbeschreibung*, 1666, I, 661 ff. Praetorius dates it 1520 and insists upon its truth.

[3] Cf. Witzschel, *Sagen, Sitten u. Gebräuche aus Thüringen*, ed. Schmidt, Pt. II, Vienna, 1878, No. 71.

[4] Cf. Nos. 12, 379, 383, 392, in the same collection (with the references given by Kuhn).

daughter of a king, and frequently the only heir. She always has great treasures in her possession. We find the story definitely attached in some cases to the daughter of Hippocrates (2, 3, 4), but even then the reward of success in loosing the spell, is joint rule with the maiden of the isle she inhabits. — This accords well with the account in Car., LD, and BI, in which we have the woman in serpent form, the daughter of a king, the heir of his lands, of exceeding beauty.

2. *The Cause of the Transformation* is usually not told. In some cases it is a retribution for sin. In 21, it is because of the young lady's former pride. In 16, it is because of her vanity and avarice when alive, for here, as in 29, the punishment is one inflicted after death. In some (e.g., 20) the curse seems to have been given by her father, that she might guard certain treasures. In others it is pure malice. A stepmother is envious of her stepdaughter's beauty in the English ballads (5, 6). Diana is angry with the daughter of Hippocrates (2). In 32 we have a definite magician who has carried the princess off from the kingdom of her father and kept her transformed with him. — In Car., LD, and BI, the princess is thus kept transformed by a magician, and here because she has refused to accede to his wishes. There is no case of two magicians or two persons causing the spell except in LD and BI, and there this number is probably due to a misunderstanding on the part of the author of their original (see pp. 126, 164).

3. *The Animal* into which the woman is transformed is always of some hideous or fierce sort. If there is but one form, it is oftenest a serpent. The other single forms are toad, dragon, bear, black wolf, etc. In the early forms, the maiden usually takes but one shape; but in the later usually three, a kiss (or three kisses) being required to be given in each form. In 12, we have frog, wolf, snake; in 13, maiden, snake, toad; in 20, toad, snake, lion; in 21, snake, toad, maid; in 24, snake, beast of prey, dragon; in 25, snake, bear; in 26, frog, snake, dragon; in 32, serpent, salamander, toad; in 33, maiden, bear, ox. In some cases (as in 31, the toad) the same animal grows bigger and bigger until the third kiss is given. In 11, we have first a woman without fingers and with a dragon's tail, then the same with bat's wings, finally with toad's head as well. In 30, it works the other way: on the first kiss the head is made natural, and

on the second, the body; the third completes the retransformation. Usually, however, the third form is the hardest and the one before which the rescuer quails, although he has been brave up to that time. In 13, the final test is made more severe by representing the devil as constantly snapping with shears at the cord from which is suspended a millstone over the head of the toad which is to be kissed.

In Car., LD, and BI, there is but one animal, a serpent (a *guivre* in BI). In LD and BI, it is said to be wondrously glittering, shedding light in the place. This feature is also in 29. In BI it spews fire from its mouth, as in 13, 24, 27. In LD, it has a woman's face, and in BI a beautiful mouth. This reminds us of the Mélusine stories, which are much mixed up with those we are discussing (see 11, 22). In them, the upper part of the body of the princess is beautiful, the lower part of serpent form. Almost invariably the princess, even when transformed, is able to talk as a human being, and converses with the hero. In our poems this feature occurs only in Car. In LD and BI, she says nothing while in serpent form. Often she can take human form, part of the time, by day, or on certain days, or at certain hours (28, 29, 30, etc.). Not so in Car., LD, or BI; but compare the father in Wig. Usually in the tales she urges her rescuer to be brave (this only in Car.).

She is frequently a "white maiden" (13, 18, 19, 23, 25, 26, 27). In *Orl. Inn.* (10) she is dressed in white when released from the spell. In Car. also all the women are transformed into "bestie *bianche* cosi belle" (ii, 45, 7). In several cases she is provided with a bunch of keys (12, 13, 18, 19, 27). This seems to have connection with the fact that in these forms (as in most) she controls a hidden treasure. In 15 she has a single golden key which she would lay on her rescuer's tongue, and which would open the door to her treasure. In 16 one of the conditions is that he take the golden key from her tongue. In 25 this last feature also appears. It is possible that we have here the reason for the words in the English ballad (6):

> She has knotted the keys upon a string,
> And with her she has them taen. (St. 2.)

Rarely do these hideous creatures seem to be in any way harmful. In 6, however, the venomous serpent is the plague of the country and has to be fed with vast quantities of food, and it is said of *Weisse*

Frauen that, although when let alone they are quite harmless, when angered by remarks of passers-by they often draw very close to the latter, breathe upon them, and cause them sickness or death.

4. *The Place of Abode*, when mentioned definitely, is generally a cave (e.g., 2, 6, 10) or underground dwelling (22). In many cases it is at or hard by a ruined castle (11, 14, 16, 18, 25). Sometimes the enchanted women are met in a forest (9, 11, 12). — In Car., LD, and BI the serpent dwells in an enchanted city. In Car. the inhabitants also are transformed into different kinds of animals, and the city is in ruins. In BI we are told that the magicians came one day, enchanted the five thousand inhabitants, and destroyed the city by their terrible enchantments. In Car. the dwarf points out to the hero the ruins and tells how a noble castle has been reduced to this form "perllo incantesmo." He directs his attention also to the transformed inhabitants who he says "mostreranti tutte i' lor dolore," and who appear to see the hero gladly. In LD the serpent comes out of a window in a stone wall, in BI out of an *aumaire*. These seem vestiges of the cave idea. In Car. there is no hint of this. As in many other stories, she seems free to wander about the castle.

5. *The Rescuer* in all the early forms has to be a knight or king's son. In Maundeville, indeed, it is told how a man is sent back to his ship to be made a knight so that he can make the attempt. In the later forms, however, the situation is completely changed. The rescuer is invariably of lowly station, induced to undertake the disgusting and perilous task by the desire of gaining treasure, not of gaining honor. He is, for example, a bailiff's son (11), schoolmaster (12), keeper of a vineyard (15), glazier (16), herdsman (17), shepherd (18, 24), tailor's son and simpleton (22), peasant (25), villager (29), orphan beggar (31), servant (32), — in one case even the daughter of a herdsman (28), in another, a servant-girl (34).

In many cases the rescuer has to be specially destined for the task, most frequently one who has been rocked in a cradle made out of a certain tree[1] (24, 25, 27, 28, 33; cf. 30). In the English ballads none but Owein, a definite knight, can do the deed. This shows us how essential is the feature emphasized in LD (2131 ff., cf. 1736)

---

[1] On this requirement cf. further Kuhn, *Westfälische Sagen*, p. 243, No. 276, and note; Wolf, *Hessische Sagen*, No. 49, etc.

that only Gawein or one of his kin can succeed. In BI the knight has only to be one of the best at Arthur's court: nothing special in Car. as to this. Other requirements in the stories are that he should be of a definite age, twenty (in 31), eighteen (in 28). More important, however, is the fact that in several cases it is essential that he be pure in body and never have sinned with woman.[1] This fits admirably with the hero in Car., LD, and BI. Indeed, it may have been one element in causing the combination of the *fier baiser* with the Perc. story. Our hero is brought up alone in the woods, entirely ignorant of the existence of other human beings except his mother. The innocent youth goes to court, but starts off immediately from there. On his way, in Car. and BI, he nearly gives way to the temptations of the enchantress; but her sorcery preserves his purity for the nonce. If this suggestion be sound, a new significance is added to these enchantments. The author of LD does not seem to have understood this feature, for, in his vague, general remarks, he laments the fact that LD was not "chast,"[2] although nothing definite is told of the youth's amour.

6. *Conditions of Change.* In the early forms and some of the later (1–4, 7–9, 16, 17, 29), only one kiss seems to have been necessary, as in Car., LD, and BI. Very often, however, three is the required number (5, 11–14, 20–27, 30–32), usually given on three separate days. In 11, we have three kisses on each of three successive occasions (cf. 32). Frequently they must be given on certain days or at certain times of the day: in 11, at nine in the morning; in 12, between twelve and one at night; in 26, 27, between eleven and twelve in the morning; in 15, precisely at midnight; in 25, at noon; in 21, on three consecutive Friday mornings; in 24, on three *Johannistage*. In 20 the princess appears only every tenth year on Easter morning; in 23, once in twenty-five years; in 18, once in a hundred years. The kiss is almost invariably on the mouth (not

---

[1] Cf. J. W. Wolf, *Beitr. zur deutschen Mythologie*, II, 245.

[2] Could it be that the "traie and tene" which the English author makes LD suffer because of his lack of chastity indicates some penance the hero had to undergo for this sin before he could free the enchanted princess? We may note that in some forms of the story, when the rescuer departs from the conditions imposed, he is finally able to redeem himself, but only after undergoing great hardship (cf. 30, 31).

so in 4, 11, 24). In most cases the freeing of the maiden by kissing is entirely at the will of the rescuer. If he refrains from giving the kiss, — if, indeed, in some cases he even shudders or shows his repugnance, — the opportunity is lost. If there are three kisses, all three have to be given. Two are of no avail, and often bring down evil on the head of the rescuer and the serpent as well. In 29, the serpent lifts its head up even with the man's mouth, and waits for the kiss; but he lacks courage, and the maiden is not retransformed.

Car. agrees with the great majority in requiring the kiss to be given by the rescuer, while LD and BI differ. In LD, the serpent comes towards him and he is kissed " er he it wiste." In BI, as it approaches, it fascinates him by its look, then it darts to him and kisses him. In both he is thus an involuntary instrument in the matter. There is support for the giving of the kiss by the dragon in LD and BI, in the story of Espertius, and that told by Kreutzwald (23), which, by the way, preserves many features agreeing with our group of poems. The kissing by the hero certainly puts the latter's bravery in a much clearer light, and is in itself more natural, besides being the account given in the great majority of the stories. It would thus appear that in this point Car. represents a more primitive form of the story than LD and BI. In LD we have here also a feature which appears to have been original: viz., the snake's coiling about the hero's neck (2112). This is found in the story just referred to (23) and in 13 and 15.

Car. and BI agree in making the hero draw his sword to defend himself. This occurs in two old versions, 6 and 10, which see. In both of these, moreover, he is told to put it up: the serpent will do him no harm. In Car. and BI, the animal shows this by its humble bows. In 15, the man uses his sword and the maiden is not freed. There is no case in which the rescuer does not dread the approach of the hideous beast. In Car. and *Orl. Inn.* he, moreover, expresses his fear.

7. *The Breaking of the Spell*, which brings about the lady's return to human form, is in most cases immediate (1–5, 8–10, 31, 32, etc.). Car. and LD agree in this primitive feature. In BI, however, she first withdraws as a serpent to her *aumaire*. The English ballad (5) has both forms, immediate and delayed change (cf. also 7). In 23, again, we have the rescuer, as in BI, going to sleep, and awaking to

find a beautiful lady beside him. In LD, much is made of the fact that after the change she is entirely naked; this feature is the same in 6. In *Lanzelet*, she has first to bathe in a stream, and then the change at once takes place (cf. 20, 21). This feature is well founded in popular belief.[1] In Car. there is a great tumult when the spell is broken; this is an additional feature in which 23 agrees.

We may note here that lack of courage in the would-be rescuer is sometimes followed by evil effects. In 2, the two sailors who fail meet their death. In 10, if Brandimarte had not put back his sword, he would have died. In 20, the men are cursed to the ninth generation. In 24, the unsuccessful man soon dies, and in 29 he soon disappears after his failure. In 11, he is poisoned when he undertakes to wed. With these may be compared the words of the princess in Car., who, when freed, tells the hero, "Tu sarai l'amor mio fino" (ii, 65, 8). Indeed, it seems as if in some cases the undertaking of the task were a pledge to marry the maiden when she is transformed. The breaking of promises to preternatural beings often meets with dire results.[2] After one unsuccessful attempt, the entrance to the cave or castle becomes invisible in 6 (note), 22, 26.

8. *The Result*, when the spell is broken, is that the rescuer is generally offered the hand and treasures of the princess, who expresses her gratitude to him. When her father is a king, the young man later becomes the ruler of her land, and they have descendants (cf. 30, 31). In 1, Lanzelet takes the king's daughter to Arthur's court. — Car., LD, and BI agree in making the princess express her gratitude to her deliverer and offer him her hand and kingdom. They both go to Arthur's court, marry, and rule over the wife's land.

In Car. the people resume their natural shapes and the city is restored. This reminds us of the story told by Toeppen[3] of a handsome prince transformed into a hideous animal and immediately changed back when voluntarily kissed by a beautiful maiden, "und

---

[1] Child, *Ballads*, Pt. II, 338 (*Tam Lin*), where other references are noted (cf. IV, 505; VI, 505).

[2] Cf. Child, *Ballads*, Pt. II, 372.

[3] *Aberglauben aus Masuren*, Danzig, 1867, pp. 144–5. Professor Child cites this feature from other forms of *Beauty and the Beast;* Mikuličić, *Narodne Pripovietke*, p. 1, No. 1; Afanasief, VII, 153, No. 15; Coelho, *Contos populares portuguezes*, p. 69, No. 29.

im Schlosse lebte Alles wieder auf, was bis dahin sich nicht geregt hatte, die Eltern und Geschwister des Prinzen und alles Gesinde. Der Prinz umarmte das Mädchen und erzählte ihr, dass er verwünscht gewesen sei, und nur ein Kuss eines reinen unschuldigen Mädchens bei einer abschreckenden Gestalt hätte ihn erlösen können." They are, of course, married and live happily.

WIGALOIS.

The relation of *Wigalois* to the poems which we have already examined is not easy to determine. The first one to discuss at any length the relation of the German poem to its original was Meisner.[1] In his opinion, Wirnt had before him "eine französische schriftliche aufzeichnung des Wigalois" (p. 23), which he had translated aloud to him by a squire, inasmuch as he himself was not familiar with French. Kölbing[2] agreed entirely with Meisner in this view. He, however, made a much more thorough examination of the question, and concluded that as LD, BI, and Wig. were unlike in so many points, Wig. at one time agreeing with LD, at another with BI, and as both Wirnt and the author of LD appeared to follow their sources with little change, there must therefore have been *three French poems* dealing with the same subject, all of which were, however, based directly or indirectly on one common primitive form.

Mebes[3] was the next to take up the question. Unfortunately he does not appear to have seen Kölbing's important article, and did not let LD influence his judgment in the matter. Indeed, he dismisses the English poem from his consideration with these words (p. 4) : "Eine eingehende Vergleichung dieser Redaction mit dem

---

[1] *Wirnt von Gravenberg, Beitr. zur Beurtheilung seiner literarhistorischen Bedeutung*, Breslau, 1874, pp. 19-25.

[2] *Engl. Studien*, I, 166 ff. See for other matters, the dissertations of Pudmenzky, *Ueber Wirnts Ausdrucksweise*, Halle, 1875; Eckert, *Wirnt v. Grav. u. sein Sprachgebrauch*, Stettin, 1875; Medem, *Ueber das Abhängigkeitsverhältniss Wirnt's von Grav. von Hartmann von Aue und Wolfram v. Eschenbach*, Danzig, 1880; etc.

[3] *Ueber den Wigalois von Wirnt von Gravenberg und seine altfranz. Quelle*, Neumünster, 1879; cf. Kölbing, *Engl. Studien*, IV, 182; Foth, *Litbl. f. germ. u. rom. Phil.*, 1880, col. 114.

Bel Inconnu von Renaud de Beaujeu zeigt unzweideutig, dass sie nach Renaud de Beaujeu gearbeitet ist, jedoch nach einer andern als der von Hippeau veröffentlichten Handschrift." He sums up the results of his investigation in the following statement (p. 20) : "Der Wigalois von Wirnt von Gravenberg ist nach dem Bel Inconnu von Renaud de Beaujeu gedichtet. Wirnt hat für den einen Theil seiner Dichtung ein Bruchstück einer Handschrift des Bel Inconnu besessen, während er den andern Theil seiner Dichtung nach der mündlichen Erzählung eines Knappen, der sich des Inhaltes des Bel Inconnu nur dunkel erinnert verfasst hat."

In recent years scholars who have dealt with this subject have usually accepted Mebes's view. Paris,[1] Mennung,[2] and Kaluza[3] all agree that, for the part of Wig. which clearly belongs to the Desc. cycle, Wirnt had a fragment of a manuscript of Renaud's poem before him, and that for the rest of his narrative he relied on the story of the squire.

It is necessary to observe, in the first place, that, despite the confident statements of Mebes, Bethge, Kaluza, and others to the contrary, there can be now no doubt that LD is not based on BI. It is important for our argument to have this point settled in advance.

In exact terms Mebes's theory is that for vv. 1518-3285 (43, 14-87, 21) of Wig. Wirnt had a fragmentary manuscript of BI (containing BI, 1-315, 2471-2726, 687-1850) before him, but that for vv. 3286-11708 (*end*) he depended on the oral narrative of a squire. (The introduction in Wig., i.e., vv. 1-1517, Mebes leaves out of account.)[4] Wirnt resorted to the squire, Mebes thinks, to supply the lacunæ of the manuscript, and the squire (to whom the imperfect manuscript had probably belonged, and who had himself merely

---

[1] *Rom.*, XV, 21, note 4; cf. *Rom.*, XX, 300. Paris speaks elsewhere (*La Litt. franç. au Moyen Age*, 2d ed., 1890, § 58) of Wig. as an "imitation allemande" of Renaud's poem.
[2] Der Bel Inconnu, pp. 58 ff.
[3] In *Litbl. f. germ. u. rom. Phil.*, 1891, coll. 84 ff.
[4] According to the concluding paragraph of his essay (p. 20), though in another place (p. 4) he mentions vv. 1-1517 as a part of the poem that seems to have been composed, like vv. 3286-11708, "nach der mundlichen Erzählung des Knappen."

heard the rest of the story of BI by word of mouth) remembered astonishingly little of what Wirnt desired to know. Mebes is not always quite clear, but he seems to suppose that this supplementary narrative of the squire's was not very long or very full, and consequently to ascribe the abundance of details (foreign to all other versions of the story) which vv. 3286-11708 (by far the larger part of Wig.) contain, to Wirnt's own attempt to fill up holes in the squire's tale.

The portion of Wig. which, according to Mebes, was derived from the fragmentary manuscript of BI, contains the following adventures: At the Court (II; p. 6, above);[1] Adventure at the Ford (III; p. 12, above); Adventure with the Giants (V; p. 18, above); Dispute about the Dog (VII; p. 32, above); Sparrow-hawk Adventure (VI; p. 25, above). The supplementary oral narrative then furnished what remnants Wig. 102,21-106,30 shows of the Adventure with Lampart (IX; p. 42, above)[2] and what is left of the Rescue of the Enchanted Lady (X; p. 47, above). The squire, however, remembered "nur in den allgemeinsten Zügen" what he had heard. He knew nothing of either the first or the second visit to the Ile d'Or,[3] and hence Wig. has no mention of the *fée*. Similarly it is to the squire's confused and defective memory that we must ascribe the complete omission of the most striking feature of the whole story, the *fier baiser*, as well as a number of other extraordinary variations in the catastrophe.

In Wig.: (1) The princess has herself suffered no bodily injury from the magician.[4] It is her father who has been transformed into

---

[1] Mebes would have done better to designate v. 1564 (44, 20) or perhaps 1554 (44, 10) as the beginning of the part of Wig. derived from his hypothetical manuscript; but the difference of these few lines does not affect the argument.

[2] Mebes does not expressly mention this passage, but it falls within that part of Wig. which he refers to the squire's story, and Mennung (p. 61) lays great stress on it. See a full discussion of the latter's argument, below, p. 229.

[3] His ignorance appears to be ascribed by Mebes partly to his possessing a (hypothetical) manuscript which belonged to a different class from that of which the Duc d'Aumale's is a member, partly to his own forgetfulness (pp. 13, 15); but this is a detail of no importance in the argument.

[4] Hence there is no *fier baiser*. Wig. has to slay the great serpent *Pfetán*, and this adventure, which is one of the two things necessary to the relief of the princess's country and the securing of her hand, is thought to be a dim reminis-

an animal. He seems, however, to have had the power at certain times of changing back to man's shape. Moreover, even as an animal, he is able to show by his actions that he is friendly to Wig. (Cf. Car.)[1] (2) Larîe has been removed with her mother to the city *Roimunt* (= *Künigsbcrc*). Wig. comes there, is welcomed, falls desperately in love with the princess, and is promised her hand if he is successful in overcoming *Rôaz von Glois*, the enchanter. (3) Rôaz comes out of a door, preceded by a magic cloud invisible to Wig. but visible to those with the enchanter. He wishes to overcome Wig. by cunning; but the knight's cross prevents the cloud from coming nearer. (Cf. *Peredur*.)[2] (4) Strangely enough, Rôaz has a loved one, Japhîte,

---

cence of the enchanted princess. It is to be observed, however, that *Pfetân* is not a result of the magician's arts. In fact, he is the magician's enemy and wastes his country (123, 26-31). There is great confusion here.

[1] Larîe's father is said to have been treacherously killed at his castle of Korntîn by the magician, who, as the occupant of a fief in the neighborhood, seems to have been his vassal (97, 10 ff.; 204, 21). The dead king's soul (125, 31) in the form of a beast with a leopard's head appears daily before the castle of Roimunt and takes the road to Korntîn (101, 27 ff.). Wig. follows the beast, whose bearing is friendly, to the castle of Korntîn (117, 16 ff.). Before the castle is a kind of park (on a rock), on reaching which the beast becomes a beautiful man (121, 4). The man explains, in effect, that he is doing purgatorial penance and that he is released therefrom for a certain time each day, this park being the place of his respite. He tells Wig. of the serpent and of Rôaz, and informs him that every night he, and the knights slain with him in the traitorous onslaught of Rôaz, suffer torment in Korntîn castle, which he and the knights (whom Wig. has seen jousting with heated weapons before the castle) enter at the end of his conversation with Wig. Korntîn castle and its environs, it is plain, have become a demesne of Purgatory (125, 31 ff.). This accounts for the fact, which Wig. has learned at Roimunt, that Korntîn appears to be on fire every night, but that in the morning it always stands uninjured as before (112, 33 ff.). This burning castle is thought by Mebes to be a reminiscence of the squire's of the brilliantly lighted hall of the *gaste cité* in Bl. It is to be observed that Wig.'s fight with the dragon takes place in the Korntîn territory, but not in or near the castle, and that his combat with the enchanter Rôaz takes place at the castle of Glois, the home of Rôaz, which is at some distance from Korntîn castle (161, 26 ff.).

[2] All this takes place at the castle of Glois (see preceding note). The cloud contains the devil to whom Rôaz has sold himself (188, 13 ff.). Before he enters Glois castle, Wig. has to overcome a dwarfish knight who guards the road (169-174), a monster, Marrîên, half man and half horse (178, 27 ff.), and two old knights. Of the latter, one is killed and the other, Count Adân, is wounded and

thoughts of whom inspire him in the fight with Wig. When he is killed, her distress is indescribable. She finally dies of grief beside him. (5) There are no dwellers in Glois but women,[1] for Rôaz is jealous lest any one come between him and his wife. These five features are enough to show that the whole conclusion of the story has been altered. (6) There is a general conversion to Christianity after Wig.'s victory.[2] (7) News comes to him while he is on his way to the court that his mother is dead. Gawein[3] laments her loss. She sends her son a ring as her last gift in witness of her love. (8) When they reach the court, Arthur takes Gawein and his son into the hall and honors them. (9) After the festivity, when Wig. and Larîe depart, Gawein rides back part of the way with them, and there is an affecting parting. (10) Larîe bears Wig. a son, whose name becomes widely known as *Lifort Gawanides*.

All or most of these changes Mebes would ascribe to the error of the squire's memory. He thinks, however, that the account as just summarized (in text and foot-notes) betrays sufficient resemblance to that in BI to show that the squire's narrative was based on that poem, if one further passage, which he regards as particularly important, be considered. This is as follows:

In BI the voice of the Fairy of the Ile d'Or (see 4903-10), who is invisible, tells the hero after his fight with the giant that he was baptized by the name of Giglain, and that he was wrongly called by Arthur, Li Biaus Desconeus; that Gauvain was his father, and the Fée

---

promises fealty to Wig. (185, 8). As to the lights in the hall at Senaudon, the twelve candles borne by the maidens at Glois (187, 32-35) furnish a better comparison than the nightly burning of Korntîn castle.

[1] With the exception of those mentioned in the preceding note.

[2] This conversion takes place at Korntîn castle (242-243), where the marriage is celebrated. Korntîn has suddenly ceased to be a place of purgatory. Larîe's father has informed Wig. that his own term of penance was on the point of expiring (125, 31-37), and we must suppose that the castle has resumed its former appearance (222, 13-18; 226, 7-18; 231, 30 ff.).

[3] Gawein has unexpectedly appeared at Korntîn castle while the wedding party is there (244, 18 ff.). Mebes remarks that, after the enchanter is overcome, Larîe declares to her assembled vassals, "ganz wie bei Renaud," that she "Wigalois, der im Gegensatz zu der Darstellung Beaujeu's sofort einwilligt, heiraten wolle" (see 240, 7 ff.). It must be remembered that there is nothing about the *fée* in Wig. from beginning to end.

Studies on the Libeaus Desconus. 213

à Blanchemal his mother; that the latter had given him armor and a sword, and sent him to Arthur, who had entrusted to him the task of helping the maiden (3205-15). This Wirnt narrates "in fast gleicher Weise" (according to Mebes), thus: Wig. after his fight with the dragon [in no way connected with the enchanter] lies stunned on the ground for a long time. When he later recovers consciousness he finds himself naked (for his clothing has been stripped from him by a man and woman who have robbed and well-nigh killed him), and cannot make out where he is. He tries to remember and says: "If I remember correctly, my mother was Queen Flôrîe of Syria; my uncle was called Jôram, who was strong and wise and won the victory over all the knights at Karidôl; my father was Gâwein, and was one of the best knights in the world; Larîe was the name of 'diu frouwe mîn,'" etc. (150, 30-151, 6). This agreement Mebes cites as "characteristisc hund von nicht zu unterschätzender Bedeutung." But the merest glance shows that the two passages have little in common. All the circumstances are entirely different. Wig. learns nothing whatever of his parentage that he did not know before. Indeed, there is no question of his gaining information; he is merely recalling, while in a semi-conscious state, his own earlier experiences.[1] But BI, in the passage cited, is having his parentage, of which he is ignorant, revealed to him by a magic voice. Mebes might have found a far better parallel in the account which the father of Larîe, changed for the nonce from his animal form, gives Wig. of the latter's birth.

With regard to the numerous adventures[2] which the last part of Wig. (that is, the part that follows the sparrow-hawk [parrot] adventure) contains, — altogether many thousand lines affording material quite foreign to our cycle, — Mebes supposes that they were inserted by Wirnt to make up for what seemed to him lacunæ in the squire's story.

Obviously Mebes's opinion that what he regards as the squire's

---

[1] Wirnt is here imitating Hartmann's *Iwein*, 3505 ff.; see Bethge, p. 59.

[2] Such are: the fight with the rival suitor (87, 33 ff.); the part played by the lord and lady of Joriphas (127, 5 ff.); the stripping of Wig. by the poor man and his wife (138, 10 ff.); the fight with the wild woman Rûel (162, 20 ff.); some of the features in the fight at Glois; the campaign of Wig. against Liôn (250, 15 ff.), which occupies about 1500 lines. Mebes does not specify these adventures: indeed, his language on this whole matter is very vague.

narrative was derived from BI, depends for its acceptance on the acceptance of his theory that in the previous part of the story (i.e., Wig. 43, 14-87, 21) Wirnt was drawing from BI. For Mebes expresses in the most emphatic terms his sense of the dissimilarity of Wig. to BI in that part of the former which he supposes was founded on the oral narrative. We must then consider whether there is any proof that Wirnt knew a fragmentary manuscript of BI, and, in the next place, whether Wirnt's poem was based on BI at all.

Mebes quotes four passages of some length from Wig., with the corresponding passages in BI, as fair specimens of those correspondences between the two poems that have convinced him that Wirnt had a manuscript of BI. Of these four parallels we need consider but one, — that which Mennung (pp. 58, 59), who accepts Mebes's view, has selected as in itself convincing. This is Wig., 53, 24-54, 12 : BI, 2487-2514. After a long comparison (the very elaboration of which suggests that the resemblance is not quite exact), Mennung concludes that no one will doubt that the one is, in Mebes's words, only a "ziemlich getreue Uebersetzung" of the other. Surely, however, there is ample room for doubt. The point under discussion, I repeat, is not : Did Wirnt have a French or any version of the Desc. story as his original? but, Did he have before him a manuscript of the particular poem BI? When this is remembered, it is impossible to call the passage in Wig. a "pretty close translation," or, indeed, a translation at all. When a Middle High German poet translates, he does so unmistakably ; indeed, his words can even be used for the textual criticism of his original. In the present instance there is no real verbal agreement between the two passages : the German throws no light whatever on the readings of the French text. Imagine a textual critic using Wig. 1930 ("ichn weiz ab wie sîn name sî") to determine the text of BI, 2501 ("Et Lampars a à non li sire").

But Mennung makes another remark on these passages : "Hierbei," he says (pp. 59-60), "ist ein besonderer Nachdruck darauf zu legen, dass die Uebereinstimmung sowohl eine qualitative *als auch vor allem eine quantitative ist, denn die 28 frz. Verse entsprechen den 29 mhd. genau.*" The fact that one poem takes twenty-nine lines to describe what in another, dealing with the same event, occupies twenty-eight, surely proves nothing unless there is a line-for-line agreement, as is not the case in the present instance. But the force of Mennung's remark disappears altogether when we observe that the "quantitative agreement" is not true of the messenger's speech as a whole, for in BI Hélie goes on with fifteen and a half lines more in which she adds important information. The only fair basis for a quantitative comparison would be the whole of the messenger's speech in each case. The additional lines are too significant to have been omitted by a close translator or by any translator. Hélie explains that, if a knight is defeated, the citizens all gather and throw at his face

>   torces enboées
>   Qui sont de la boe loées,
>   Et puis pleins de cendre et d'ordure (2517 ff.);

while the result in Wig. is merely:

>   so muoz er danne blôzer wider
>   scheiden gar ân sîne habe. (54, 8-9.)

As to the three other parallels adduced by Mebes, they are not near enough to give ground for the opinion that Wirnt used any part of a manuscript of the BI of Renaud. Of course there is some resemblance in each case, for both poets are telling the same story; but this very fact makes the resemblances even less significant. A slight resemblance was inevitable. The agreements must, in a case like this, be very decided to establish the borrowing of one specific version of a story from another.

The parallels adduced by Mebes and Mennung are thus shown to be quite insufficient to support their view that Wirnt had a manuscript of BI before him.[1] Indeed, they might well be held to prove the opposite view. It seems clear that in the part of Wig. which resembles the Desc. poems Wirnt was not following a manuscript of any of the extant poems of our cycle.

But what relation does the general form of the story as told in Wig. bear to these other Desc. poems? Meisner and Kölbing thought that Wirnt had before him a French working-over of a primitive poem, which he followed throughout. This view is, however, entirely untenable, as will appear later. Nearly all other investigators of this subject, for example, Mebes, Mennung, Paris, Kaluza,

---

[1] Cf. Bethge, *Wirnt von Gravenberg*, pp. 24 ff.

and Bethge, have been confident that Renaud's poem was the one to which Wig. went back more or less directly. It is essential, then, that we should examine this opinion.

It is not going too far to say that, if Wirnt followed Renaud, he must surely have shown traces of the latter's marked peculiarities and have agreed with him in some points in which Renaud varied from his original. If he has done this, the question is at once settled in favor of Bl as the source of Wig.; if not, this theory has no prop. We remember that the incidents due to the relations between Bl and the enchantress occupy by all odds the leading place in Renaud's poem. They must have been unquestionably the parts most easily remembered,[1] and yet they are not even hinted at in *Wigalois*. Further, the other important change which we know Renaud to have made, is the introduction of the squire Robert, who is ever at hand, always doing or saying something; but he is not mentioned in Wig. If Wirnt had him in his original,[2] he has with great care cut him out of the story, so that he has been able to make it more primitive and simpler, more like LD and Car.

But, if we examine the poems more closely, we find that Wig. agrees with Bl, as opposed to LD in the following points:

(1) The dwarf at court does not object to the sending of Wig. His singing a song will not, it is to be hoped, be urged as an objection. (2) The messenger and dwarf ride away without Wig., who follows later and asks to be allowed to accompany them. In LD all three leave the court together. (3) It is said that on the evening of the fight with the giants the nightingales were singing and the moon was shining. (4) Wig. inquires of his companion if she hears the cries of the maiden in distress. LD says nothing to Elene at this time.

---

[1] Even as late as 1777 the Comte de Tressan picked them out for narration. Bethge also argues that it is inconceivable that Wirnt or his squire could have forgotten these parts of the story. He explains their omission as due to moral scruples on Wirnt's part. "Wirnt," he says, "ist ein äusserst sittenstrenger mann, er vermeidet alles was auch der grösten prüderie irgend anstössig sein könte," etc. Golther, *Gesch. der deutschen Litt.*, I, 226, adopts this somewhat amusing explanation.

[2] I say Wirnt's original, for it matters little here whether we believe he had a manuscript before him or was following the tale of a squire. If the latter, then I mean the form of the story which the squire learned.

(5) The dwarf stands up for Wig. against the messenger's chiding. (6) The little dog is said to be mostly white. (7) The sparrowhawk adventure is preceded by the meeting of the hero with a beautiful young maiden, "evidently of king's kin," riding along alone. She is in great sorrow because she had been deprived of the prize of beauty, which was justly hers. There is no such character in LD. (8) The hall of the enchanter becomes suddenly dark, and Wig. cannot see his hand before him. (9) After the fight Wig., exhausted, goes to sleep, and, when he awakes, the daylight has come. (10) He has his wounds washed and bound up. (11) The place is purified from enchantment.

On the other hand, Wig. agrees with LD as opposed to BI in the following points besides those already mentioned :

1. It has an account of the youth of the hero and gives good reasons for his coming to Arthur's court. In BI he appears there suddenly, and we know nothing of his early life nor of what has attracted him thither.

2. He is courteous in his demeanor and shows due respect to the king. In BI he rides into the hall and remains obstinately on horseback before the king until he is granted an unreasonable request.

3. We all know him from the first to be the son of Gawein. In BI this is first revealed after he has gone through many adventures.

4. The king asks him his name at once and the stranger gives him the name by which he is known. In BI it is not until they are seated at the feast that the king thinks it well to find out. He then sends Beduier to inquire quietly, and the speeches of Arthur to Beduier, Beduier to BI, BI to Beduier, and Beduier to Arthur are all given.

5. The stranger wishes to be made a knight.

6. He is given over to Gawein for instruction in knightly ways.

7. The feast is prepared for the young knight. In BI they are at table when he comes.

8. He is given a sword, shield, and spear, together with rich apparel. BI comes armed, and nothing of the kind is bestowed on him.

9. The messenger rides a white horse (cf. *Lai de Tyolet*).

10. The dwarf is gifted in music.[1]

---

[1] Cf. also the description of the dwarf who accompanies the maiden in *Durmart*, 1786: "A grosse vois venoit chantant." Cf. also *Perc.*, 18785 ff.

11. There is no specific mention of what the hero must do. In BI it is said he will have to perform the "fier baiser."

12. The hero offers his services immediately without giving the others a chance. In BI, Arthur looks about waiting for some one to present himself.

13. In the fight with the giants, when the hero is aroused he starts off at once and alone to the fight. In BI he has to wait until he has overruled all Hélie's objections and crossed himself, and until the whole company is got in motion. Then follows Robert, who acts as guide. When they see the maiden, BI has a parley with Hélie, who tells him all about the giants and advises him not to go unless he wishes to be killed. The companion has no objection to his going in LD and Wig.

14. At the conclusion of the fight Arthur is remembered: in one case the heads are sent, in the other the young lady is taken to him; in both mention is made of the joy at Arthur's court. Arthur is not spoken of in BI in connection with this adventure.

15. The hero's companion expresses a desire for the little dog, and he catches it and presents it to her. In BI she herself dismounts and gets it, being able to catch it because it has a thorn in its foot.

16. The dog comes alone. In BI it comes, with other dogs, pursuing a stag.

17. The companions go on "mit grôzen fröuden," or telling tales of knightly deeds. In BI the owner of the dog appears at once.

18. The hero meets the owner's threats with ridicule. In BI he begs his companion to give the dog back.

19. He finds to his dismay that the magician with whom he has fought and whom he has left lying on the ground, has been carried off mysteriously.

20. Only one sword can harm the magician.

21. The hero himself announces the latter's death.

22. The young woman whom he saves from her trouble goes with him to Arthur's court.

These agreements between Wig. and LD in points in which the latter is at variance with BI are very striking, and seem to me to put out of the question the theory that Wirnt was following Renaud's poem, even in a second-hand account. Taken in connection with the agreements between Wig. and BI as opposed to LD (pointed out above, p. 216), they suggest the theory that Wig., in those parts of the poem which resemble the other members of the Desc. cycle, is derived either from the common original of BI–LD, or from some form closely allied to that original.[1]

We must consider what bearing the proper names in the three poems have on this theory. As we have seen (above, pp. 59, 60), there are one hundred and forty names in BI which are not in LD. None of these are in Wig. either. There is no name in the borrowed part of Wig. which is in BI and not in LD. Indeed, if I mistake not, *Erec, Kay,* and *Miljanz* are the only names in the whole poem which are in BI but not in LD, and in no case are the actions of these characters in any way similar. In BI, Kay is Arthur's seneschal, and Melians is mentioned once among the knights at the tournament. In Wig. they are two of those who fight unsuccessfully with the owner of the girdle. As for Erec, he is mentioned in BI but twice, once in the list of those at court, and again in the list of those at the tournament. In Wig., Erec, Lanzelet, and Iwein are the knights who are associated with Gawein to go and congratulate the boy on his victory. In BI, "Lasselos dou Lac" and Yvain are both mentioned in lists of warriors, but nowhere are they associated with Gawein. In LD, however, Gawein, Iwein, and Launcelet are three of the five knights who are sent to get the boy ready to start out. Obviously the argument from proper names does not interfere with the theory suggested, but on the contrary strengthens it.

As to the large part of Wig. (some 9000 verses) which does not correspond to the Desc. poems, what shall we say? Are we to agree with Mebes that it was in this part of the poem only that Wirnt depended on the narrative of his squire? And if so, are we to suppose that the faint reminiscences of the Desc. story which these lines contain are all that Wirnt derived from the squire or, with Mennung, that most of the extraneous matter came from the squire's stores of information?

The author of Wig. opens his poem with some account of himself,

---

[1] Kölbing, *Engl. Studien,* I, 121–69, long ago pointed out some of the agreements between Wig. and LD in important points in which LD and BI differ.

giving his name and asking leniency of his readers " wan ditz ist sîn êrstez werc " (8, 40). He explains to us :

> ' nu wil ich iu ein mære
> sagen. *als ez mir ist geseit.*' (8, 31-2.)

In many other places also he refers to an *oral* account for his source, and he appeals to his authorities thirty-four times in all. Such references may be in general merely conventional phrases, and much weight cannot be given them. Without exception they either take up a whole line or the latter part of one, and are thus convenient rhyme-resources. It is, however, very striking that, in the part which shows pretty close relation to the Desc. cycle, there is practically not a single reference of this kind. In the first 47 columns which precede the main event with which the Desc. stories begin, we have 10 references to a source. Then come the 58 columns which correspond to our cycle, and in these there are but three such references.[1] Immediately after the resemblance ceases, they begin again, and before the poem closes we find 21 more. It certainly looks as if the poet felt himself on fairly secure ground when he was following, more or less closely as his fancy dictated, the Desc. story; but as if in all the rest, where he used no such guide, he felt he had to prop up his account by appeals to his authorities. We cannot but feel that our author "doth protest too much." He knows his narrative is rambling and extravagant, and he betrays over-anxiety lest his readers get the impression that he is inventing. So far no one has been able to say definitely where Wirnt got all his new material.[2] The introductory part shows some resemblances to other stories of the Arthur cycle ; but the latter part is mostly foreign to it.

This continuation is full of stories, such as were especially common

---

[1] Just at the beginning there are two in the part where the two accounts overlap, but in both cases they are used to explain the introduction of features not in the Desc. poems. The first (48, 5) tells how lavish Arthur was with his presents to his guests; the second how the dwarf rode behind the maiden wherever she went, with his hands on her shoulders. Moreover, just at the end an episode foreign to our cycle is introduced before the last corresponding adventure is told, and there too we have an appeal to authority (102, 6) when the author tells how the dragon emits all-destroying fire from its mouth. See Mennung's list (p. 64; cf. p. 61); cf. also 9, 5; 23, 24; 138, 7; 204, 20.

[2] See Bethge, *Wirnt von Gravenberg*, kap. ii.

in the East, telling of marvellous monsters and monstrous marvels. Indeed, the combination of the several parts forms a very incongruous mixture. We read (p. 257) of the arrival at a place of Gawein, Erec, Owein, and Lancelot, in the same breath with that of the different kings of Asia. The Queen of Persia begs Wig. to go home with her a few days after he has left Karidôl. No regard is paid to limitations of time and space. Syria, Lybia, and India are near at hand. Larîe, the princess whom Wig. marries, goes with him to Arthur's court on an elephant, in true Eastern fashion; and so on. It is my belief that Wirnt is himself responsible for this conglomerate. He probably gathered in materials from different sources and joined them together; and parts may be sheer inventions of his own. Meisner's view,[1] that he followed closely an old French original throughout, merely begs the question.

Wirnt himself, however, asserts that his poem follows the oral narrative of a squire.[2] Speaking of Gawein's defeat by an unknown knight and Arthur's sorrow because of it, he evidently realizes that it was a perilous thing to depart from the traditional view, which always represented Gawein as invincible, and so he adds:

> ez enquæme ouch niemer für mînen munt,
> hiet mirz ein knappe niht geseit
> ze einer ganzen wârheit,
> wider den ich alle wîle streit. (20, 15 ff.)

The object of this is of course to inspire us with confidence in the narrator, who thus assures us that he has allowed nothing which is at variance with accepted views to pass into the book without being well attested. In concluding he again speaks of the squire as his authority:

> Ich wil daz mære volnden hie,
> als michz ein knappe wizzen lie
> der mir ez ze tihten gunde.
> *niwan eines von sinem munde*
> *enpfie ich die âventiure.* (297, 22 ff.)

---

[1] See above, p. 208.
[2] There is a paper MS. of Wig. of the year 1468 in the British Museum (Addit. 19,554); see Ward, *Catal. of Romances*, I, 398 fl. The hero there gives his name as *Wigaleis von Galoys* instead of *Gwi von Galois* in the printed editions. At the end the author says he had learned the story from a "maister," not a "knappe."

It is of course possible to regard all this as merely a literary subterfuge, but I see no reason for such incredulity. If we accept the author's statement so far as to believe that he derived a part of his poem from the squire, it must surely have been not the part foreign to our cycle, but rather the Desc. part[1] which the squire is responsible for. This[2] is the only part of Wig. which can really be called *the story*. The rest is mainly a hotch-potch of miscellaneous adventures added, with the idea of lengthening and, doubtless, as the writer thought, of improving his narrative. When, then, Wirnt says that the story was told him by a squire, we must understand by that the parts which correspond to the account in the Desc. poems. Moreover, if Wirnt was only told the story by word of mouth by a squire, who may himself have received it in like manner, and who at any rate could hardly have remembered it exactly, this accounts for the variations of Wig. in the Desc. part from any other account of our hero's adventures. It might well account also for the almost complete omission (in the Desc. part) of the names familiar to us in both LD and BI, and therefore in their original, as contrasted with the plethora of strange names in the continuation.[3] I open the German poem at random, and find in cols. 257–8 the following names: *Korntin, Riâl, Jeraphin, Zaradech, Panschafar, Llamère, Roimunt, Êlamie, Marin, Liôn, Adân von Âlarie, Darel, Gâmer, Ariûn, Medarie, Belacûn, Bejolarz, Lêodarz, Môrâl, Ursin, Ambigâl, Sâlle,*—twenty-three names unknown to our cycle in less than fifty short lines. Under ordinary circumstances, this absence of names in one part of a story and abundance of them in another would be taken to indicate that in the one case the author was following an oral account, and in the other a manuscript; and yet it is precisely the opposite view which is maintained in this case by Mebes and those who agree with him. Surely Wirnt could not have had any object in deliberately concealing or changing the names of his characters if he had had these in a manuscript before him.

---

[1] This is the part which Mebes and those who accept his view regard as derived from a MS. of BI. I have tried to show that this theory is untenable.

[2] With the few bits of genuine Desc. matter in the non-Desc. portion. These bits may also be ascribed to the squire, though not in the form in which we find them.

[3] Strangely enough, the messenger, who has no name in the body of the narrative, receives one at the beginning of the continuation (107, 5).

We must conclude, therefore, that it was the Desc. part of Wig. which the German poet learned from the squire.

Even in the part in which Wirnt adheres in general features to the Desc. poems he does not do so closely.[1] He is ever ready for digressions of his own of all kinds. He expands and works over the original story at will (witness the account of the sparrow-hawk adventure), introducing new features which could never have belonged to the French original, and leaving his own personality very clearly stamped on the whole work.[2] When Wig. sees the young lady in the power of the giants, Wirnt makes him stop and soliloquize at length how much joy men would lose if there were no women. When he makes the giant promise to go to Arthur, he takes thirteen new lines to explain how men kept their oaths in former times. When he sees the maiden in distress because she has been deprived of the prize, riding alone, he takes the opportunity of introducing another discussion about women and the manners in olden times, which he spreads over thirty-eight lines.

These are only examples of the way in which Wirnt regularly treats his subject. He is no mere translator. He purposes to work in his own opinions, and feels no necessity of following closely the story which he is using to serve his purpose. It is possibly to this individuality and to the conversational element which he introduces into the poem that it owes the wide popularity attested by the frequent mention of the poem in other works, the numerous manuscripts, and the existence of *Volksbücher* in other languages as well as German, treating the same subject.[3]

But, even if we agree that the Desc. part of Wig. was told Wirnt by his squire, the question still remains : What form of the story did the latter know?

I have already suggested that this part of Wig. is based on the

---

[1] Cf. Paris, *Rom.*, XV, 21.

[2] It should be observed that Wirnt tells his story in such a way that there are no breaks discernible to a reader unfamiliar with other works of the Desc. cycle.

[3] Schönbach (*Haupt's Zt.*, XXIV, 168) knew twenty-four manuscripts and fragments of Wig. For references by Wirnt's contemporaries and by later writers, see Pfeiffer, *Vorwort*, p. xvi, and Meisner, *Wirnt von Gravenberg*, cap. i. Sarrazin, *Quellen u. Forschungen*, XXXV, 7, points out that *Wigamur* shows the influence of *Wigalois;* cf. Golther, *Gesch. der deutschen. Litt.*, I, 245.

original of LD and BI, *or on some form closely allied to it*. I have put in the italicized phrase in order to avoid being too definite in a matter which is purely hypothetical, and in which the facts may well be more complicated than one is disposed to think them at first sight. I cannot refrain, for example, from calling attention to the fact that Wig. has points in common with the late prose redaction of Renaud's poem; and, more important still, with Car. also. The former will be noted in the section dealing with the Claude version (p. 239, below). Let us now see wherein Wig. and Car. agree as opposed to LD and BI.

(1) In both Wig. and Car. the mother plays an important part. She tries to dissuade her son from leaving her; and when he insists, she herself procures him an equipment. (2) The boy is informed by his mother who his father is before he goes to court, but this knowledge is concealed. He bears, however, a definite name from the start, not one given him by the king. The information given him by his mother of his parentage affects his conduct from first to last. (3) He has many admiring friends in the city where he dwelt before going to Arthur. (4) He does not ask for a promise that an undefined adventure be given him to perform. (5) The messenger does not chide the king after the latter has given his decision that the young knight is to go. (6) The hero fights first with the giant seated by the fire. (In LD and BI with the other.) (7) The princess whom he marries bears him a son, of whom it is specially noted that he became celebrated. (8) There is only one enchanter. (9) In addition to this, Wig. and Car. show a striking agreement in the combat between the hero and the single knight; cf. Wig. 55, 7–14, 19–21, with Car. ii, 23.

This conflict varies greatly in LD and BI. In the latter the part corresponding occupies 56 lines (425–480); in the former, 72 lines (337–408). In both the knight is not killed, but compelled to beg for mercy, and allowed to live only on condition that he give his promise to go to Arthur. Further, in Wig. and Car., when the knight is seen to be dead, one of the hero's company is in great alarm lest they pay dear for the deed. In Wig. the messenger exclaims:

> 'nu nemt war
> welch ein mort ir habt getân!' (55, 24–5.)

and says they must hurry on to escape vengeance. In Car. the dwarf exclaims, "omè ! che à' tu fatto?" (ii, 24, 1) and tells Car. that he has slain a great lord. Pucci here, however, introduces new features of his own, as we have seen (pp. 15, 186).

Of course these agreements may be accidental; but they seem to indicate that there were other versions, varying more or less from those few that we can definitely establish. It may be that the changes are only due to different manuscripts of the same version. Gordon de Percel (l'Abbé Lenglet-Dufresnoy), in 1734,[1] knew a quarto manuscript of "Giglan fils de Gauvain en vers." It is evident we have not all the materials at hand for a complete solution of the questions which arise.

It is important now to examine more carefully some of the incidents which Wig. and LD have in common (cf. p. 217, above). This comparison will, it is hoped, not only strengthen the contention already made as to the closeness of relationship between Wig. and LD, but also serve to correct some wrong impressions which have obtained heretofore.

First, then, let us compare the first adventure which each hero has after leaving the court. It will be remembered that in both poems the messenger chides the young knight and does not hesitate to express her disappointment.

1. Together, they approach, however, a place where a knight is wont to fight with all who pass, and the messenger explains in LD that " þis pase kepeþ a kniȝt, þat wiþ ech man will fiȝt." (286-7.) He is an exceedingly good fighter and is always victorious. LD, however, is not afraid, but declares that he will fight at all hazards. In Wig. also the messenger tells the hero of a knight, " des hûs ist hie nâhen bî " (53, 29), whose custom it is to fight with every one who comes there. She advises Wig. to avoid a fight; but he will not listen to her.

2. When this knight (in both LD and Wig.) sees them coming, he starts for them straightway. Cf. LD, 313-4, with Wig. 54, 24-26.

---

[1] *De l'Usage des Romans*, Amsterdam, 1734, II, 245. Pointed out by Bethge, p. 7, note 1. Mennung's statement (p. 2) that Gordon de Percel knew *four manuscripts*, comes from a misapprehension of the phrase "in 4. manuscrit."

3. In LD the conditions of the fight are explained by the knight:

'Who so rit her day oþer niȝt,
Wiþ me he mot fiȝt
Oþer leve his armes her.' (316 ff.)

In Wig. the situation is influenced by the introduction of a character istic of the fight with the steward later. Every one who asks for lodging at the castle must fight with the lord, and, if he wins, he gets all his heart desires; if he loses, he must suffer a penalty. It is important to observe, however, that the penalty is as follows:

'stichet ab in der wirt nider,
sô muoz er danne blôzer wider
scheiden gar ân sine habe.' (54, 7 ff.)

In the corresponding place in both LD and BI (the fight with Lampart) defeat will expose the knight to the insults of the citizens, who will pelt him with "foul fen." In BI, on the other hand, *in this first adventure*, there is no such condition as that in Wig. and LD. We merely read that the little company comes to a ford on the other side of which is a lodging in which a knight "atendoit l'aventure" (329). Hélie sees him making ready, and warns BI not to go over, "que tu jà ne soies ocis" (373). BI crosses, nevertheless, and is stopped by the knight, who explains:

'Folie fu del gué passer;
Je vos l'ferai cier compérer.' (395-6.)

The knight then explains the situation thus:

'Avant n'irés-vos, sans bataille;
Del gué passer est tels l'usages;
Ensi l'a tenu mes lignages;
Et je certes plus de VII ans
Maintes gens i a fais dolens,
Et maint bon chevalier de pris
I ai abatu et ocis.' (414 ff.)

There is thus no mention of any penalty for defeat, or of any way to avoid a fight. The knight's family has merely had for a long time the pleasant custom of killing all other knights who passed the ford, and he himself has done his duty in the matter faithfully for seven years.

It is clear that we have in this one incident an important argument against the view that Wirnt knew Renaud's poem, for we have a striking agreement of Wig. with the English poem in a point where it varies from the French of Renaud. And yet, be it noted, this is the very passage, and the only one, which Mennung picks out to prove that Wig. is taken from Renaud's poem.

Moreover, it is evident that the feature of asking for lodging was not originally present here, but is introduced from the later adventure with Lampart, for we see that in Wig. the conditions and situation do not fit. Wig. does not ask for lodging at all. As in LD, the knight sees him coming and makes for him.

> Er wânde im solde gelingen
> als im ofte ê was getân. (54, 29-30.)

He is on the lookout for knights who happen to be passing and is ever ready to fight. As in LD also, he sees LD and his companions before they see him. How stupid, then, to have the fight depend on the asking for lodging! Moreover, the companions do not stop after the fight; they continue their journey as in LD and BI. It may be noted also that there is no question of a *gué* in LD or Wig.

We thus see that Wirnt introduces at the proper place the fight with the single knight, making it the first adventure after the hero leaves court; and his account, moreover, agrees in details with that given in LD, and is opposed to that in BI. The opinion, then, which has heretofore prevailed, that Wirnt omitted this first incident, is erroneous. All he has done is stupidly to introduce here a characteristic of a later incident, and yet not make it fit. He tells the second incident in its proper place, but is careful to avoid repeating himself, as will be seen if we compare the adventure with the steward in Wig. with that in LD and BI.

An adventure foreign to our cycle intervenes between the sparrowhawk episode and that with which we have to deal. Afterwards when Wig. and the messenger are riding along together, the latter informs the hero that they are near the city of her mistress, tells him of the enchanter, informs him how the distress was brought about, and instructs him how to perform the adventure. They soon come before the beautiful city and see a knight riding out armed. Wig. asks who he is, and the messenger tells him that he is " truhsæze hie "

(103, 21). He and Wig. fight together on the plain; but the contest is undecided. Finally the knight, recognizing the merit of his opponent, comes to Wig. and bids him welcome (104, 8). Then he sees the maiden whom his lady had sent to Arthur for aid (104, 11). He welcomes her also, and all ride together to the castle. They are joyfully received. The messenger tells of her journey and Wig.'s bravery, and there is great rejoicing.

In LD also, whilst LD and the messenger are riding along, the latter gives the hero information as to the "steward" or "constable" of the castle which they are approaching, and which belongs to her mistress. As in Wig., after the fight which ensues between this knight and LD, the former bids the latter welcome (1739; cf. 1751). When he sees the messenger, his joy is increased, especially when she gives an account of the bravery of LD and his victories on their way thither. Cf. the following passages of Wig. and LD (BI is quite different):

>Owê, waz dâ wart gesaget
>mære von ir reise!
>si zalte manege freise
>die si von vorhten leit
>dô ir geselle streit.
>. . . . .
>ir getwerc daz pfert für si reit
>und fuorte den sitech unt den hunt.
>. . . .
>diu magt begunde mêren
>dem jungen riter sînen pris:
>si lobte in manegen wis
>. . . .
>er wolde verliesen sînen lîp
>durch si, das wær im gedâht. (105,39–106,24.)

and

>Anon þat maide Elene
>Was fet wiþ kniȝtes ten
>   Before sir Lambard.
>Sche and þe dwerȝ bedene
>Telde of six dedes kene,
>   þat he did þidirward,
>And hou þat sir Libewe
>Fauȝt wiþ fele schrewe
>   And for no deþ ne spard. (1753 ff.)

Up to this time LD has known nothing definite of his mission, and, like Wig., he therefore inquires about it. In each case he is told the name(s) of the enchanter(s) and the method of enchantment, and vows to go to the rescue. We read also in Wig. of the information given to the hero of the people of the enchanted city.

> ' man hœret dâ niwan wê! wê!
> schrîen die langen naht.
> . . . . .
> ez ist uns ein swære
> daz wir des niht mügen gesehen
> wâ von ode wie ez sî geschehen.' (113, 5-11.)

With this should be compared the information given to LD.

> ' Ofte we here þ her crie,
> But her to se wil i3e,
> Þer to have we no mi3t.' (1801 ff.)

We thus see that we have here in Wig. the fight with the steward in its proper place. The feature as to the conditions for obtaining lodging, being told before, is of course not repeated. The agreements with LD, as opposed to BI, are again remarkable. We have in both, for example, the bidding the hero welcome, the joy of the people, the recounting by the messenger and the dwarf of the knight's brave deeds on the way, his willingness to risk his life, his being told the name(s) of the enchanter(s) before he enters the city, and the information given him at the castle that they can hear the cries of the people of the enchanted city, whom they cannot see.

It is interesting now to see what Mennung has to say about these two adventures, for they play an important part in his argument. He is of the opinion that Wirnt did not include in Wig. any incident parallel to that with the first knight in LD and BI, but that he related "ein und dasselbe Abenteuer" (viz., that with the steward) twice. The reason for this repetition, he thinks, is easily seen. "Auf der einen Seite folgte er der korrekten schriftlichen Vorlage, und daher die genaue Uebereinstimmung der mitgeteilten Textstücke, auf der andern hingegen den dunkeln Reminiscenzen des Knappen, der das Abenteuer derartig vortrug, dass Wirnt die Identität beider Quellen nicht erkannte. Dass dieser Irrtum eintreten konnte, lag einesteils daran, dass der Knappe weiter nichts mehr wusste, als dass Guinglain mit dem Truchsess der zu erlösenden Jungfrau gekämpft, andernteils aber auch, dass der Stand dieses Gegners in der schriftlichen Vorlage erst ganz spät nach dem Kampfe genannt wird. Brach die Vorlage vorher ab, so konnte Wirnt nicht wissen, dass es sich in beiden Berichten um ein und dieselbe Person des Seneschalls oder Truchsesses handelte. Dieser bedeutungsvolle Irrtum spricht nach meiner Ansicht sehr für die Benutzung zweier verschiedenen Quellen." (P. 61.)

How unfortunate this ingenious explanation is, will surely be apparent to all. In disproof of Mennung's last conjecture we may note that the position of the hero's opponent in LD is told before LD goes to the castle. LD inquires about the castle in the distance, and Elene tells him that no knight can get lodging there

> 'For doute of a stiward,
> þat men clepeþ sir Lambard,
> Constable of þis castell.' (1576 ff.)

And we remember that Wirnt is following a version very near this and very unlike BI. Moreover, a comparison of LD and BI shows that in the former the characters are almost always named when they appear first, while Renaud repeatedly makes the mistake of not telling their names until long after, in some cases not until they are to be dismissed from the narrative. (E.g., Hélie, Tidogolain, Orguillous de la Lande, Margerie, Giflet li fius Do, Malgier, Mabon and Eurain.)

4. I should like also to call particular attention to the agreements between Wig. and LD, as opposed to BI, in the adventure with the dog. To this end compare the following passages:

> an der selben stunde
> lief vor in ein bräkelin,
> daz niht schœners mohte sîn.
> daz was blanc über al:
> niwan ein òre was im val,
> daz ander ròt alsam ein bluot.
> des wart diu maget wol gemuot:
> wande si des selbe jach
> daz si nie deheinez gesach
> daz ir z'ihte mære
> wider daz selbe wære.

Studies on the Libeaus Desconus. 231

and

> des wart der riter harte vrô.
> daz hundelin vienger dô
> und leit ez für si ûf ir kleit.
> des wart diu maget vil gemeit,
> mit grôzen fröuden si dô reit. (60, 23 ff.)
>
> As þey ride talkinge,
> þey siʒe a rach come flinge
>   Overþwert þe way.
> Þan seiden eld and ʒinge,
> From her ferst ginninge
>   Þey ne siʒe never non so gay.
> He was of all colours
> þat man may sen of flours
>   Betwene midsomer and may.
> Þe maide saide also snell:
> 'Ne siʒ I never no juell
>   So likinge to my pay.
> God wold, þat I him auʒte!'
> Libeans anoon him cauʒte
>   And ʒaf him to maide Elene.
> Þey ride forþ all sauʒt
> And telde, hou kniʒtes fauʒt
>   For ladies briʒt and schene. (1069 ff.)

With this ending cf. also

> Die strâze riten si als ê.
> ir fröude was dô michels mê
> denne ir dâ vor wære.
> Mit manegem guoten mære
> vertriben si die selben zît. (62, 16 ff.)

In BI the whole of this episode is changed, and certainly for the worse. We must, however, say that BI shows some likeness to Wig. in a place where the author of LD is in no way opposed, but contents himself with generalities. The dog is thus described in BI:

> Plus estoit blans que nulle nois;
> Orelles noires comme pois,
> (Celi qui fu au lès senestre;)
> De l'autre part, sor le flanc destre,
> Ot une tace tote noire. (1275 ff.)

This agreement is not by any means exact enough to warrant us in assuming translation; and LD hints at the same features clearly. On the other hand, it will be remembered that in BI Hélie herself alights and catches the dog, being able to do so because it has a thorn in its foot, etc.

In Wig. and LD they ride on; but soon the owner appears and demands his dog. When it is refused, he begins to threaten; but the hero is defiant. Cf.

> Er sprach : ' Wie getorst ir ie
> gevâhen mînen schœnen hunt?
> heizt in lâzen an dirre stunt
> balde ûf die strâze nider,
> ode irn kumet niemer wider
> mit deheinen iuwern êren,
> und müezet wider kêren
> mit ungesundem lîbe.'
> ' diu rede zæm einem wibe'
> sprach her Wîgâlois der degen.
> . . . . . .
> 'swaz ab uns dâ von geschiht,
> wirn geben iu des hundes niht
> durch bœse rede noch durch drô.'   (61, 24-62, 3.)

and

> ' Frendes, leteþ him go!'
> Libeaus answerde þo :
>   ' Þat schall never betide !'
>   . . . . .
> Quoþ sir Otes de Lile :
> ' Þou puttest þe in greet perile,
>   Biker ȝef þou abide.'
> Libeaus seide : ' Be seint Gile!
> I ne ȝeve nouȝt of þy gile,
>   Cherl, þauȝ þou chide.'
>   . . . . .
> ' Þer of do þy best
>   Þis rach wiþ me schall wende!'   (1105-31.)

We need not enter into the variations in BI. Suffice it to remember that BI even pleads with Hélie to give the dog back.

In LD after this adventure we read:

    Libeaus rod many a mile
    And siȝ aventurs file
    In Irland and in Wales. (1300 ff.)

With this cf.

    Mit fröuden riten si dô dan.
    der getwerc einez in began
    sagen schœniu mære,
    wer sîn herre wære
    der in dar hêt gesant,
    und wie ez stüende in Îrlant. (87, 22 ff.)

The passage in LD is hard to understand. How could LD ride about at this time, and see terrible adventures in Ireland and Wales? The idea is preposterous. The passage is probably due to a misunderstanding of the original, which we may suppose was somewhat like the passage in Wig. just given. It is well to observe, at any rate, that there is no passage in BI in which Ireland is mentioned in this way. In fact, the name occurs only twice in the poem, in both cases merely as the name of the land from which come two kings mentioned as taking part in the tournament.

There is surely no need to continue the discussion. It must now be clear (1) that Wirnt in writing *Wigalois* had no knowledge of Renaud's poem, and (2) that the form of the story told to Wirnt by his squire (i.e. what we have called "the Desc. part" of Wig.) was drawn either from the common source of LD and BI, or from some form closely allied to it.

This theory will be seen to differ in almost every particular from that of Mebes. It is also very dissimilar to Bethge's view. Bethge first placed,[1] as he thought, "über jeden zweifel" the opinion that "kein andres werk als der BI Renaulds de Beaujeu die quelle Wirnts gewesen sein kann" (p. 77). He then declared (p. 77): "Wirnt hat nicht das französische gedicht selbst gekant oder gar wie herr dr. Mebes wähnte teilweise in einer handschrift vor sich gehabt, sondern er folgte wie er selbst angibt der einmaligen mündlichen erzählung

---

[1] *Wirnt von Gravenberg, eine literarhistorische Untersuchung*, Berlin, 1881. See the disparaging review by Rhode in *Engl. Studien*, VII, 150 ff.; and cf. Paris, *Hist. Litt.*, XXX, 187, n. 1; Kaluza, *Einl.*, p. cxxxii.

eines knappen die von anfang an ungenau war und gegen das ende hin immer lückenhafter und verworrener wurde. Die abweichungen des deutschen gedichts von dem französischen beruhen zum teil auf vergesslichkeiten teils des dichters teils seines gewährsmannes zum teil aber auch auf absichtlichen veränderungen, auslassungen und zusätzen Wirnts."

Bethge, then, holds that the squire's story (which, in his opinion, was derived from BI [1]) was confused and defective, especially toward the end, and that Wirnt himself did not remember well what the squire told him. The variation in the catastrophe of Wig. (including the omission of the *fier baiser*) he ascribes to lapses of memory on the squire's part.[2] The *fée* episode he supposes was omitted by Wirnt on moral grounds. My opinion, on the contrary, is that Wirnt followed the squire's story more or less closely until he reached the catastrophe, viz., the disenchantment of the princess,[3] but that at this point he decided to lengthen the narrative according to his own fancy. He therefore foisted in various incidents taken from various sources or drawn from his own imagination, and postponed the catastrophe until he had thus conducted the hero through a series of disconnected adventures. He then wound up the story proper in a way which resembled remotely the conclusion of his original,[4] and

---

[1] It is true Bethge says (p. 17): "dass der knappe eine ältere französische bearbeitung kante ist ganz sicher zu widerlegen; eine solche hat es niemals gegeben"; and again (p. 19): "nirgend vor Renauld de Beaujeu wird von Guinglain oder Libiaus gesagt oder gesungen"; but these opinions are plainly erroneous. Rhode (*Engl. Studien*, VII, 150 f.) advances the argument that if Renaud's poem had been the first on the subject it must have jumped into remarkable popularity all at once, to have been worked over after so very short a time by the German poet.

[2] Bethge, like Mebes, supposes that most of the additions in the non-Desc. part of Wig. were made by Wirnt rather than by the squire, but he ascribes a considerable activity in this regard to the latter also (p. 51). The additions were, he thinks, in great part made to fill up gaps in the squire's imperfect story.

[3] It will be remembered that in my opinion the squire was not following Renaud's poem, and that therefore the return visit to the Ile d'Or, the tournament, and the rest of Renaud's additions were unknown to him, and consequently to Wirnt. Bethge did not learn of the existence of Car. until he had finished his essay, nor does he give any evidence of having carefully compared LD with BI.

[4] Bethge's idea that the variation at this point is due to the squire's weak memory is peculiarly improbable. The incident of the *fier baiser* is certainly too striking to have been forgotten either by the squire or his master.

inserted a long adventure after the narrative had really come to an end.

If the conclusion at which we have arrived as to Wirnt's source is correct, the agreements of Wig. with BI as opposed to LD, and with LD as opposed to BI, are accounted for, and Wig. becomes an important factor in determining what were probably the features in Version B. We must ascribe to Version B at least two important features in which Wig. agrees with BI and is unlike LD, viz., the messenger's leaving the court without the young knight (p. 158, above), and the meeting with the young woman which leads to the sparrow-hawk adventure (p. 165, above). Moreover, I am of the opinion that the squire's story included a short introduction telling of the youth of the hero, and that Wirnt amplified this by means of another story with which he was familiar. Bethge, of course, considers the introduction in Wig. to be entirely an addition made by Wirnt, inasmuch as Renaud's poem (the only Desc. story, according to Bethge, which the squire could have known) contains nothing that could have suggested it.[1]

We must now give some account of the part of Wig. which precedes the boy's reception at court.

After a long introduction, in which Wirnt tells us his name and somewhat of himself (1–144), he opens the narrative by a description of Arthur and his glorious residence at Karidôl (145–247). The king had a custom not to sit down to meat until he had had some adventure.[2] Once it was past midday before any offered itself. An unknown red knight rides up and begs the queen to accept a beautiful girdle with magic powers,[3] which he reaches up on a spear to her; if not, to choose a knight to fight with him. On Gawein's advice she returns it in the morning, and the stranger rides off to the plain to await adventure (248–435). One after another the knights are conquered, and finally even Gawein has to yield (436–618). He goes

---

[1] Mebes also seems to ascribe the introduction to Wirnt, but he is confused on this point (see p. 209, above).

[2] On this common feature of the Arthur poems, see Child, *Ballads*, Part II, p. 257, note ‡. Cf. Löseth, *Tristan*, p. 280; Freymond, *Zt. f. fr. Sp. u. Litt.*, XVII, 46, etc.

[3] Cf. Cuchulinn's girdle, theories as to the connection of which with Siegfried's invulnerability may be seen in Zimmer, Haupt's *Zeitschrift*, XXXII, 319.

with the unknown knight to the latter's land, being given the magic girdle whilst they are on their journey. He is well received by the king and queen, and by their wonderfully beautiful niece, whom it takes over five pages to describe (619-950). Gawein is in raptures when the king tells him he may have her to wife. They are married and live together happily. Gawein becomes famous in the land; but after half a year longs to see his old companions. He leaves his wife sorrowful, although he promises to be but a very short time away, and in twelve days is at Karidôl. His coming causes great joy. Soon, however, he decides to return, and leaves the court secretly. As he has left the magic girdle behind with his wife (instructing her that if anything happens to him, it shall be given to his child, if a son), he cannot find his home again, and after a year's vain searching goes back to Arthur (951-1220). Meanwhile his wife, Flôrie, has given birth to a son,[1] to whose training she gives her most assiduous attention, with the result that all love and honor the boy for his virtue and powers. He is told of the bravery of his father, and determines to go in search of him. His mother tries to dissuade him, but finally tells him more of his father and gives him the girdle. He takes leave of her in sorrow (1221-1410). On his way he meets a messenger sent by Arthur to summon knights to a tournament at which three thousand are to be present. The boy is shown the way to the court, and finds a great celebration going on (1411-1475). Beside a linden he sees a beautiful variegated stone, which has such powers that no one can touch it unless he is without sin.[2] He ties his horse to a bough and sits down on the stone. Nobody at court can do this but Arthur, not even Gawein. News of this marvel is at once brought to Arthur,

---

[1] Wirnt is not alone in making *Gawein* marry a beautiful princess *Flôrie*, and have by her a distinguished son. This is the case in Version P of the *Livre d'Artus*, which has just been made accessible by Freymond. Florée is there the daughter of King Alain of Escavalon, and before the birth of her son it was prophesied by Merlin that he should become a brave knight of the Round Table. As the editor says (p. 50, note 2), "Eine ganze Reihe von Punkten in unserem Text erinnern, was ich hier nicht weiter ausführen will, an ähnliches in den verschiedenen Versionen des Guinglain." A number of these will be found noted in their proper places.

[2] On this feature see Child, *Ballads*, Part II, 257 ff., especially 269, note ‡; also IV, 502; VI, 503; VIII, 454; IX, 212. See also Bethge, p. 44.

who starts off with the ladies and knights to verify the report. The boy is given a hearty welcome by the king and queen. Arthur asks him what he wishes and who he is. He replies that he cannot tell who his father is. (In Car. also he knows his father's name, but conceals it.) He gives his name as *Gwî von Gâlois*, and makes his request:

> 'mit minem dienest wold ich
> erwerben des ich ie hân gegert:
> ob ich der êren wære wert
> daz ich rîter würde hie.'

His request is granted; he is given over to Gawein for instruction; a feast is made in his honor when he is knighted, after which Arthur distributes presents freely to his guests (1475-1716). At the next solstice, when they are again at table, the messenger and the dwarf appear.

The introductory part in LD is told very briefly. In BI it is omitted altogether. It is therefore likely that the author of Version A, knowing that this part of his story was familiar to his hearers or readers, passed over it lightly, merely outlining the story, and hastening on to the part which he was to develope in a new way. In Car., as I have pointed out, the author reverted to the story of Perceval's youth as he found it in a late prose account;[1] in Wig. to some other story of a young knight coming unknown to Arthur's court, and later performing wonderful feats. This story Wirnt probably treated freely, as he did the rest of his material.

We have, for example, in *Mériaduec* or *Li Chevaliers as deus Espees*[2] some features in common with the introductory part of Wig. and with later incidents in the other poems of our cycle. The following resemblances to Wig. are noteworthy:

(1) *Mér.* opens with a description of a great feast at Arthur's court at *Cardueil*, where all the knights are gathered. (2) The king is worried because no adventure has yet offered itself, and it is time to begin the feasting. (3) A stranger comes to the court in possession of a wonderful girdle and sword. (4) All the knights in turn try to perform the task she assigns; but one after another they are baffled. (5) A boy, who has been in Gawein's charge and is not twenty-

---

[1] Cf. Paris, *Hist. Litt.*, XXX, 239, note 1. [2] See *Hist. Litt.*, XXX, 237 ff.

two years of age, comes to Arthur and begs to be made a knight.
(6) All marvel at his beauty and courageous appearance. (7) He
is knighted with due religious ceremonies, and provided with the
best of armor.

Mér. also presents the following points of resemblance to LD and
Bl : (1) A young woman and a dwarf come to the court. The former makes Arthur accede to an undefined request before she will
dismount. (2) A repast is made ready. (3) The young knight begs
to be allowed to undertake the adventure she has proposed. All are
surprised at his temerity; but the king accedes to his request.
(4) This boy knows neither who was his father nor what his own
name is, and is known at court merely as *le biel vallet*, the only name
by which his mother had called him. He has been brought up by
his mother in ignorance of his parentage, and has received no definite
name. (5) The young knight rides in quest of adventure. Every-
where he is victorious, and his fame reaches Arthur's court, whither he
sends those whom he conquers to promise submission, and say they
were sent by the *chevalier as deus espees*, the name first given him at
court. Amongst his adventures are: (*a*) his assisting a woman in
distress, whom he meets in a forest lamenting the death of her lover
(7770 ff.); (*b*) his forcing *Gerflet li fius Do* to go to Arthur (8739);
(*c*) his conquering a red knight *du val Perilleus*, who is Arthur's
avowed enemy (10918). But it should especially be noted that in
this poem (6) Gawein frees a beautiful young lady from the necessity
of marrying a knight whose offer she has refused and who has therefore
besieged her. The time is just about come when she must give in.
Gawein succeeds in his fight with the knight, and sticks his opponent's
head up on a pole with those of forty-four other knights whom the
latter has conquered. There is great joy in the castle when the people
see themselves freed. After a rich meal, Gawein betakes himself to
bed. The mother brings her daughter to the room and gives her
over to him. After a part of the night spent in embraces, Gawein
will fulfil his further wishes, but is prevented by the young woman's
withdrawal. (Cf. *Peredur*.) (7) It is at the wish of the king that
Mér. marries the beautiful queen of Caradigan, whom he loves.
There is a great celebration and feast at their wedding. They then
leave the court for Caradigan, where Mér. is made king. The lady
is called *Lore* (cf. *Larie*), and bears Mér. children.

THE FRENCH PROSE REDACTION.

The French prose redaction of BI made by Claude Platin, is known to me only from the analysis of the Comte de Tressan,[1] and from the account of it given by Paris.[2] Platin professes to have translated from a Spanish poem; but, according to Paris, this statement must be understood as referring to that part of his work which is taken from the Provençal *Jaufré* (Platin having mistaken Provençal for Spanish).[3] The only source admitted by Paris for the Desc. part of Platin's version is Renaud, and, Paris tells us, he follows his original in general pretty faithfully. The analysis of the Comte de Tressan, however, has "l'inexactitude et les enjolivements qui caractérisent les 'extraits' de ce galant vulgarisateur."

To Tressan, then, we infer, must be due the remarkable form of the story in the "extrait," — the entire omission of the *fier baiser*, the match-making of Queen Guinovere, the death of the *fée de la Blanchevalée* (as the lady of the Ile d'Or is called) from sorrow at Giglan's inconstancy, the introduction of episodes foreign to our cycle, such as the fight between Gawain and his son, and the like. We infer also that the boy's bringing up "dans un lieu désert et éloigné du commerce des hommes" was introduced, say from the *Perceval*, by the Comte de Tressan; and that the account of his coming to court, begging a boon of Arthur, etc., was shifted by him from the Desc. part to that devoted to Geoffroy de Mayence.

[Just in time to be noted here a communication from the author, now in Paris, has been received, in which he gives additional details about the contents of Platin's work. He has examined two editions of it in the *Bibliothèque Nationale*, one lacking the last page, the other dated 1539 and published at Lyons, not, however, by Claude Nourry, but by Hilles et Jaques Huguetan frères. "The analysis of the Comte de Tressan," writes Dr. Schofield, "bears little likeness to the romance itself, and a careful reading of the latter shows that on the whole Claude's redaction follows Renaud's poem very closely." There is not space here to note differences in details. — *Eds.*]

---

[1] *Bibl. univ. des Romans*, October, 1777, pp. 59 ff.
[2] *Rom.*, XV, 22-24; also *Hist. Litt.*, XXX, 196-199.
[3] Cf. Grässe, *Die grossen Sagenkreise des Mittelalters*, 1842, p. 225.

WOLFRAM'S PARZIVAL.

The bearing of the results of the present investigation[1] on the important problems in connection with Wolfram's *Parzival* and the Grail stories in general is obvious. I refrain from entering into these questions now because they do not affect my conclusions in the more definite problems with which we are dealing, and because I hope before long to publish a careful examination of the whole matter. I shall only say now that in those poems which seem to depend on Chrétien, the young knight, when he comes to court, rides abruptly before the king and makes his rough demand; while Wolfram agrees with LD, Car., and Wig. in that the boy first salutes the king and his courtiers suitably and then proffers his request. We have, moreover, in Wolfram an adventure which is remarkably like two episodes found in LD only. Parzival goes to a castle, where he is well treated, and his wounds received in a recent fight are attended to. Fine apparel is given him. The knight of the castle offers him the hand of his only daughter, and his lands after him; but Parzival is unwilling to marry, and, after a stay of a fortnight, rides away.

In LD after the fight with the giants, LD goes to the home of the rescued maiden, where he receives rich apparel. The knight offers him the hand of his only daughter, and his lands after him; but he replies that "nouȝt wive ȝet I ne may" (741), and leaves them. After the fight with Sir Otes he goes to the knight's castle, where he is well received.

> He dede him helen his wounde,
> þat he was hol and sounde
> Be þe fourteniȝt ende. (1279 ff.)

Then the hero takes his departure. These two episodes united present all the features of the account in Wolfram. It is curious to note also that the knight in LD who offers his daughter's hand to LD is there, and there alone, called *Antore*, and the only name I have noticed in any of the Perc. stories at all like this is *Antanor*, which

---

[1] See also Mennung, p. 40.

is in Wolfram, iii, 1099. We may add also that Parzival, when asked his name, replies as follows:

> 'bon fiz, schier fiz, *beà fiz*,[1]
> alsus hât mich genennet
> der mich dâ hcime erkennet;' (iii, 722 ff.)

and that when he first goes to court all marvel at his beauty. One knight, for example, exclaims:

> 'owôl der muoter diu dich bar!
> i'ne gesach nie lip sò wol gevar.' (iii, 903-4.)

LATER HISTORY OF THE ENGLISH ROMANCE.

The English romance was undoubtedly very popular, as is evident from the number of references made to it in later works. It was a doubtful honor to have it included by Chaucer in *Sir Thopas* as one of the "romances of prys," but still this shows how well it was known. In *The Squyr of Lowe Degree*, as Kaluza points out (p. clxiv ff.), our hero is mentioned, attention is directed to a specific scene in LD, and an extract given from the poem.[2] The name of the hero is also mentioned in *The Carle of Carlile*,[3] and, as Ritson notes, III, 253,[4] by Skelton and Henry Crosse.[5] Professor Kittredge calls my attention to the following passage in the *Weddynge of Syr Gawene*:[6]

> Syr Gawen gat on her *Gyngolyn*,
> That was a good knyght of strength and kynn,
> And of the Table Round.

---

[1] In Wolfram, ix, 1225, we also have a *Lybbeâls*, one of the Grail knights, who, curiously enough, comes from the land of *Prienlascors*, which is said to be from the Prov. *priendre las cortz*, and to mean " der die Höfe der Fürsten aufsucht " (Bartsch, *Germanistische Studien*, II, 149).

[2] See vv. 78, 611-632; Hazlitt, *Early Popular Poetry*, II, 26, 46-47; Ritson, *Anc. Engleish Metrical Romanceës*, III, 148, 170-171.

[3] Ed. Madden (in *Syr Gawayne*, p. 188), v. 55; ed. Hales and Furnivall, *Percy's Folio Manuscript*, III, 278, v. 33.

[4] *Phyllyp Sparowe*, 649-650.

[5] *Vertues Common wealth or the Highway to Honour*, 1600. Cf. Hales and Furnivall, II, 414.

[6] Vv. 800 ff. (Madden, *Syr Gawayne*, p. 298 *x*).

R

There is still another interesting reference to our hero in the interlude *Thersites*[1] written by an unknown author, and acted in 1537. Thersites boastfully challenges the knights of the Round Table:

> 'Where arte thou Gawyn the curtesse and Cay the crabed?
> Here be a couple of knightes cowardishe and scabbed!
> Apere in thy likenesse Syr Libeus Disconius,
> Yf thou wilt have my clubbe lyghte on thy hedibus.'

I should like also to call attention to the fact that an incident in LD (viz., the fight of the hero with the heathen giant Maugis, who had beset the lady of the Ile d'Or, 1321 ff.), is, it seems, clearly preserved in the semi-historical ballad of *The Earl of Westmoreland*, sts. 54 ff.[2] In both poems: (1) A Christian knight comes from a distance to a place where the people are all in fear of a heathen warrior. (2) The land is ruled by a woman, and none of her following dares oppose the heathen. (3) The knight determines to meet the giant, and his determination causes joy among the people, whose sympathies are all with him. (4) The giant is "both fowle and uglye for to see." (5) When he sees the young knight approach he greets him with derision, for he thinks him no match. (6) In LD (and this is important) the hero is a child, and in the ballad he has a child's voice. (7) He replies, however, that he is ready for his opponent, and does not fear. (8) They fight by the water's edge. (9) In the first encounter they both break their swords; they continue the fight on foot. (10) Thus they keep up the struggle for a long time, dealing each other severe blows until both are weary. (11) Finally the young man cuts off the heathen's head, which (12) he takes up and carries off. (13) The people of the city come to meet him "with a fair procession." (14) The lady-ruler receives him in person, and at once offers to marry him and give him control of her land. (15) He, however, is obliged to refuse and depart from her.[3]

---

[1] Child, *Four Old Plays*, p. 58; Pollard, *English Miracle Plays*, etc., pp. 130 ff.

[2] Child, *Ballads*, Pt. VI, 421-23.

[3] We may also compare with LD's fight with Lampart (1681 ff.), sts. 27-29, 31, of *Hugh Spencer's Feats in France*, Version B, Child, Pt. VI, 280; see particularly LD, 1705 ff.

APPENDIX.

PROPER NAMES IN LE BEL INCONNU.[1]

A

1. *Adant*, 2167.
2. *Agolans* (rois d'Escoce), 1814, 5159.
3. *Aguillars*, 31.
4. *Aguissans* (li rois), 5815, 5867, 5871, 5877, 5931; cf. *Aguizans* (rois d'Escoce), 5372; *Aguisel* (le roi), 5971.
5. *Aies* (land of Elin?), 521, 960, 1100, 1120, 1149, 1165, 1183, 1193, 1213; *Sire des*, 5031; *cil de*, 5915.
6. *Alixandre* (gold of), 3419.
7. *Almaine*, 3479.
8. *Amangons* (rois), 47, 5162, 5172, 5452, 5735, 5747, 6016.
9. *Ample bois* (dus de l'), 5399.
10. *Aquins d'Orbie*, 50.
11. *Arés* (rois), 42.
12. *Artu(s)*, 15, 32, 83, 251, 406, 410, 475, 479, 1177, 1455, 1785, 2075, 2690, 2881, 3205, 3213, 3287, 3332, 3378, 3580, 3854, 4882, 4965, 4985, 5012, 5153, 5440, 5472, 5497, 5801, 5809, 5861, 5981, 6000, 6004, 6067, 6072.
13. *Atels* (le roi, Tors li fius de), 5487.

B

14. *Baladi(n)gan(t)* (li vallés de), 46, 5408, 5548, 5561.
15. *Balant* (Brus de), 5562.
16. *Ban Regomer* (li rois), 5384.
17. *Bans de Gomertel* (rois), 5737.
18. *Baradigan* (li rois de — Caraan —), 5380.
19. *Baudris*, 5606.
20. *Beduiers*, 37, 61, 105, 109, 119.
21. *Beduer de Normendie*, 5480.
22. *Bel fil*, 124.
23. *Bel leus*, 1488.
24. *Blances Mains* (la fée as), 3211, 3650, 3878, 5111 (?).
25. *Bliblis*, 4260.
26. *Blioblièris*, 333, 431, 459, 517, 535, 824, 1201, 5029, 5913.
27. *Blonde Esmerée*, 3638, 3804, 3842, 4963, 5466, 5793, 6002, 6009, 6053, 6066.
28. *Braimant*, 3013.
29. *Bretaingne*, 3484, 3569, 3632, 5736.
30. *Bretons* (les), 5695, 5762, 5767.
31. *Bruians des Illes*, 5454; (li rois) 5601, 5605, 5619, 5654, 5961, 6017.
32. *Brus de Balant*, 5562.
33. *Bues de Gonefort*, 35.

C

34. *Cadoalens* (li rois), 5657.
35. *Cadoc* (le roi), 5694, 5702, 5708.
36. *Caraan* (rois de Baradigan), 5381.
37. *Carados*, 44.
38. *Caraés*, 41.

---

[1] Those numbered in black-faced type are also in LD.

Appendix.

39. Carentins, 44.
40. Cartre (Gervis de), 36.
41. Catehuels, 5486.
42. C(h)arlion, 11, 2691.
43. Cil à la cote mautaillie, 49.
44. Clarie, 877, 1216.
45. Coudrins d'Illande, 5603.
46. Constantinoble, 4667.
47. Cornouaille, 1844, 3010, 5394, 5448, 5594.

D

48. Dius, 8, 308, 310, 312, etc.
49. Dinaus, 43.
50. Durains (roi), 5428.
51. Dunebrie (Geldras li rois de), 5390.
52. Do (Gifles li fius). See *Gifles*.

E

53. Elaine, 4258.
54. Elemagne cité (roi de), 5848.
55. Elias (li dus), 5414.
56. Elins (li blans, Sire des Aies (?)), 521, 959.
57. Enaud (rois), 38.
58. Enée, 4262.
59. Eoars (li biaus), 48.
    Epire (?), 5219.
60. Erec, li fius Lac, 39.
61. Erec d'Estregales, 5479.
62. Erians, 36.
63. Escoce, 1813, 1828, 5372, 5867.
64. Espai(n)gne, 3485, 5760.
65. Esqes d'Estrans, 50.
66. Estregales (Erec d'), 5479.
67. Eurains, 3341.

F

68. Fineposterne (Grahelens de), 5424.
69. Flore (le duc de France), 5482, 5872.
70. Floriens, 34.
71. France (Flore le duc de), 5872.
72. François, 5482.
73. Frise (bon ceval de), 5780.

G

74. Gale li cals, 5162, 6020 (*cauf* (?), 41).
75. Gal(l)es, 3358, 3431, 3813, 4964, 5123, 5129, 6079.
76. Galouin (le rice conte), 5775.
77. Galigans, 2485.
78. Gandelus, 5432.
79. Gascont, 1699.
80. Gaste cité, 1224, 2751, 3363.
81. Gaudins (li rois d'Illande), 5444; cf. le roi Gaudi, 5617.
82. Gauvains (li niés Artu), 37, 102, 261, 266, 3190, 3200, 3209, 5010, 5110, 5139, 5154, 5158, 5472, 5477, 5772; *li cortois*, 93; *li bials*, 3483; *dans Gauvains*, 3334.
83. Geldain (li rois), 5725, 5749.
84. Geldras (li rois de Dunebrie), 5390.
85. Gervis de Cartre, 36.
86. Gifles (li fius Do), 1788, 1789, 1795, 1808, 1820, 1824, (D'eu (?)) 5035, 5964, 6017.
87. Giglains, 3207, 3224, 3227 (104 times).
88. Gohenet (li rois Hoel de), 5376.
89. Gomertel (Bans de), 5737.
90. Gorhout (Gormans de), 5434.
91. Gormans (de Gorhout), 5434.
92. Grahelens de Fineposterne (freres de Guingamer), 5424.
93. Graies (li bons chev. de), 522, 1099, 1110, 1119, 1194.
94. Gramadone (ridden by Celui des Aies), 1123.
95. Gringa(r)s, (roi) father of the enchanted princess, 173, 3283, 3948, 5193.
96 (?). Gué Périllous, 319, 533, 997, 1202, 5914.
97. Guingamer (freres de Grahelens de F.), 5426.
    Guinglains (see *Giglains*).

Appendix. 245

98. *Guinlains (de Tintaguel)*, 51.
99. *Guivres* (li rois : qui ot amenés les Irois), 5388-9; *li sire des Irois*, 5729.
100. *Gunes* (niés d'Oïrecestre), 5476.

H

101. *Haute Montaigne* (cil de la), 5418.
102. *Hélie*, 193, 719, 814, 829, 1000, 1003, 1031, 1220, 1827, 1852, 1929, 1975, 2284, 2292, 2335, 2681, 3391, 3402, 4895.
103. *Helin* (de Graies ?), 1110, 1194-5, 1214; cf. 1119.
104. *Hoel* (li rois de Gohenet), 5376, 5484, 5595, 5656, 5668.
105. *Horels* (li rois), 34.
106. *Hungrie*, 4150.

I

107. *Illande* (Gaudins, li rois d'), 5445; (Condrins d') 5603.
108. *Ille Noires* (sire de l'), 5423.
109. *Ile d'Or*, 1914, 3653, 3773, 3886, 3902, 5228.
110. *Irois* (Guivres li Sire des), 5389, 5729.
111. *Isex la blonde*, 4260 (cf. 5492).

J

112. *Jhesus*, 2167.

K

113. *Kahadist*, 5398.
114. *Kais, li senescals*, 53, 63, 5161, 5574, 6019.

L

115. *Lac* (Erec li fius), 39.
116. *Lais hardis de Cornouaille*, 5394.
117. *Lampars*, 2501, 2564, 2576, 2590, 2598, 2658, 2662, 2680, 2682, 2687, 2702, 2721, 2737, 2764, 2772, 2823, 3402, 3505, 5470, 5790, 5795, 5964, 6019.
118. *Lasselos* (Lancelot) *dou Lac*, 40, 5412.
119. *Lavine de Lombardie*, 4261.
120. *Libiaus Desconneus*, 131, 201, 277, etc. (56 times).
121. *Libnus*, 5496.
122. *Limors*, 3889.
123. *Lindezie* (Yvains li rois de), 5369, 5659.
124. *Lombardie* (Lavine de), 4261.
125. *Londres*, 5040, 6001, 6007, 6064.
126. *Los* (freres d'Artu), 33.

M

127. *Mabons*, 3321, 3342, 3460, 4904.
128. *Mainet*, 3013.
129. *Malgiers li Gris*, 2171.
130. *Marcel* (le cors saint), 1605.
131. *Margerie*, 1639, 1642, 1684, 1809.
132. *Marie* (mère de Deu), 2645.
133. *Mars* (li rois), 47; (de Cornouaille) 5448, 5593.
134. *Martin* (saint), 903.
135. *Melians de Lis*, 5435.
136. *Montbestée* (l'ille de la — dwelling of the fée who made the mantle of Bl. Es.), 3264.
137. *Montesclair* (le rois de), 5212; (li Sors de) 5400, 5411, 5517, 5543.
138. *Mordrès* (li rois, freres de Segrantés), 45, 5474, 5637.
139. *Morge* (la fée), 4263.
140. *Morholt* (le grant), 3011.

N

141. *Nantes* (Hoel de), 5484.
142. *Norgales* (li riches dus de), 5478.
143. *Normendie* (Beduer de), 5480.

O

144. *Oduins* (li cuens), 43.
145. *Oïrecestre* (Gunes niés de), 5476.
146. *Olivier*, 3012.
147. *Orbie* (Aquins d'), 50.

148. *Orguillous de la Lande*, 1472, 5033, 5915.

P

149. *Paris*, 4259.
150. *Perceval li Galois*, 5406.
151. *Puceles* (castel as), 5208, 5360.

R

152. *Renals de Biauju*, 6105.
153. *Riciers* (quens), 38.
154. *Robers*, 273, 505, 509, etc. (44 times).
155. *Rege cité* (li rois de la), 5386.
156. *Rollant*, 3012.
157. *Rose espanie*, 1709.

S

158. *Sa(i)gremors*, 5905, 6020; (brother of Clarie) 879.
159. *Sainte-Marie* (mostier), 4936.
160. *Salebrant* (Willaumes), 523, 961, 1197.
161. *Segrantés* (freres de Mordret), 5475.
162. *Segurés*, 45.
163. *Senaudon*, 3361, 3822, 6078, 6085.
164. *Sors* (de *Montescler*), 5400, 5411, 5517, 5528, 5536, 5543, 5549.

T

165. *Table Réonde*, 222, 245, 5496.
166. *Tesale*, 2258.
167. *Tidogolains*, 256.
168. *Tintaguel* (home of Guinlains), 57.
169. *Tors* (li fius le roi Arés, Atels), 42, 5487.
170. *Tristans*, 35, 3011, 5210, 5488, 5518, 5521, 5530, 5531, 5541, 6018.
171. *Truerem* (li quens de), 5420.

U

172. *Uriens* (brother of Arthur), 33.

V

173. *Valcolor* (le roce de), 992.
174. *Val(l)edon*, 5209, 5211, 5441, 5499, 5980, 5998.

W

175. *Willaumes* (de Salebrant), 523, 961-2, 1020, 1052, 1076, 1087, 1197-8.

Y

176. *Yder(s)* (li rois), 5430, 5460, 5553, 5564, 5579.
177. *Yvains* (li rois de Lindezie), 5369, 6018.

www.ingramcontent.com/pod-product-compliance
Lightning Source LLC
Chambersburg PA
CBHW020801230426
43666CB00007B/797